ONE LIFE,
MANY WORLDS

ONE LIFE, MANY WORLDS

MY JOURNEYS THROUGH THE HEAVENS AND HELLS OF EXTRATERRESTRIAL WORLDS

JULLIENA OKAH

TATE PUBLISHING
AND ENTERPRISES, LLC

Published by Tate Publishing & Enterprises, LLC
127 E. Trade Center Terrace | Mustang, Oklahoma 73064 USA
1.888.361.9473 | www.tatepublishing.com

Tate Publishing is committed to excellence in the publishing industry. The company reflects the philosophy established by the founders, based on Psalm 68:11,
"The Lord gave the word and great was the company of those who published it."

Book design copyright © 2015 by Tate Publishing, LLC. All rights reserved.
Cover design by Rtor Maghuyop
Interior design by Jomel Pepito

Published in the United States of America

ISBN: 978-1-62854-341-4
1. Body, Mind & Spirit / Parapsychology / Esp (Clairvoyance, Precognition)
2. Body, Mind & Spirit / UFOs & Extraterrestrials
15.07.13

DEDICATION

I dedicate this book to all the nonhuman beings who have helped me to weather my crises and have guided me all this time to this day. I am thankful for those nonhuman beings who gave me the supernatural experiences that led me to a deeper understanding of the spiritual path that God intended for me to know.

I am also dedicating this book to all people who struggle on their paths to understanding the mysteries of life.

ACKNOWLEDGMENTS

Writing my first book in English and not in my native Japanese has been an incredibly difficult challenge during the past seven years. So many people contributed in various ways to the completion of this 'labor of love' and I would like to thank them all from the bottom of my heart. If I have overlooked mentioning anyone please attribute it to the pressures of publication and know that you are not forgotten.

Most especially, to my editor, Barbara Ardinger, Ph.D., a successful author herself, I express my gratitude. She worked on my book for three years. Her work was amazing. She was for me through this difficult process.

My sincere appreciation goes to my friend actor/comedian/writer L.G. Ross, who did not give up on me. An enormous help from the beginning to the end of this project. I also thank dance critic Hal de Becker who has written for publication in New York City, Las Vegas. He postponed his own writing commitments in order to read my manuscript and provided valuable suggestions.

I would like to acknowledge the newspaper writer Bondo Wyszpolski in Los Angeles and the photographer Gloria

Plascencia, Art director Benoit Menasche, who is the leader of my various art exhibitions in Florida, my violinist friend at the MGM showroom band Helene Honda, author of "Allegro", a memoir of the Japanese in America, the scientist John Dodds who has authored scientific papers and is an excellent proofreader, who had been giving me special help on producing my book and giving me so much advice for many years. I would like to show my great gratitude for their heart filled help. There were so many professional writers who participated past seven years and I am grateful for all their help.

My sincere appreciation goes to Mr. Goi and Monk Kiriyama, two spiritual leaders in Japan who gave me great insight and contributed profoundly to my life. My thanks as well go to Tanahashi the German philosophy professor who contributed deeply to my path.

Professor Walter Barylli, former concert-master of the Vienna Philharmonic Orchestra, Sandor Deki Lakatos, world-renowned virtuoso gypsy violinist and Lee Liberace also have my gratitude for so generously helping me pursue my international musical career.

I would like to say thank you to all the cruise ship companies, theaters, and agencies around the world that employed me so I could sustain my independence to write this book.

I also wish to thank everyone at Tate Publishing for their help and support. I am so grateful for their confidence on my book.

My most heartfelt thanks belongs to my parents who gave me education and loving support, particularly my mother whose own spiritual path affected my life so profoundly.

Finally, to the extraterrestrials that guided my life and brought me this far I can never thank you enough.

Faith is to believe what we do not see, and the reward of this faith is to see what we believe.

—St. Augustine

TABLE OF CONTENTS

PART 3

INTRODUCTION

Without ever seeing, hearing, or touching him, most people in this world believe in God or some other deity. Some people devote their lives to this unseen, higher being.

But what if one's spiritual odyssey was motivated by other forces, namely aliens?

It has been said that the facts often distort the truth, and the truth can, at times, be stranger than fiction. Such is my story. It is less a biography than the story of a journey of faith and spirituality. It is an odyssey that asks readers to suspend their disbelief and accept at face value that what I am saying is an actual recounting of my life, a true story understandably motivated by fantastic and unimaginable events that are still affecting me today. What you are reading I am disclosing for the first time. Some may dismiss it as a dream, others as the ranting of a crazed woman.

I don't care. It happened.

PRELUDE

What a glorious day it has been! It's 2008, and I'm sitting on the quiet beach in Nice, where tourists enjoy respites from their hectic lives. On this autumn evening, hardly anyone else is here. Waves stir the emerald water, and a cool breeze from the Alps blows across a translucent blue sky. It's nature whispering ever so gently, reminding me that I am more than the life I have made for myself. Most of my life is hectic. I live in New York City and travel around the world on cruise ships on which I entertain passengers with my one-woman musical show. I have been a professional solo violinist all my adult life. But when I come to the French Riviera, I shut off all communication with the outside world and enjoy the silence as I stay alone in my small hideaway home across the street from the beach.

The sky starts to turn a rosy pink as I gaze at it, and the sounds of the calming waves speak softly to me. I feel like I'm dreaming with my eyes open. I love to play these calming sounds on my violin. The music I've been playing all these years is often accompanied by drums and horns. The stage lights flash; the smoke machine shoots smoke. I've always enjoyed those performances, but here

I'm in a different world, the most beautiful spot on the planet. How I love to express these colors on canvas and these sounds in my music. I am fascinated by the beauty here.

Nestled between Cannes and Monaco, the Alps and the Mediterranean, Nice is a beautiful artists' haven. Picasso, Matisse, and Chagall lived here and were inspired by the scenic views and the Mediterranean climate. In 1988, the first time I visited this place, I could not resist its allure either. Now I come here whenever I can. Nice became special to me because in September 2001, without any prior interest or training in art, I became a painter here. I must have been inspired by the great painters who came before me or perhaps just by seeing these brilliant colors of southern France.

But, truth be told, it wasn't the beauty of this city that brought me to Nice. The appearance of alien vehicles and their incredible events brought me here. It happened late in October, 1988, while I was vacationing here. In that evening, while I was strolling on the beach, I knew intuitively there would be a visitation that night. It was three o'clock in the morning when three alien vehicles (what most people might call flying saucers), appeared in the sky above me and awakened me. They were shooting their beams directly at me. They were bright, white lights. The next day, Nice became my home. I have come to realize that every time an alien vehicle appears to me, my life and career will change.

In this day, in 2008, I am sitting on the beach and watching an amazing sunset. As the sun melds into the horizon the sea and sky blend, I am contented. The color turns to golden pink. I seem to be having an illusion of entering a different world. The most beautiful world! The golden world I once visited. Suddenly, my memory flashes back. The extraordinary memories involving the beings in another world! It was the memories of my childhood in Japan.

PART 1

First Encounter

It was after the Second World War, when Japan was recovering from its devastation, that I was born in the sacred city of Kyoto. It was my mother's hometown and the city in which her ancestors had lived for a thousand years as they served the emperors. Today, Kyoto is a major tourist attraction. It is also the only major Japanese city not left in ruins by the war because the American general, Douglas MacArthur, decided not to destroy our important cultural treasures. We can never thank General MacArthur enough for his consideration.

When I was three years old, our family moved to Tokyo because of my father's bank business. Japan needed to rebuild, and my father had to reestablish the bank in Tokyo because most of the city had been bombed. Although all our relatives still lived near Kyoto, we relocated to a smaller city named Sakuradai, which was north of Tokyo in the eastern Nerima-ku district. Surrounded by rice fields and forested hills, Sakuradai was in better condition than other parts of Tokyo. We lived a fairly primitive, but peaceful, life in Sakuradai.

I was the middle child. My older sister, Kiyo, set the standards by which my younger sister, Chizu, and I would always be measured. My father, Shinn, was disappointed that he had no sons. He was an exceedingly serious man and the manager of the local branch of the conservative Sumitomo Bank. Although he was number one at work, he was secondary at home as he was often pushed aside by the demands of four females. Father was the breadwinner, but mother ruled at home. My mother, Sachi, devoted herself to her daughters, primarily to get us a good education. We four females stuck together and laughed a lot. Most of the time, I was the first person to laugh. Father was a Buddhist, and although Mother had grown up in a Buddhist family, she had changed her faith to Christianity after the war when western religions were not common in Japan. She respected the teachings of Buddhism all her life, but she raised her daughters to be Christians.

I was an adventurous girl, a tomboy, active, and extroverted. From my early childhood, however, a defective heart valve restricted my activities. Because of the destruction of the war, many Japanese had deficient immune systems. My heart valve defect was no doubt caused by germs invading my body. Though our parents were healthy, my sisters also had various medical problems, and I had the worst health in my family. My mother consistently warned me against overexertion and told me not to stray far from the house. But I always wanted to go a little farther away and see and do new things.

When my health permitted, I tried to be outdoors as much as I could. I enjoyed the company of boys and loved to do boy things rather than girl things. Playing house, dressing up dolls—those were not for me. Climbing the jungle gym and playing hide-and-seek were more to my liking. But although I had many boy and girl friend, I often played alone. I have been that way all my life because I love freedom. Freedom allows me to accomplish things quickly. I enjoyed exploring new places and trying new things. That has always been my nature.

After school, I normally came home and practiced the violin and the piano. My mother's mother, Aiko Abe(I've changed her name to protect her privacy), had been one of the most famous concert pianists in Japan, and so my two sisters and I were required to learn music, whether we wanted to or not. At that time I had very little interest in music, and practicing made me yearn to be outside.

I MEET THE DISK CREATURES

My first encounter happened when I was six years old and ventured into an area where I had been told not to go. Although 700,000 people live in and around Sakuradai today, in the early 1950s, it was a small rural community. Crime was unheard of back then, and lessons like "Never talk to strangers" did not apply. In fact, we were encouraged to talk to people, whether we knew them or not. Despite my tomboy demeanor, I was essentially shy, so my parents urged me to be open and friendly when I met people. As a whole, Japan is considered a very safe place to live, even in the twenty-first century. That is one of the reasons why my first abduction was not a terrifying experience. I did not know fear or danger. I was bold.

One Sunday afternoon when I went outside to play, I set out alone toward the open fields, a little further from the house than my mother permitted. Father loved walking in nature. He often took my younger sister Chizu and me to these fields on a Sunday afternoon for few hours. They were the closest place to our home where we could spend time in undisturbed nature. The fields were large, though we could see farmers' houses here and there. On this weekend, however, my father was away on a business trip. Spring had arrived. I had to go to the fields.

Despite the relative safety of rural Japan, the local families had good reason to warn their children to avoid the wild fields. A mental hospital was situated on one side of the fields, and there was a forest on the other side. The forest was another place we were told to stay away from. Even during the day, the forest was dark and a child could easy get lost there. North of the forest was a juvenile detention hall. Anything could happen to children who went to the fields alone. The distance between the fields and my home was about a thirty-minute walk, though many times, I rode my bicycle to get there. Usually, when I ventured into those fields, I told no one because I did not want my parents to scold me. How could I not go to visit this heavenly scenery? The cherry blossom season did not last for long.

I have always been a person who loves nature. I have always been happy surrounded by flowers. Yellow rape flowers blanketed the fields. Cherry blossoms bloomed along the riverbank. The combination of yellow, pink, and green looked like heaven to me. Life was being reborn after the long winter, and I soon found myself near the Shakujii River and the forest, drawn to the cherry blossoms like a bee to pollen.

That Sunday afternoon, I stopped walking when I noticed two yellow butterflies flying very close to me. I watched them and then greeted them.

"Hello, there," I said. "Are you two sisters or friends?" I have always loved to talk to animals, even insects.

I looked at the flowers, thinking the butterflies were going to land on the petals.

But something about the flowers didn't look right. Not sure what I was seeing, I leaned closer to see better. Something had already landed on the flowers, but it wasn't a bird or insect I recognized. What I saw seemed to be small for animals, but big for insects, about half the length of my hand, maybe a few inches in diameter and half that in height. There were several of them, and each one was light, silvery white, shiny, and transparent in places. They were perfectly round with a raised center. I never had seen anything like them in my life. They were hard to see, but the closer I looked, the more of them I could see. I counted perhaps ten of them quietly sitting on top of the yellow flowers. They must have had little density, for the flowers did not bend under their weight.

With some hesitation, I raised my hand to touch one of them, but before my finger came close to the nearest one, it moved to another flower. It moved so fast I didn't see it fly or even hop like a cricket. I withdrew my hand, but I was fascinated. I tried touching another one, and it jumped away too. I doubted my eyes. The little white disk was gone but not gone, just on a different flower. My goodness, they were quick! And they were absolutely silent. I knew they weren't insects or birds because I saw no heads, feet, or legs, no eyes or noses, either. I thought they could see me. And they were alive.

I thought I should let them know that I was their friend, so I started by asking them the questions important to a child. "What are you? I've never seen you before. Do you live here?"

They seemed to hear me. They jumped up an inch, but softly, a little, cautious jump. That made me happy. Butterflies did not respond like these disk creatures did. Looking up, I saw more of these disk creatures floating in the air. They must have just come, but I hadn't heard them approaching. I watched them curiously for few minutes. No movement. My curiosity turned to interest. I felt compelled to catch one or more of them. I wanted to take them home so my parents could tell me what they were, and I could keep them in a cage and take care of them, like pets.

I gingerly moved toward the nearest one and cupped my hands, ready to catch it. But when my hands were just inches away from it, it disappeared right in front of me! What had happened? Had I missed seeing it? Could anything move that fast? I tried to capture another one, but it disappeared too. I thought maybe they were blending in color with the flowers. They were hard to see.

Soon, I spotted another one and—*wham!* My hands closed together like a trap. I felt the little disk creature fluttering against my palms. I was careful not to crush it. I opened my hands a crack to see if it was all right, but when I looked through the space between my thumbs, I didn't see anything. The disk creature wasn't there! I knew I had caught it. I'd felt it tickle my hands. I tried catching another one. There was no mistake. I definitely felt the tickling sensation again. But when I looked? Nothing! I carefully closed my palms together, but I did not feel anything. The disk creature had disappeared in my hands. I frowned. What a puzzle this was.

I looked around. And in the blink of an eye, the world I knew changed. I felt something, a huge tugging, a kind of suction as if by an enormous vacuum cleaner. It was pulling at my head and arms, my whole body. I lost my balance and felt myself being pulled skyward. I no longer felt the ground underneath me.

All this happened within a few seconds. I screamed in horror. Suddenly, I seemed to be spinning through a spiraling tube. I blacked out. I don't know how long I was unconscious, but I do remember feeling the walls around me come to an end as I was expelled into openness.

Now I felt motion. I was moving. I was flying! I found myself with the ability to fly like a bird. So high and so fast, I could fly! I tested myself by waving both arms. The more I moved my arms, the faster I flew. When I looked up, I felt myself rising higher. The same thing happened when I looked down. I flew lower. Wherever I was, I was in a great white light and it was too bright to see clearly, but pretty soon, I could see a colorful city below me. Now I had complete control over my flying ability. This was ecstasy. Not only did I have an absence of any physical discomfort, but I also had a total absence of physical awareness. My muscles did not tire when I waved my arms to gain speed. If I was traveling fast in the sky, I guess I should have been cold, but I had no awareness of being cold. I was enjoying refreshing comfort.

I felt magical wonder in every cell in my body. I have come to believe that this happened in my spiritual body because I was unconscious all this time. But this sensation of flying is something that is hard to forget. It was completely different from a dream of flying.

This wondrous experience ended all too quickly. I felt myself being pulled down toward the ground. How disappointing it was to become aware of my heavy body, to know that my arms were not wings. After experiencing ecstasy in an unbound spiritual body, I sadly felt the limitations of my physical body again.

The disappointment instantly woke me up.

My head was not functioning normally. My mind felt vacant. I was numb. I was lying on what seemed to be a table. I could see that I was in a huge room surrounded by circular windows that allowed dim light to filter in. There was no furniture that I could see, just a lot of funny-looking machines.

Something was wrong. I frantically tried to push myself up, but I couldn't move. Against my wishes, I felt myself becoming sleepy. Thoughts of flying again entered my mind. I told myself that I might wake up and find myself back in the beautiful fields.

I don't remember flying again, and I don't know how long I was asleep, but when I woke up, I was still lying on the table. I hadn't gone anywhere. Now I became aware of electronic vibrations that seemed to be coursing through my body. If this wasn't a dream, how was I ever going to get home?

When I tried to sit up, however, my body felt weak, as if my muscles hadn't been used in months. My body felt like a tree trunk. Something about this room made me feel heavy. My head felt strange. I felt no emotion, no fear.

Slowly, I sat up and looked around the room. It seemed to have more breadth than height, and it was filled with unfamiliar equipment. Our village had very few electrical machines (not even washing machines), and because I had so little exposure to the industrialized world, I had no idea what this equipment might be, with its lights blinking on and off. The ambient light that filtered in through the windows around the room was a dull silver-white, but the lights on the panels of the machines looked like a Christmas display. Otherwise, the dark room lacked color.

My mother had warned me not to venture too far from home. But I *had* gone very far. I was sure I was in big trouble now. How long had I been asleep? I had to get home!

When I slid off the side of the table, my legs were hardly strong enough to hold me up. And even if I had the strength to run away, where could I run to? I saw no doors in that room full of machines.

FACE TO FACE WITH OTHER BEINGS

Then I saw them. They were standing maybe eight feet away from me, but they had been so still, so quiet, that I hadn't noticed them. Maybe I had mistaken them for part of the room.

My heart almost stopped. They were tall and slim, yet sturdy in build. And they were not Japanese. I had never seen people like them before. In fact, I had never seen any foreigners, and at age six, I had never heard of aliens. I must say that these people looked nothing like the aliens we see in books and movies today, nothing like those child-size beings with big heads and strange eyes that Hollywood dreams up. Had they looked like those beings, I would have been greatly frightened. My first impression was that they were human. I would say that the aliens I was seeing were more Caucasian than Asian, though I make this guess because of their height and structure. Their appearance was not threatening, even though they were staring at me in an unblinking silence and there were no smiles on their faces. Their appearance and clothes were the same grayish silver as the room. They wore clothes that were tight on their bodies, like a second skin. The material of their clothing looked like soft, shiny metal. They were all about the same height. I did not see any hair on their heads and bodies. Maybe their skintight clothes also covered their heads. It was difficult to tell where their clothes ended and their skin began. The lack of light prevented me from seeing them clearly. I didn't count them, but I think there were perhaps ten of them, and I think all of them were male. I say this because they carried themselves in a strict, authoritative, no-nonsense stance, something I associate with men.

I guess I should have been scared. I was far away from home, alone in a strange place, surrounded by aliens. Yet I don't recall feeling any fear. I'm not sure if my calmness was due to their nonthreatening demeanor or something else, perhaps the vibration I'd felt while lying on the table. Or perhaps it was the innocence of childhood. Children can often trust adults without knowing better. I had not been taught to distrust strangers and had not yet experienced the ugliness of people who wished to do me harm. I didn't know why, but their presence was so calming that I felt I didn't have to be afraid of them.

Who were these people? I had seen pictures of people from America, India, and Africa in books and knew people had different-colored skin and hair. But these people...I couldn't compare them to anyone I'd read about. They must have come from a country I hadn't learned about in school.

As I stared, one of them took a step forward, very slowly and calmly, and then he extended his hand toward me. When his palm was facing on me, suddenly I felt peaceful, as if I were hypnotized. I wanted to ask the obvious questions: "Who are you? Where am I?" I don't know if I actually asked anything, but to this day, I remember what I heard.

We have come from a faraway place.

He spoke Japanese! I didn't expect them to talk to me in my native tongue. When he spoke, I could hardly see movement on his face. I did not notice if he had a tongue or teeth.

We have traveled to Earth with a special purpose.

What? Traveled to Earth? My six-year-old mind knew nothing about basic astronomy. Did they really come from so far away? Now I understood why they looked so different.

This may sound funny, but I thought they were rather nice-looking and I also thought they were middle-aged, neither old nor young. By now, I wasn't sure if they were human or not.

The being spoke again. *We've known you for a long time, Kayoko* [my Japanese name].

He knows my name! How could they know me? At that moment, I experienced some fear. I knew I had never met them before. And "for a long time"? How was that possible? I was only six years old. My head started spinning. At that moment, I believed they somehow knew me better than I knew myself. That was a scary thought! Even more mystifying was my distinct notion that I also knew them. That was the oddest feeling I would ever have. Where and how had I met them before?

He spoke again. *We are contacting other beings. We are here to guide and help you.*

My imagination was going wild and not necessarily in a good way. Back home, I had a special instructor who came to my home to teach me to play the violin. My mother had told me, "We are getting an instructor. You must respect him and be well behaved because he is coming from far away to help you."

Now here I was, being told by these tall persons that they had also come from far away, that they, too, were here to guide and help me. What were they teaching me? Then I began to wonder—did my mother have something to do with this?

My mother brought her children up with Christian values. I began to wonder if religious teaching was the motivation here. Maybe this was not an accidental encounter. Maybe it had been planned. But by whom? I knew about heaven and earth, and these beings said they were not from earth, so they must have come from heaven. Mother had been always praying to God for help. He must have sent these men to me. That could be the only explanation for my encounter with these beings. Now I knew I really must behave well. I looked at them with awe. I felt a great benevolence emanating from them.

I had learned about angels and heaven. I could tell these beings were not from earth, but they didn't look like the pictures of angels. I wanted to ask if they were servants of angels, but I do not remember if I asked or not. Then I heard something from one of the beings even though I didn't see him move his mouth. It was as if I could hear what he was thinking before he spoke. Something peculiar happened. I felt like I'd gone to a different world. I was immersed in memories of something I had forgotten long ago. I seemed to be experiencing an ancient time. And then suddenly, I lost consciousness.

Then I heard a clear voice that brought me back to myself.

WE WILL BE BACK

With no recollection of how it happened, I suddenly found myself back in the forest near the river where I had been walking before I was taken. I opened my eyes and found myself standing there, my mind vacant. I had no idea how long I'd been gone, though I was aware of how weak I felt. I felt pressure inside my head. My entire body felt different, though I didn't feel any pain. I fell to the ground. The words *We will be back* was so clear to my ears.

My first thought—as I believe anyone's first thought in such a situation would be—was, *Did I dream all that? Had I fallen asleep? Did I fall down? Hit my head?* I touched my head. It felt fine.

My mind was in a state of chaos. I knew *something strange, something inexplicable, had happened to me.* Random thoughts collided with one another like spilled water. Soon, a volcano of memories erupted inside my brain. The never-before-seen beings. The strange room. The funny machines with all their blinking lights. That weird tingling I'd felt in my body. I looked around. Where were those tall, silver beings? How had they sent me back to the field? In my mind, I could still see the room and its machines. I looked around. Surrounding me were the yellow flowers I remembered. Only a short time ago, I had been with strange beings in their machinery room. At least, I thought it was a short time ago. I looked up at the sun ducking behind the clouds. Was it still Sunday afternoon? I felt like I had been in that room for a long time. I had also slept. Was it tomorrow? My father and mother were going to be so angry with me. I started to walk home, slowly because I needed to piece together everything I remembered before I walked in the front door.

I had just met people not of this earth, beings who said they were my friends and were guiding and helping me. I had never before had adult friends. All my friends were my age. Suddenly, I felt like I was grown up. I had learned so much, more than I had ever learned in school, or ever could learn. I consider this a sort of enlightenment that my six-year-old sensibility understood but could not articulate. I had been given knowledge without being consciously aware of it. Yes, I felt wise beyond my years.

Bit by bit, more of my memories were coming back. I recalled the words I had heard. There were not many words, but I felt I had learned a lot from them. I knew something very important thing had happened to me. Was there anything missing in my memory? There must have been much more I'd heard, but as soon as I came close to grasping it, I lost it again. What was most important, what I remember most clearly, was that these friends, these old friends who remembered me from long ago, who came to help me, had said *they would be back.*

Now I felt unabashed joy. I liked these beings. I could not be happier. I'd had some scary moments in their room, yet this new, exciting adventure made up for some strange physical feelings. I made up my mind that what had happened was too real to be anything but real.

I was buoyant, filled with energy. I couldn't wait to get home to tell this exciting experience. My pace quickened. As I entered my backyard, I could see my mother through the kitchen window. She looked as busy as usual, preparing dinner, not looking like a mother frantic over a missing child. *Good*, I thought. It was still

Sunday. I had not been gone longer than normal. Now I could tell the whole family about my wonderful adventure.

I ran into the kitchen. Mother was standing at the counter, chopping vegetables. I was out of breath and taking gulps of air as I spoke.

"Mom—guess what happened today!"

She didn't even look up from the vegetables. "You're late. Hurry up. Take a bath."

"Mom, listen! I met some people who came from another world and became friends with them."

"What are you talking about? Father has come back from his trip. We will have dinner soon. Take your bath."

"I will, but I have to tell you this first! They are adult men. They've known me for a long time. They came to me for a special purpose and said they would guide me. And they said they'll be back."

Mother never moved away from the counter. I asked if I could have a glass of water. She stopped cutting the vegetables long enough to give me a glass of water.

We are here to guide and help you. These words still echoed in my mind. I believed Mother had been involved in securing help for me from my new friends. Holding the glass of water, I waited for her to explain what kind of help I would be getting.

Then I began to wonder, *was I the only one getting help?* Or was Chizu going to get instructions too? All our lives so far, whatever I got, she got too. Maybe Kiyo, my older sister, would be excluded from their instructions. She was nine years older than me, and she was getting different tutors. Mother had not asked me if I liked the beings or not, but I was sure she would tell me to behave myself well because they had come from far away to train me.

"When did you tell them about me?" I asked my mother.

"What are you talking about?"

"You asked for help from far away, right?"

"What are you talking about?"

"The arrangement you and Father made for us."

"What arrangement?"

"For having the different people. You told me the other day that you might get another tutor for us."

She looked at me and finally noticed the grass stains on my clothes. "Did you go to the field?" she asked. "Take off those dirty clothes and wash yourself now."

She sounded a little mad at me, and I could tell she knew nothing about my encounter. I was as lost as I could be when I left the kitchen. If Mother had nothing to do with my encounter, then who had arranged it?

On my way to the bathroom, I saw Chizu sitting in the living room playing with her favorite dolls. Chizu is two years younger than me, and we often played together. Kiyo almost never played with us, though she cared for us as an older sister does. She mostly stayed by herself and studied a lot. We'd had one more sister born after Kiyo, but she had died during the war before I was born.

"Chizu," I said, "listen to what happened to me today."

I told her that if she had come along with me, she would have had the same experience. I always liked to take Chizu with me, but she never wanted to go very far. Not only that, she was much more obedient than I was. She listened to our parents and did what she was told without question. I always tried to point out to her that when we are more adventurous, exciting things can happen. What had happened to me this afternoon had been a missed opportunity for her.

Chizu hung on to my every word. I knew she was not as brave as I was, so I avoided telling her the scary parts of my adventure. But I did describe my fantastic flying experience. I told her the parts I knew would capture her interest. Even at age six, I used selective storytelling to keep Chizu as an ally.

Mother heard me talking to Chizu and came into the room and shouted to me, "I said wash up quickly."

After I took my quick bath, I saw Father in the dining room. He always had a happy face when he was holding hot sake. Dinner was the time when we related our day's events, what we did. My heart was pounding with excitement and it showed.

"What happened to you today, Kayoko?" Kiyo asked. "You look like you're ready to explode."

I saw the disgust appear on my mother's face, but I ignored it and told my family everything I remembered. I told how these beings I met were different because they came from far away. Except for Chizu, no one responded.

"People not of this earth?" Father asked after a minute. "Where are they?"

"I don't know." Not the best answer, but an honest one. "But they live far away from earth."

"Where would that be?" Kiyo asked.

"I wish I did know," I said. "I will ask next time when I meet them."

"How do they know you for a long time?"

"I thought Mother told them," I said. "They were very intelligent."

"You could hear the voice without him talking? How is that possible?"

Nothing made sense to them. I had nothing to support my claims. That's when I started to realize how hard it would be for me to convince anyone I was telling the truth. Mentioning the disk creatures and how they disappeared from inside my hands was no help at all.

"What were those creatures?" Kiyo asked.

"I don't know. I've never seen them before."

"Neither have I," she said.

"I was trying to catch one and show it to you but—"

"Yeah. They disappeared." Kiyo sounded disgusted. "She's crazy."

"You are not supposed to go to the fields," Mother finally said. "You went into the fields after lunch and took a nap. You dreamed all this."

She had a point: I often fell asleep after lunch. My weak physical condition caused me to fall asleep easily. But I had not fallen asleep in the field. Yes, I had slept in the machinery room, but what happened to me was not a dream, I knew it wasn't.

My story was soon concluded when Kiyo started to talk about something else.

I couldn't believe this was happening to me. How could a six-year-old make up such a fantastic story? Imagining a room full of electronic machines. We didn't even have television until several years later. I had never heard of science fiction.

I must admit that one reason for my family's negative response was that this was not the first time I had told them a fantastic story. Since I was only two or three years old, I had been talking about coming from another world and needing to go back. I kept saying this so often that my family was familiar with it. But what I said was true. I have always felt that I came from another world and my heart missed that world. My family obviously thought I was just telling another story like my usual ones. My parents had been encouraging me not to think and talk about fantasy worlds. Whenever I talked about something different, they tried to ignore me. They thought it wasn't healthy for me to be caught up in thoughts about nonexistent worlds. They wanted me to stay in the real world.

"They will be back!" I protested to my family. "They said they would."

With those words, I stormed out of the house and ran to the garden, where I sat on the swing and looked up at the night sky. My family's reaction disturbed me, but I was not disheartened. I looked up the starry sky and smiled. My real world transcended my home, my school, even all of Japan. Knowing my friends came from "far away" excited me. My fascination with the universe began that night.

While I believed my new friends had come from some place far away, I also believed they lived near my home. That round room with its electronic machines, I believed, was their workplace.

I could not stop thinking about them, and soon, I started thinking of them as *the others*. I tried to think in positive terms, but my parents' disbelief still crept into my mind. How could I ever convince my family?

There was one hope: Chizu. If she could come with me, be my witness, she was all I needed. She was not as excited now after seeing the reaction I'd gotten from our parents, but she agreed to come with me to the fields. To avoid another scolding, she and I made a secret agreement not to tell our family.

After school the next day, I considered skipping music practice and heading straight for the fields, but to avoid being punished, I went home and practiced the violin and the piano for thirty minutes. Chizu and I created a cacophony of shrieking on our violins. Each note I played was noise to my ears. Mother told me that I was not improving and really needed to concentrate, but I didn't care. I was consumed with the notion that my new friends, *the others*, were waiting for me.

Back in the fields after we finished practicing, Chizu and I looked for the disk creatures first. I had brought a clear, plastic bag and a net to capture them. Hours passed. We saw neither the disk creatures nor *the others*.

"Don't they know we were going to be here?" Chizu asked.

I was thinking the same thing. She was starting to become impatient, and I was worried that my friends weren't coming back, at least not today. I told her we'd wait a little longer, then we'd go home. Maybe *the others* would be waiting for us tomorrow. I hoped they would honor our patience by showing up tomorrow.

At school the next day, my mind was in a different place. *We will be back.* Their words kept echoing in my head.

Our teacher, Ms. Tada, was talking about geography or geology or something *geo-* when I heard the word *earth* come out of her mouth. *Earth.* That brought me back from my daydream. Suddenly, I was energized. I raised my hand.

"Where is the other world far away from the earth?" I heard my classmates laughing, but I didn't care. "What about life *other* than on earth?" I was persistent. "Someone lives on these stars, right?"

Now many heads turned back to the teacher. I was glad my classmates seemed to be taking an interest in my question.

Ms. Tada looked thoughtful. "What you're asking falls under astronomy, not biology," she said. "But let's go ahead and talk about astronomy for a little while."

I was glad because she took my questions seriously, even though this question had nothing to do with what she was teaching at the time. This was a different reaction than my family had given me. I liked school. I liked Ms. Tada.

"We don't know if there is life on other planets. It's hard to believe, though it is possible." She gestured at the chalkboard and all the empty space on it. "Space is huge." She drew a tiny circle. "This little ball is our planet. This big circle is the sun." She tapped the empty space around them, and said, "There are billions stars and planets that we do not know anything about. Even here, here on earth, we haven't found all life yet."

She pointed to Japan on the globe in the front of the room. "If we travel to the south by ship, many days later, we land in a country called Australia. It's like another world to us. The people there are very different looking. Most of them are taller than us and hardly anyone has black hair. They speak a different language. We cannot communicate with them. And right next to us is China." She pointed to that large land. "They look similar to us, yet the languages we speak are different."

I listened carefully to her words. I was wondering how *the others* looked so different, yet could speak Japanese.

The bell rang, and my classmates started to spill out of the classroom.

"Ms. Tada," I said, "is it possible for someone from far away from earth to come here? I know we can't go to them, but if they are smarter than us, can they somehow visit us?"

"I don't know," she replied. "I'm not qualified to answer that.

"If they did visit us, could they speak Japanese?"

"I don't think so." She smiled at me.

Now she had me feeling uncertain. *The others* had spoken to me in Japanese. I had understood them perfectly. Perhaps, I thought, they might have learned Japanese while they were here. I just thanked my teacher and left quickly.

Though Chizu had been somewhat put off by the failure of *the others* to show themselves, she was also eager to go to the field a second time in the hope that they'd arrive today. She had asked Mother to put a ribbon in her hair today. I suppose that when I told her I thought they were good-looking, she wanted to be equally good-looking for them.

Our second day's search for the disk creatures was not successful. They really didn't matter very much, though; *the others* were the ones who said they'd come back. We kept looking up at the sky. Chizu even called out for them to come down to us.

I told her not to yell. "They were adults, quiet persons. They came to guide me. I think you were also included. We must show them respect." Deep inside, I wanted to scream out too. As I saw the sun approaching the horizon, I started to worry that they might not come again. Then I began to wonder where their home on earth was. If I knew where they lived, I could visit them.

Next few days, I led Chizu to different parts of the fields. I also started to feel that I should expand my search and go into the forbidden forest. The Shakujii River flowed at the edge of the forest, as if it were a final barrier. But rivers have always attracted me. I didn't mind crossing rivers, but I knew that was one place where Chizu would refuse to go.

It was the last time my sister came with me, and I was disappointed. By the end of the week, my own confidence was waning. When they said they were going to return, I thought it would be soon. In a few days. A week at most. I would not stop making myself available to *the others* to come back, but I was losing my original fervor. I looked out the window at the night sky and asked them to come to my house. Or just to leave me a note telling me where to meet them. I couldn't keep going to the fields. The June rainy season started. And then, the hot summer arrived.

So far, Chizu was the only person on my side. I had not told my other playmates and classmates about my adventure, but now my thinking was starting to change. If I told my friends, I would have more witnesses. The more the better. I decided to ask my friends to make an expedition to the forest with me, but then I changed my mind, because now I was becoming angry at *the others*. They seemed to have forgotten me. Chizu knew I was still going to the fields in search of *the others* when the weather permitted, and she often asked me what had happened. What could I tell her?

As weeks turned into months, my excitement faded. Though I trusted them, even without knowing them well, I started to feel waves of disappointment at being deceived.

ENCOUNTER IN THE FOREST

Because of our health problems, Mother often took Chizu and me to the clinic. I remember one day when Kiyo took us because Mother was busy. The clinic was located on the outskirts of the forest, about a forty-minute walk down a dirt path between the rice fields and the edge of the forest.

In times past, whenever I had walked along this path, I could not help but wonder about the mysteries inside the forbidden forest.

On our way back from the clinic on this day, the forest captured my attention. Looking at the tall trees, I felt like they were drawing me closer to them. Suddenly, I heard someone calling to me. I stood still and listened.

"What are you doing there?" Kiyo asked. She came to get me and pulled on my hand.

"Can you take me inside the forest?" I asked her.

"You know we cannot go there."

"Just a little bit?"

"No. There is nothing fun in there. Only scary things."

"Like what?"

"Bats," she said. "I'm afraid of bats."

"Can we stay here for a little while?"

My older sister was becoming annoyed. "Why?"

Now my younger sister spoke up. "Kayoko is looking for aliens,"

"Oh, no. *Please.*"

"Just a little while?" I begged. "Please?"

She relented. "Just a few minutes. But don't go into the forest!"

My sisters left me alone and went to pick small flowers growing on the other side of the path. I went a little closer to the edge of the forest. I knew something was in there.

Then I heard Kiyo calling me again. "Do you want to stay there alone in the dark? We're going home."

We started to walk toward our home, but to this day, I have not forgotten the uncanny feeling I had standing near the trees. I was quiet all the way home.

A few days later, something else happened. It was a miserably hot September evening, and I was alone in the small playground near my house. We were told to not go outside during the day because many children were getting sunstroke. After a painful hour at the violin, I had escaped, if only for a little while. I was adding the finishing touches to a sandcastle I was building in the sandbox when I closed my eyes and imagined the prince coming from the castle. I opened my eyes.

There was no castle. No sandbox. I looked all around me. I was standing in the midst of bushes and trees, as if I had been dropped there. There was no path, no clear way to get into or out of this place. *Where was I?*

The air felt cool on my skin, which made me think I was in a forest. But what forest? Despite thoughts of going to look for *the others* in the forest by my home, I had never ventured there. It was forbidden. The rice fields in the village were tended by farmers, but the forest remained wild and uncultivated. Even the bamboo trees in the forest were left untouched, and bamboo shoots were an important food in Japan.

If this was the forbidden forest, I was in big trouble. I had been playing peacefully in a sandbox, and now without having taken a single step, I was standing in the middle of nowhere. This was inconceivable. But this was not the time to sit down and consider my quest. If I didn't get out, I might be in real trouble. I heard birds flapping their wings. Their cries were sounds I had never heard before.

"Can anyone hear me?" I screamed and screamed.

No one answered. I was alone, lost in the forest. I panicked. I started to walk, pushing through the underbrush, having no idea where I was going. Anything was better than just standing there, even though I might have been going further into the forest. The thick foliage kept this place in perpetual darkness. The heavy layer of leaves made it difficult for me to walk. It seemed as if the forest did not want me to leave. Tears welled up in my eyes.

What if it got dark before I got out of there? Would I spend the night here, uninvited, a lost child, undesired, or worse, desired by the animals that come out at night? Fear captured me. I pushed myself in the direction of sunlight, any light. Passing another bush, I looked up to see what new obstacle I had to fight to get past.

That's when I saw someone standing in the distance among the trees and bushes. I didn't know how I'd gotten here, but with God's help, I had found someone. I was so relieved.

"Hello!" I called out. I walked faster toward him.

The person just stood there. I called again. There was no sign of a response. There was no movement. As I got closer, even though he was still too far away for me to clearly see his face, it hit me who this was. One of *the others*! I was thankful to find someone who could help me. Seeing one of *the others* was the last thing I could have imagined, but this was unmistakably the being who had spoken to me. It was him, I knew it was. They were back! No, I was back. They were here all the time. The forest was their home. I knew it! They had brought me to them again.

He stood alone. My tears of desperation turned to tears of joy.

Though I was bursting with joy, he didn't look glad to see me. Then he held out his hands, palms toward me, just as he had in that round room. I felt a pleasant warmth pass through me and immediately calmed down.

I knew now it was *him*, the one who had brought me here. I should have known that that was the reason why I was suddenly no longer in the sandbox. Only *the others* could do such things. But this was different. I had not flown, had not spiraled through a straw as I had the first time. This was a different form of travel, one I didn't understand. I didn't have to understand it. They were super beings who came from far away. Their ability to do things was beyond human knowledge. I didn't know if an adult could understand their ways, so how could I? I was glad to be outside during this encounter and not in that round room full of machines. This time, I would stay wide awake and remember everything.

By the time I reached him, he had lowered his hands. I saw a clearing behind him in the distance, a big, open field. It was bright. There were no trees. This image has always been starkly clear in my memory. I believed this had to be the place where these people lived and worked. I didn't see their workplace with the machinery room, but I thought it must be close by.

ANCIENT MEMORY

Suddenly, I didn't feel like a little girl anymore. I should be older, as old as the wisdom I had acquired. This was the same strange sensation I'd felt in their machinery room. This sensation is hard to explain because it was so different from any other feelings I'd ever had, but something that seemed to involve huge, long, ancient memories. I felt like I was immersed in a different time again, as if I were transported into some other world, sometimes in the past. My eyes implored him to take me with him to his world, to not leave me behind. How much I had longed and waited for him to come. I knew this was the reason he had come to me from far away from the earth. I belonged to his world. Yes, that was my true home. I should not be on earth. It was at that moment I realized that not one word had been spoken all this time. My friend and I communicated without words. I closed my eyes just as the tears spilled forth. I was deliriously happy.

When I opened them, I was looking at bright light coming through the branches of the trees. As the light of the setting sun hit my eyes and blinded me, I covered my eyes and turned away. I did not know what happened afterwards, but when my vision cleared I found myself standing alone in the same rice field near the forest where I had seen the disk creatures.

My friend was gone.

I suppose I should have felt shock and confusion. I should have asked myself if I had been dreaming. But I knew I had not been dreaming. This was real. I had the intelligence on my side. If this had been a dream, I would have awakened in the sandbox in the playground. I still remembered the big clearing I'd seen in the forest. I had no way of knowing that place unless I'd been inside the forest. But again, I had no proof to show that my friends had come back and taken me to the forest from the playground and then left me somewhere else.

It was a puzzle. I lay down on the grass and looked up at the sky to calm my mind. I thought about the disk creatures. They were puzzling. They instantly moved from one place to another in no time.

One thing became clear to me. This place near the forest was the home of *the others*. That was the reason why the adults always told us to stay away. I could not say for sure, but I think something must have happened in the forest that made it off-limits. I had finally learned the true reason for my obsession with this dark, forbidden forest. No one else was interested in it, but now it was clear that my curiosity was not merely childish interest in an adventure. In my heart, I knew something was there. And I was right. My instinct was right. *They* had been calling me. I must have been hearing my friend's silent voice. The voice from the forest was *him*. My curiosity had been about *the others*. Even years before I met them, even when I knew nothing about them, secretly, somewhere in my heart, I knew them. I also understood my attraction to the rice fields. The fields had led me to *the others*.

They said that they had known me for a long time. Maybe I had been their child once. That would explain the reason they came to me and would guide me. But my friend did not take me home to his world. This made me very sad. When I asked him to take me, I heard, *Not yet*.

This was the first time I ever heard these words, *Not yet*. But I would hear them later in my life. Almost every time I saw their vehicle, I would scream, "Take me with you." Their reply was always *Not yet*.

I was disappointed and contented at the same time. My friends had kept their word. As promised, they had returned. My trust in them was serious.

That was a great discovery of personal growth. Though I was dying to share my experience, the more I thought about it, the more discouraged I became. This was stranger than last time. My story this time included the forbidden forest. I decided that I better not tell anyone.

I went home, and later, I went with my family to an amusement park where the Buddhist festival called Obon was taking place. Obon is a religious celebration of the deceased that is held every year on the evening of the full moon in September. Families wearing their casual kimonos bring flowers, incense, and food to the shrine in the temple. Lanterns fill the park, and there are games for the children—puppet shows, cotton candy, and other happy things. There was music and people dancing. The Obon festival was always fun, but this year, nothing appealed to me.

My mind was filled with *the others*, with my otherworldly friend, who had opened up the new world to me. This was the world I had forgotten, but now it was suddenly brought back to my consciousness. This was a grown-up feeling, something I felt only twice, only when I was with *the others*. I realized that when I was with *the others*, I was a different person, and I possessed powers I never knew I had. That's why I did not feel I was a little girl. This was reincarnation, but not human reincarnation. I was not human. And the world I really lived on was not the earth.

Since that day, and even to this day, this memory is still in me and ruling my life.

Uisiting Golden World

If my encounters with the beings from another world had happened later in my life, if I had been an adult, my reaction would have been very different. As adults, we rationalize the things that happen to us. We seek to explain and understand what we consider to be "not normal." Reasoning is not, however, fully developed in a child's mind nor are they as suspicious as adults. Something that may be an unbelievable fantasy to an adult is often accepted as reality to a child. As a six-year old child, I appreciated the world through a child's eyes and from a child's point of view and did so with wonder and amazement. I took the encounter in the forest as part of my life and never knew it was unusual until years later. I made no judgment and had no expectations. I just accepted.

What happened in the forest was unimaginable. But my later experiences went far beyond any storybook tale I had ever heard. When I look back at my life, I think that this next otherworldly event must have been the whole purpose of my encounters with aliens. It must have been planned for some reason by some *other* intelligence. Perhaps it was God's plan for me. After my first encounter with *the others*, my life began moving in a direction I would have never imagined.

Mother often read to us, and there is one Japanese fairy tale that I remember very well. This is "Urashima Taro" a story in which a man whose name is Urashima Taro finds a utopian land under the ocean. Although the story was written in a style for children, it appears in one of the important classical Japanese books, the *Mannyoushu*, which is a collection of Japanese stories that date to AD 720. It is said to be a true story.

Urashima was born in the eighth century in the Kagawa district on the third biggest island in central Japan. The Kagawa district faces the inner sea between the biggest main islands and is not too far from Kyoto. The children's story tells us that a turtle takes Urashima to the sea god's palace. Urashima helped the turtle earlier, and so the turtle comes back to thank him by inviting him to the palace. He rides on the turtle's back as the turtle swims under the ocean and takes him to the fantastic heavenly world where beautiful fairy beings live.

Although all the books that tell this story relate it to the sea, adult books say it is a ship that takes Urashima to utopia and that the sea palace is not under the water but beyond the ocean. Many books also connect the story with UFOs and say that unearthly beings are on the ship. Those beings are described as servants of the palace. The children's book says that the turtle is a queen of the palace who changed her figure in order to come to earth.

Who would expect to see a fantasy world coming to life? I still do not understand precisely what happened to me, just as I have never understood the event in the forest. But the fact is that my subsequent otherworldly experiences have ruled my entire life. Both my career and my spiritual understanding have been built on what I learned on the other world.

After my experience in the forest, I did not go to the field as often as I had before. The fields were too far away for everyday activity. But one day, I had had an awful day at school, having failed the audition for the school's Christmas concert. I played both piano and violin, but I was not selected. One of my classmates did not even have a piano at home, yet she passed the audition. After all the musical education I had received, I was still not good enough even for the school concert. I felt terrible about myself. I didn't want to go home.

It was Saturday, a beautiful autumn day. After school lunch I took the long walk to the field. My thoughts turned to my friends, *the others*. I was still clinging to the hope that they would return to me and take me to their world. Once I reached the field, I stood still and looked up at the sky.

Competition is not for you.

The voice came from the sky. This was the first time I heard something like this, but I would hear this same voice again. It always comes from high above my head and only when I am alone. The voice always gives me some message. On that day in my childhood, however, I knew immediately that this voice was him, one of *the others*.

Competition is not for you.

These words literally moved me. I suddenly found myself back in the huge machinery room I had visited before. This time, I had no feeling of being sucked into the sky. It was more like the way I had been taken to the forest. But again, I was afflicted by the same drowsiness. I knew I had been asleep.

This time the room was brightly lit. I thought it must be nighttime outside for the room to have so much artificial light. I tried to look around, but the bright light prevented me from seeing very much. And I still couldn't keep my eyes open. Last time I was here, I could barely see *the others* until they stepped forward, but now, even with the room brightly lit, I still couldn't see if they were here or not. I walked unsteadily to the nearest window and looked out. It was dark, as black as tar. I curled my fingers around my eyes like binoculars to shield them from the bright light, looked out again. Was this a night sky? There were no stars, no moon.

Just as I was wishing I could see something, light miraculously appeared outside the window. It happened so fast, my heart nearly stopped.

What I saw was a golden world. My view was saturated with gold. Shining, dazzling gold. Within seconds, as if my eyes were a camera, the view zoomed in. Now I could see details. I was looking at a huge, widespread expanse, bigger than any city or field I had ever seen. Here was a city of gold! Everything was brilliantly golden. Even the sky appeared golden, as if the city glowed so much with the gold that it filled the air. My jaw dropped. I could not speak. There was no one to talk to, but even if there had been I had no voice to express what I felt.

And that is the last thing I remember of that visit. At that moment, everything stopped. I suspect I was awake for just a few minutes, but it was probably less, before I started to succumb to drowsiness. It was spreading through my body. But who could sleep while coming face-to-face with heaven? That's what this place had to be. *Heaven.* I had been told heaven was impossible to imagine. But, this was it and it was truly unimaginable. Falling asleep was the last thing I wanted to do, but I couldn't help it. Since that day, falling asleep at a crucial time has always been a concern of mine.

And so I slept. I thought maybe I was dreaming. I must have been dreaming.

And I woke up refreshed, as from a much-needed nap. I was fully conscious, my senses were heightened, and my physical being, every part of my body, had changed dramatically. I had never felt so wonderful. It was as though I didn't have a body. For me, this lack of any physical awareness defined perfection.

MY SHANGRI-LA VISION

Next, I found myself actually standing in that beautiful, shining, golden city. The first thing that struck my eyes again was that unexplainable color. When I saw it from above, the city appeared completely golden. But now, up close, it was not exactly all gold. I could see a dozen variations of orange, purple, all the colors of the rainbow, plus exotic colors like turquoise, emerald, aquamarine. Yet it all seemed to be brushed with gold. The colors were more transparent than solid. But how could that be? This place had to be solid. I was standing in it. A better description would be to say that the color itself was somehow solid, like a light bulb is solid, though from a distance, it appeared to be a ball of light. It was also similar to the feel of a kaleidoscope that has some depth. And the bright lights here were not harsh, but extremely comfortable and soft to look at. It was very different from the bright light that had filled the machinery room.

Another way to describe this city might be to call it a manifestation of Shangri-La, the secret city in James Hilton's novel "Lost Horizon". As I stood there, I remembered the story of Urashima. I thought that was fiction. But was I wrong? If that sea god's palace existed, then this golden Shangri-La might really exist too. *It does exist*, I said to myself. *I am looking at it now.* Maybe fairy tales and legends are based on some truths.

And the buildings! They were all huge. Their architecture was beyond human imagination. Some of the buildings looked partly faded, as if instead of a roof, the top opened up then blended into the golden atmosphere. The roofs of other buildings looked like they extended into the sky, staircases to heaven. In the distance, I saw huge round buildings suspended in the air. Some were moving slowly and methodically. I was dumbfounded.

And then, I noticed something round hovering in the sky, not nearly as big as the buildings. And it didn't look like it was made entirely of color like the city did. It had circular windows. Yes—it was the room I had just been in. It had rows of windows. I was looking up at the ship, at the workplace of *the others*! At least, I think that's what it was. This was the first time I had seen it from the outside. The first time I was inside the vehicle, I assumed it was colorless, dull silver at best, but from the outside, it looked just like the city, a kaleidoscope of colors in the shape of a golden saucer. Perhaps what I was seeing was the reflection of the light that bloomed from the city.

The others had not lied. They had said they came from far away. It was their airship that had come for me and brought me to Shangri-La. I had left my world. I was standing on the surface of another world.

Without taking my eyes from the scenery I begun walking, marveling at everything I saw. I was so excited my breathing became rapid but effortless. The air was unusually easy to breath. I knew Earth needed plants to make oxygen, yet I saw no plants, not even trees. The air felt amazingly fresh and because I was breathing such pure air, my body felt energized. My walking too was effortless. I felt almost lifted up, as if some kind of compressed power had entered me, pushing me upwards as if floating. Maybe, I thought, gravity here was not as heavy as gravity on earth. I was feeling rapturous, renewed, energetic, ecstatic. Yes, "ecstasy" is the word that best describes what I felt. I was so thrilled by my surroundings, and feeling so healthy that I wished to stay here forever.

Where I was standing must have been in the center of the enormous city. As immense as it was, however, I had no feeling of being crowded. It was spacious. But then, it occurred to me that I saw no people or animals walking around. How strange! Where were they? It was quiet and calm, yet the city was alive and vibrant.

What kind of intelligence could have built such an artistic golden city? If some beings had constructed this city, it meant their technology had to be more advanced than ours on earth.

Soon, I did see some beings. And they were not like *the others* at all. I began to see many stunningly beautiful beings, maybe fifty or more, floating in the distance. Every one of them wore a soft, flowing gown. I cannot say they were gaseous creatures, but they seemed to project a kind of glow, an aura that if captured on film would look like a mist or a haze. I intuitively felt they were highly developed spiritually. They were heavenly creatures.

THE TEACHINGS OF THE HIGHER BEINGS

I must have entered a gate or door without noticing one, for I now found myself inside a huge hall. I did not see a ceiling. Perhaps no roof existed or it was too high for me to see or maybe it was transparent and blended into the atmosphere. I could see the outside, and what I saw seemed to be nature. It seemed as if the huge city and nature somehow overlay each other. I started to wonder how I could be in the middle of a city and see nature outside or around it. I had walked only a short time, or at least that's how it seemed to me. But then I thought I might have been instantaneously transported to some other location, just as I had been in the forest.

The scenery was heavenly. I could see a lake, waterfalls, and a river winding across the hillside. I saw beautiful birds in the sky that seemed to be diaphanous, like so much of this golden world. The atmosphere was dreamy, almost transparent yet filled with brilliant colors. As I was gazing at it, I felt a power arising out of it. Something about it inspired me, made me feel exalted. I felt I was being instilled with wisdom and even a degree of genius.

In that moment, one of angelic beings, a male, began talking to me. *We are high, spiritual beings that abide in a totally different realm*, he said. *We possess abilities that allow us to see the past, the present, and the future. We can also see the progression of the universe. There are many beings that exist in this universe. Our spiritual level determines our next destination. Our purpose is for the enlightenment of others, to bring them to a higher state of being. We will be guiding you.*

I gazed up at this angelic being with awe but also with some confusion. I understood his words, but all I could think was, *I'm only a little girl, barely able to make it through school.*

That very day, I had failed my audition at school, and next, I had felt endowed with a level of genius, but now, I was experiencing a feeling of inferiority. *The others* on their ship said that they had come to guide me. I felt grateful to be receiving such guidance, but I had no idea how to process what was happening to me. While I was thinking these thoughts, the angelic being spoke again.

There are projects that you need to work on for your purpose in this life. Your life will not be easy. Therefore, we will help you.

I became keenly aware that I understood this with a perception beyond my years. If I had had the same experience as an adult, I might have been overwhelmed, and worried about my difficult life and all that might now be expected of me. But the fact is that, somehow, I understood it then much better than I do today. *And that is the mystery.* I did not feel that I was an ineffectual little girl. I felt confident. In retrospect, I think that perhaps I was imbued with this confidence by some sort of telepathy or hypnosis, much like I had experienced with *the others.* What I remembered most clearly—what I remember to this day—is that I was told again that I would be receiving the help.

I also can never forget these words of this angelic being:

You have something you are obligated to do.

Even though I never said one word to the angelic being, I felt a deeper communication with him than with the beings I had seen on the ship. I felt that these new beings cared about me. The words this angelic being said to me took root in the deepest recesses of my soul. This was something that could never be changed.

On that day and without my knowledge, my path through life was laid out.

I RETURN HOME: PROBLEMS WITH FAMILY AND FRIENDS

We will be back.

That is the last thing I remember.

When I opened my eyes again, I was standing in the same open field as before when I had been transported to the golden city. The vision of the golden city was still flashing in my eyes. I was not able to make sense of anything. My head was groggy. I had to sit down and rest. When I saw sunset approaching, however, I forced myself to stand up, but halfway up, I fell back down and landed on my tailbone. Ouch! Gravity was pulling at me. The ground was hard. I was still feeling the sensation of the lesser gravity of the other world. I had never thought about gravity till this day, but now, I had something to relate it to my physical body. I felt a little pain in my bottom. That brought me back to earthly reality.

I was still feeling the perfect health I'd experienced in the other world but I realized that now, back on earth, my physical body would not remain as it had been in the other world. I still could not remember everything that had happened to me, at least not with my mind. But my body remembered it: I found myself having difficulty breathing because of the difference in the air.

The city! The golden city. The colors! I was remembering more and more. *Angels! The words of the angelic beings. Words spoken to me.* Something to do with a spiritual path. Yes, now I remembered that they had said they would help me. That I had something to do. That I had a mission. I didn't remember what that mission was, but I was sure I would remember later.

We will be back. These words echoed in my head. These were the words of *the others*. Did I see *the others* from the ship again? I didn't remember. What had happened to me?

All this was too confusing for me. I covered my head with both arms and closed my eyes and struggled to pull my thoughts together. When I opened my eyes again, what I saw was the brown earth in front of me. That's when I knew I had gone to another world. *I knew it.* That golden world was not the earth. But where was it? I remembered a lecture from school in which my teacher had said if a ship kept sailing south from Japan, it would arrive in Australia, which she had said was 'another world'. But I knew it wasn't the golden world that I had visited.

The others had taken me, just like they had taken me to the forest. That must be it! I thought that round room was the workplace of *the others,* but it was their ship. I had seen their ship hovering in the sky. The ship of *the others* must have taken me there, wherever that world was. There was no question about it. *The others* had taken me to the golden world. I could not think of anything else. Just a minute ago, I had seen a clear space in the forest from above. That's what I saw when I met *the others* in the forest. Then I remembered that I had seen the golden city from above. There was no mistake. I had been flying!

I looked at the setting sun. I felt like I had been gone for days. My family must be worried sick about me. But I didn't care how long I was gone. I had visited another world!

All of a sudden, I started to get angry. Why had I come back to this village in Japan? Why could I not stay in the golden world? I looked around. I couldn't see anything nice here, just the plain yellow rice fields. Their yellow color took my mind back to that shining golden world. Here on earth, we have flat, one-dimensional colors, but the other world emanated light and the colors had depth. I used to think this rice field was a heavenly place, but it no longer attracted me. How, I asked myself, could I keep living here after seeing that amazing golden world?

Just a little while ago, I had been moving freely without any restriction, but now, gravity had taken over my body and my walking felt heavy and clumsy. My small steps moved so slowly.

I began comparing the two worlds. Somehow, I felt much more natural in their world than I did here, where I had lived for all of my seven years. It was a strange feeling not to be in their world. But I had been sent back. Now I had to face my earthbound reality. I had to regain my balance and rush home. I had no idea how long I had been gone. I had to think about how I would explain my absence.

I thought again about the story of Urashima. After he had stayed in the sea palace for a while, he began to worry about his family and decided to go back home. But when the turtle took him back to his home, he did not recognize anything. The land on which his house had stood was deserted. He didn't see anyone he knew. As in the American story of Rip van Winkle, Urashima learned that many years had passed. Time in the palace, he realized, was different from ordinary time. I thought about time too, and as I passed through fields, I looked carefully at the houses. I was relieved to see the same houses I knew from yesterday. I was not happy to be back on earth to begin with, but if I couldn't find my home, that would be a catastrophe. Everything looked the same. By the time I reached home, I felt better. Now only one thing concerned me. Was my whole family still alive?

"I'm home," I called out as I entered the garden. I rushed into the kitchen.

"You're late," my mother said in her normal voice. "I was about to ask your friends if you were still with them. Father is taking a bath now," she added. "You can take your bath after dinner."

I was surprised to hear this, but it proved that I had left this world and gone to another one and come home all on the same day.

"You didn't go too far away, I hope," Mother said.

"Did you know I went far away?" I asked her.

"You were gone all afternoon," she said. "Were you with Tetsuko? You haven't practiced the violin today. You will practice twice as long tomorrow after Sunday school."

I normally spent Saturday afternoon with my friends but I had to come back by the evening for musical practice. Then I remembered—I had failed the audition. I decided I would tell her about it after I told her my fantastic story. She might allow me to stop playing violin.

I went out to the garden and sat on the swing. I should have been excited about my fabulous experience, but I was confused. I needed to be clear about the many things in my head, especially the time issue. It seemed to me as though I had been away for days, but it must have been only six hours.

Urashima had stayed for a long time with the angelic beings in the sea palace. I wanted to stay in the golden city, but I had met the angels right away. When the angel talked to me, I was no longer enjoying myself. Urashima had all sorts of amusements that I didn't have. I was sure that was the reason I came back so fast. I had to solve this puzzle with my child's brain. Maybe it wasn't meant for me to know any more than my special purpose. I started to swing. Urashima's story said that the turtle was actually a queen of the sea palace. She changed her form and came to see the earth. Were *the others* the ethereal beings of the golden world? When they came to earth, did they change? I did not understand the connection between *the others* and the angels. There were just too many questions.

As I ate my dinner with a big appetite, I kept silently rehearsing my story. Mother noticed how much I ate.

"You skipped your snack today," she said. "Did you eat with your friend?"

"No," I answered.

In the story, Urashima ate fantastic food in the sea palace, but I had eaten nothing in the other world. I wondered why they had not fed me.

I waited after my family finished telling all their stories for the day. I needed more time to digest my story. I still could not believe what had happened to me, but I sort of expected that someone in my family would be able to explain it. Maybe my parents had had a similar experience. When Mother asked me why I was so quiet, I took a big breath and started to talk.

"Today, I went to another world. Just like Urashima Taro—"

"Oh, no, not again!" Kiyo cut me off.

Had I started the wrong way? I knew no other way to start, so I just told the truth. She said *not again*, but this time was entirely different. I ignored her and continued.

"The story of Urashima must be a true story," I said, "because today, I saw a place just like the sea god's palace. But the world I saw was not under the sea. It was the sky god's palace. Beautiful angels were flying there, just like the angels Urashima saw. Not only that, but buildings were also flying. The angels talked to me. They are very intelligent, and they said they will help me too, just like *the others* said they would." I paused.

"Is that it?" Kiyo asked.

She must have wanted to hear more. Silence filled the room. My family seemed to be fascinated. Maybe they needed some time to digest what I had said.

Finally, Chizu broke the silence. "They came to get you?"

"Yes."

"Who are *they*?" Mother asked.

"*The others*. My friends. I told you about them."

"How did you get there?" Chizu asked. She must have been sorry to have missed this adventure.

"Urashima rode on the back of the turtle, but I flew! Do you remember the fantastic flying I told you about? But this time, the room flew."

"What are you talking about?" Father said.

"Do you feel all right?" Kiyo asked.

Then they all started talking at the same time.

"Did you fall asleep again in the field?"

"You cannot mix fairy stories with reality."

"Stop living in a fantasy world."

"Not too long ago," Mother said, "you told us you met nonhuman beings. Now are you saying you met angels?" She shook her head.

That told me that Mother had never been abducted. If she had been, she would know what I was talking about. I guessed Father hadn't either. I wondered why. Kiyo definitely had not, and Chizu was too young.

Kiyo spoke up again, "You were tricked by a fox. That's what happened to you!"

Now they all laughed.

In Japan in those days, there were many stories about raccoons and foxes that lived in the fields. It was said that they tricked us by creating phenomena. *Captured by the magic of a fox* was a common phrase used to explain strange but supposedly true events. One story recently spread through our village about a farmer who went walking in the fields on his way home. He often walked at night and he knew the path very well, but that night, he suddenly found himself on a mountain. He had no idea how he got there. He struggled to find the way home, but he could not. He spent the night there. When the sun rose the next morning, he saw a fox standing in front of him. As soon as the fox ran away, the farmer found himself in the field again. There was no mountain in sight. He claimed this mountain had been created by the fox. My friend, Terada, had also told me similar story. Her uncle, who lived in Brazil, had been tricked by raccoons. He had the same kind of phenomenon. The foxes and raccoons want to feel superior to us and enjoy making people become perplexed. So they show themselves and are delighted to take the responsibility for fooling humans. It is said that animals maintain their supernatural powers only when they live in the wild.

I protested that I had never seen a fox or a raccoon, that there was no way those animals could do such sophisticated things. Could they create heaven? Speak spiritual words and messages?

Even if I was sleeping in the machinery room on the ship, my experience could not be a dream. Dreams are fragmented, but my memory was sequential and in great depth. But how could I prove it? Again, I faced the same problem I had faced the first time I was abducted. Sharing this experience was an absolute disaster. It was worse than the first time. I had no witness to corroborate my story. I left the room, feeling humiliated by the derision of my family. This monumental day had turned into another problematic day. I had not thought that I was the only one in my family who had this kind of experience.

Well, I said to myself, if my family would not accept the truth of my abductions, then I would turn to others. Ms. Tada, my teacher, came to mind. I should have talked to her first. Then I thought it was better to have someone with me when I spoke to her. I could not look to Chizu for help any more if it meant going to another world. Our parents' negative reactions scared her. This was too important to keep to myself. I needed a witness. I had wanted to tell my friends, but I decided not to because of my uncertainty. But that was cleared up now. *The others* had come back. I now had amazing evidence.

The next day, I decided to share my experience with my playmate, Ken. He was two years younger than me, but he loved adventure. He always sought new things, just like I did. We'd always wanted to explore the forest and had talked about this, but we were never able to summon up the courage to follow through on our brave words.

After Sunday school, I found Ken on the playground and asked him if he had ever been taken to another world. At first, he didn't know what I meant, and when I explained, he said no, but the look on his face told me he wished he had. When I said there might be an opportunity for him, he was enthralled. He agreed to accompany me to the forest where we might meet *the others*. We made a pact to tell no one what we were going to do. It was like we were on a secret mission.

The river was at its lowest this time of year, so crossing it was relatively easy at. The edge of the forest, the trees looked like sentinels, guarding something forbidden. They seemed menacing, and gloomy. Were they trying to warn us? We courageously entered the forest and walked for about five minutes. I found myself holding my breath, and my palms were already sweaty. Suddenly, we heard something moving in the branches above us. We looked up just in time to see several owls swooping down on us, their menacing wings spread wide as if to prove they were bigger than two little kids. I knew owls were night creatures. For them to appear in daylight was unusual. Were the owls protecting the aliens? Keeping all intruders out of the forest?

My imagination began running wild. Ken ran so fast, he fell and cut his knee. It wasn't a big cut, but he was upset. Only after we left the forest did we dare to look behind us. Nothing there. The owls must have stayed in their tree.

I had forgotten how frightened I had been the first time I ventured alone into the forest. Ken never wanted to return with me. He was still a little boy and not ready for this kind of serious adventure.

Next, I shared my story with some of my closest girlfriends, but they showed no interest in going to the forest.

"Don't you know we shouldn't go there?" one of them asked.

"Do you want to be eaten by a scary monster?" another friend asked.

"Did you ever see one?" I said.

"No, and I don't want to," my friend replied. "But I heard there was one living there. They come out at nighttime."

"Let's go in the daytime then," I argued.

"I cannot believe you'd say something like that. My mother would be very angry if I went into the forest."

Conversations like this turned me off from playing with girls. They were so girlish. I was glad I was tomboyish.

In our village, storytelling was a common entertainment for children. Every evening, a man walked down the street, ringing a bell and calling the children to come outside. About twenty of us gathered and listened to his stories. He made up his own stories and illustrated them with watercolor paintings, showing them one by one as the story progressed. Since we did not have a cinema in our area, this was the best entertainment we had. When he finished, he sold sweets to us. That was his occupation.

His stories were mostly enjoyable, but I still remember the story about the monster that lived in the forest. Our parents confirmed his story and repeated it to us children to keep us from going into the forest. The man had painted a picture of the monster. It was big and scary. In his picture, the monster stood at the edge of the forest with both arms raised to ward off intruders.

"This is my territory," it seemed to be saying. "Stay away, children!"

I wondered if the storyteller had ever seen *the others*. I knew they did not look like monsters, but I couldn't tell anyone until I had proof.

When television eventually made its way to rural Japan, people like the storyteller lost their work. One day, the man stopped ringing his bell, and I never saw him again.

Even though the forest *was* scary, I would not let fear stop me again. I needed a companion who wouldn't be stopped by fear either. I thought of everyone I knew, and in the end, only one person came to mind: a boy named Kiyoshi. A few years older than me, he was very intelligent and brave. He always looked like he was deep in concentration. I decided he might have seen the other world. When I saw him in the park, sitting alone on the bench, I approached him and carefully brought up my subject, this time intellectually and from a Buddhist point of view.

"Do you know where we go after we die?"

His family was Buddhist. I got his attention. I should have started this way with my family. Then my father might have reacted differently. Kiyoshi looked at me uncertainly.

"I saw my next life," I said. "It's a fantastic heavenly world! I may live there because I saw it."

"The next life?" he asked. "How did you see it?"

"Someone took me there. I met some beings very different. They're not human."

"What? Not human?"

"I wanted to ask you. Have you met them?"

"Not human? No. What are you talking about?"

"Oh," I said. "I thought you had." His eyes were fixed on me as I told about the golden city and told him about the disk creatures and how I was taken inside their room. I pointed into the forest.

"I want to see them again," I said, "so I'm going in there. Into the forest." I spoke very clearly.

"I want to go too,"

Kiyoshi and I immediately got on our bicycles and headed into the forest. On the way, he asked questions about the aliens' appearance. I answered the best I could. He seemed to take everything at face value. Then he said something out of context.

"You said you saw heaven. Do you think you can go to heaven after you die? You're a prankster. If you died now, you couldn't go. My mother has told me I shouldn't do the things you do."

Though that was probably true enough, but now was not the time to be reminded of my mischief. I was dismayed.

"First," I replied, "I didn't say it was heaven. I only said it was heavenly. There must be many heavenly worlds. I saw one of them. Second, I didn't say I would go there. I only said I *might* go there after I died. I won't die now. I'm going to change my ways because I want to go there." I was nearly shouting by now. "*The others* said they would guide me. They came to help me. If I follow them, I'll go to their world. Do you understand what I mean?"

I think Kiyoshi was a bit embarrassed by now.

I knew his mother told him about my history. A few days earlier, I had urged my younger playmates to enter a neighbor's garden. I had always wanted to see that garden because it was the biggest in our area, but the residents were old and did not associate themselves with many people, so hardly anyone ever saw their garden. For weeks, we had been talking about venturing in there. We tried it. And we were caught. My playmates said it was my idea, which meant I got another spanking from Father. All our neighbors found out about this. I was glad Kiyoshi was with me, but now, he had gotten me upset. We didn't say another word until we reached the river.

The river was deeper today, making crossing it somewhat dangerous. I had trouble keeping my balance. Kiyoshi helped me leap from one stone to the next, but when I tried another leap, I slipped off the submerged stone. I did not feel the sand on the bottom of the river till the water was up past my waist. The water was very cold.

"You can't go on with wet clothes," Kiyoshi said when we reached the other side.

Even though I was freezing, I couldn't afford to miss this rare chance. "This is nothing," I said. "Let's keep going."

Two courageous young persons proceeded into the forest. The sun disappeared as soon as we ventured between the hulking trees, making our wet clothes feel colder. It wasn't long before I started shivering.

We could have spent hours in the forest and not found anything, and I could not afford to get sick. When my friend said we should go back, I sadly agreed, but when I asked about our next excursion, he didn't sound as enthusiastic as he had earlier.

"The more I think about it, the more uncertain I am," he said. "Why are you the only person who has seen beings from other worlds? If they came here, other people should also have seen them."

"I thought you had met them," I said. "I've been asking people if they've seen them. I don't know many people, but I'm sure someone else has seen them. But don't tell anyone we came here. If your mother found out, I'd be in trouble again."

Though Kiyoshi never told his mother, I had to confess to mine where I had gotten wet because I ended up going to the hospital, and then I was confined to my bed at home for nearly a month with an infected lung. I regretted what I'd done, and I also had to promise that I would never go into forest again. Kiyoshi was also punished by his mother even after I said it was all my fault. She thought that being older he should have stopped me from doing such a reckless thing.

Even though I knew *the others* were in the forest, I could not look for them anymore. Since I had first met *the others* in the rice fields, I hoped to have the opportunity to invite them to my home. I thought if I could take *the others* to my home, my family would see that I was telling the truth.

I also started to think about meeting the children in the golden world during my next visit. Although I hadn't seen anyone around my own age, I assumed there were children there.

I often wondered about the disk creatures. At first, I thought they were animals or birds. But after I saw the shape of their ship in the golden world, I realized that they were the same but only smaller. I concluded that they were the babies' of the disk creatures. If not, they had to be their toys or tools.

Though my interest was in the celestial beings, my emotional attachment remained with *the others*. That was because they lived on earth near my house and had known me for a long time. We had become friends. They were the one who took me to the golden world. Also, they were more accessible than the celestial beings that were like angels and lived somewhere up high and did not descend to me. I could not really call them my friends. Even though those two kinds of otherworldly beings were different, I felt they were definitely connected.

I knew what kinds of beings lived in the golden world. They were highly spiritual and super-intelligent beings. Their high qualities attracted me at an early age, and I soon decided that if I wanted to live in their world, I needed to have those qualities, too. I knew someday I would need to work toward that goal. Also my lifelong attraction to art was influenced by my visit to the golden world. How could I ever forget the colors I saw there? I saw colors that didn't exist on earth. The seeds of my obsession with color and painting were planted back then, but, because music occupied all my time, they did not blossom until later in my life.

I don't know how I got this idea, but in those days I thought alien contacts and abductions happened to everybody at some point in their life. I never considered my abduction to be special. Meeting aliens, I thought, was normal and that other people had the same experiences as my own.

As time passed, everything I experienced on the other world became more important to me. I may have seemed like any ordinary girl, but I was led along a very different path from the other girls around me. My mysterious journey with *the others* started very early in my life. I began to see life differently. Blessed or cursed, my life would become extraordinary. The otherworldly beings significantly changed the course of my life.

Receiving Supernatural Powers

PRE-BIRTH MEMORIES

How many people have pre-birth memories? I'm not talking about memories of a past life, but of the time between a life lived and the birth into a new one. Great curiosity surrounds the notion of spirits or souls existing in humans before and after birth. I became involved in this subject when I was seven years old after I visited the golden world.

Early one morning while I was still in bed, a vision appeared in front of my eyes. It was very clear, like watching a movie, and the things I saw have never faded from my memory. I saw myself in the sky. I was looking for something. Below me was a big Japanese house with a garden. The roof was black-tiled, which was normal for an old-style Japanese house. When I spotted one rooftop, I realized this was the place I was looking for. I descended into the garden, where there were a lot of trees, well trimmed in bonsai style, and a stream running through it from a hillside. A waterfall flowed into a pond.

My body curled up somewhat as I flew, and I started to move more slowly. I saw myself pass through the roof, as easily as passing through air, and I also freely passed through the walls and moved around inside that house. I did not feel awkward doing this. It seemed natural. Then I saw several people gathered in the kitchen. I think they were the servants of the owners of the house. They wore different uniforms, some befitting gardeners, some maids, and one who looked like a cook. Some were sitting and talking quietly while others were cooking and cleaning. It was obvious that something was wrong. A dark and brooding mood hovered in the air.

I kept moving. There were many rooms in that house, but most were vacant and empty. Then I passed through another wall and came into a large room filled with people. I stopped and rose to the ceiling, but did not pass through it. I stayed there, looking down at what was going on. There were three girls and a man, presumably their father. I did not see a mother. They were grieving. I wondered what tragedy had caused such grief.

Then I saw that the furniture in the room had white paper taped to it—a cabinet, the table, the chairs, the desk, even the smaller items on the table and cabinet had paper taped to them. That paper captured my attention. A word was written in black ink on each piece of paper, and a thick black line ran from the top right side to the bottom left corner on each sheet of paper. The word was *forbidden*.

The weeping of one of the girls next captured my attention. She must have been about thirteen years old, and in that moment, a sudden awareness coursed through every vein in my body. She was my future mother! I was aware in that moment that I had come to see my future mother and her family. I, a floating spirit, gazed down at her, a child, still too young to have children. But she would be my mother. I felt the destiny of my upcoming life.

I now knew that I would be Japanese and that I would be a new branch on this family tree. Looking down at this sad family, I realized there were complications that would affect the fate of my next life. I knew intuitively that it would not be a happy life. I even sensed an omen. But I did not grieve nor was I discouraged. I already knew it before I saw this. I felt like I had already made up my mind to accept my next life's assignment.

The vision lasted only a few minutes, then it faded. What had I just seen? That was *me*. The floating being was me. That was me passing through ceilings and walls. The young girl was my mother. That was her childhood house. I had never seen such a huge mansion in my young life. I was sure it meant that the scene had happened many years ago. I tried to calculate the years between my mother's present age and what she had looked like at perhaps thirteen. This led me to conclude that this event had happened twenty to twenty-five years earlier. I was stunned. This scene had taken place before my birth. I *knew* this had happened. I had the memory and not just because I was seeing it. My vision became the tool that brought back the memory I already had. It stimulated my dormant memory.

Soon, I heard Mother walking toward my room to awaken me like she did every day. When I looked at her, I saw the face of the grieving young girl. I could not move. I laid in bed a while longer to digest the scene I had seen.

Breakfast was a busy time in our house. After Mother sent Father off to work and Kiyo went to school, the time came for Chizu and me to eat. After breakfast, I very carefully asked, "Mom, what happened in your house? The house where you grew up. Why was there white paper on the furniture?"

Mother almost dropped the plate she was holding. Her silence continued for a long time.

At last, she opened her mouth to speak, but then she closed it again. She repeated this few times. And then, forcing herself to get the words out, "What are you talking about?"

I treated this obviously difficult moment like everyday conversation. "There were many papers," I said. "They had a black line, like paint, drawn across them. And there was a word written on each piece of paper. *Forbidden*."

Mother took a step back and grabbed the kitchen counter to steady herself. "What are you talking about?"

"Something happened in your house when you were still a child," I persisted.

"What are you talking about!" she almost shouted. "You do not know this."

"You lived in real huge house with a waterfall and a pond," I continued, but that was all I said. I didn't ask any more questions. I rushed off to school, leaving her totally disoriented.

Even though Mother hadn't said anything, she had somehow said what I needed to know. Her reaction proved that what I had seen was true. That incident had really happened in her life long before my birth. She was right: I should not know this. I could not have known unless someone who had been there that day had shared their memories with me. Mother never talked about her youth. Her two sisters lived in different parts of Japan and I had never met them. Her father had died before I was born. I could not have known any of the employees in that house.

Many years later, Mother finally told me what had happened that day. Her father, Taro, had inherited an enormous business from his father but lost his business and had to sell his mansion and all the furniture. *Forbidden* was written on papers attached to everything as it was sold. They had had many servants in that mansion. Her mother Aiko, left her family. That's why I did not see her there. All the details I saw were correct.

Some months later, I had an another vision. I was in my garden, swinging as high as I could, higher than ever before. When Mother called me for tea, I stopped and just sat on the swing for a few minutes, waiting for my breath to calm down. At that moment, another moving vision appeared before my eyes.

I saw a small knoll surrounded by trees in a garden. The house there was nothing special compared to the mansion in the previous vision with the papered furniture. This house and garden looked deserted as if no one had cared for the garden for a long time. It was early morning, before sunrise, and I saw a few people running out of the house, then I heard a high-pitched siren. Mother was carrying a little girl and pushing another girl to hurry her up. She opened a thick, dark plank of wood in the earth, and they went inside the knoll. Inside, behind the door, a dark rag hung, hiding a big hole like a large animal's burrow.

Again, I was floating above the garden. As soon as they went inside the knoll, I followed them through the door. They went down a few steps. It was very dark underground, so Mother lit a lantern. The hole was barely big enough for them to sit in, no more than four feet high, and the grownups had to duck. One of the girls was about three years old, the other, perhaps five. The older girl looked scared as the siren kept wailing. The noise of the siren seemed to indicate that I was seeing something that had occurred during the Second World War.

Mother was calming the elder daughter. The younger one looked like she was sleeping. I realized that I was looking at my future family. We were all jammed up together, yet nobody noticed me. As I tried to get their attention by moving closer to the younger daughter, trying to get a good look at her face, I passed right through the elder girl. I thought maybe this would make her aware of my presence, but she showed no reaction. She covered herself with a blanket, held both knees close, and looked down in silence. She looked tired. I also saw baskets, a few small pots, blankets, toys, a tattered rug on the ground, cushions, and a child's portable toilet. I looked at the little girl. She was not asleep as I thought, and then it dawned on me that she was sick. That was why she was so skinny. Mother tried to feed her something, but she would not eat. I felt concerned for her.

This was another painful scene in the past of my future family. I knew I would be born soon. These two girls would be my sisters and their mother would be my mother. I would be entering her womb soon. I looked at her carefully. I knew this woman was the grieving girl I had seen in my earlier vision of that big house. Many years had passed, and she had grown to be a beautiful woman.

"Hello, hello," I kept saying. "Here I am. See you soon."

I didn't know what else to say to them. Mother and the girls didn't hear me, of course. Even though I knew it was my destiny to be born into this family, I wasn't particularly happy to see them. I felt a closeness with the little girl that I did not feel with the elder one. I looked more closely at her face. I could see that she was dying.

It would be a short time later when I would be born to replace her. That was it! That was all I could bear. I willed myself to leave.

My feet were still off the ground, but now, I could feel the seat of the swing beneath me. I sat there, still staring at the fading images. For a second time, I had witnessed Mother's life before my actual birth. I had been able to smell the odor in that man-made dungeon. It was the Second World War, the war when, for the first time in Japanese history, the homeland knew defeat. Even though I didn't have a physical body in the vision, I was physically close to them. I saw the sister I never had an opportunity to meet in this life.

Then I heard Mother's voice. She was calling me again. That brought me back to the present. This was her second call. When I was busy playing, she often had to call me more than once. She usually waited a few minutes before calling me again, which meant that this vision had lasted a few minutes.

When I went inside, I looked closely at her. She looked almost the same as she had in my second vision, even though she was older than she had been on that day during the war.

"Something wrong?" Mother asked.

"Nothing." Then I decided to take a chance. "Mom, did you hide in a hole in the ground during the war?"

"Yes, we did," she said. Her answer came back without any hesitation or suspicion this time. "Your father made it and told us to hide there when it was dangerous. We were lucky because we had a big yard. Some people who did not have a place to hide and…well, some of them died from the bombings."

"Was I born in that house?"

"No. We lived at that time in Osaka. But we moved to Kyoto a little while later because of my father's death. That's where you were born." She calmly continued her story. "My father committed suicide because Japan lost the war. Our family had worked closely with the emperor for many generations. In the devastation and defeat, my father took his own life. It was an honorable thing to do in wartime. I was very close to my father. My agony was huge."

"Did you have food and a children's portable toilet inside the hole?"

"Yes," Mother answered. "We had that because we did not know how long we had to stay in there. That time was one of the most difficult times of my life. Your sister Yuko died during the war. She was ill, but doctors were scarce. Most of them were called to service to attend to our wounded soldiers. We didn't have enough food either. We made a garden out of our yard and planted vegetables, but the people in the city took the vegetables away to give to the soldiers. We had to survive by eating roots. We suffered a lot.

"We have so much food now," she continued with great emotion as she was passing some sweets to us, "If we only had a little bread and butter, I think Yuko could have survived. She was weak since birth. I lost two people close to me about the same time." Then she added, "My mother, Aiko, was killed by a bomb just before the war ended."

She hardly ever talked about her mother except to say she was a famous pianist. Because Aiko left her house when Mother was a child, Mother did not have a good memory of her.

"After Yuko died, " Mother said, "we thought we had to have another child. After the war, a few years later, you were begotten."

My heart was crushed. I was a replacement for a dead sister. Now I could not speak, not only because of this horrible revelation, but also because of the accuracy of my vision and memory.

Mother was still talking very calmly. She must have thought I was asking general questions. She knew I had just learned about the war in school. It had been a common thing for people to hide in bunkers during bombings. Many still existed.

"How big was the bunker?" I asked her.

"It was very small. Just enough room for us to sit. There was no place to walk."

"Was there a door?"

"No, no door, just wood."

"That's it?"

"I covered the wood with cloth for protection against the rain that came in."

The shape and height of the hole and everything I had seen matched what Mother was telling us. I thought it best this time not to talk about my vision or anything I had seen in it. I kept my questions vague, not asking for any particulars, as I reached for more cookies.

"Where was Father?" I asked. "Did he also hide in that hole?"

"No," she said. "He didn't live with us in those days. He worked for our defense as an accountant. He was very good with numbers. Guns and bullets cost money, and your father had to keep records of how much the war cost. Like a business. The authorities appointed him to work in an office. If he had been a soldier, you two would never have been born. All the soldiers from our area died."

"Oh," I said rather absently. "No wonder I didn't see him." As soon as I said that, I left the kitchen.

"See him where?" I heard her say.

I pretended not to hear. I had enough information.

How can I explain these things? I remembered those two events very clearly. I also remember my thoughts and feelings at that time. Even though I was a spirit in my two visions, I had emotions, five senses, and a brain to think with. It was not much different from having a physical body. I was aware of everything and knew exactly what I was doing and why I was coming to see my future mother. I believe that the spirit lives on without physical body, yet has the ability to see and hear and remember just as the physical eyes and ears and the brain used to do.

But I discovered that as a floating spirit, I had a tremendous amount of knowledge. My two visions taught me that our physical brain has so much limitation, but once we lose the physical body, I assumed, we live with full knowledge. We know far more than we knew when we lived. Yet not only the knowledge, but also the understandings I had at that time surprised me. I was enlightened. Because I had seen Mother's family background and my own past life, I already knew *why* I would be born into this particular family. Viewing this history gave me the reason and the purpose of my birth. I am talking about history that goes back many hundreds of years prior to this life.

I don't feel exceptional or special. My visions felt natural. I believe that as soon as we get a physical body, we forget everything. But I was almost convinced that we all know ahead of time where we will be born, that we are already familiar with our family background. And we understand the reason and condition of our birth. I thought everyone had memories of times before their birth somewhere in their brain. Most people, however, do not remember their earlier lives. If I had not seen those visions, I was not sure if I remembered or not, but since I did remember, I concluded that everyone did, whether they knew it or not.

MEMORIES OF A PAST LIFE

When I was three or four years old, I started to see flashbacks of my previous life. These were fragmentary images, nothing like what I saw of the time before my birth. But these images brought me longings to see a place I didn't know.

I came from another place. I have another home somewhere else. I must go back.

I often said these words. They made Mother crazy. I still am not sure I was looking at a previous life or at an ancient time I experienced with *the others*. I was too young to know, but I certainly had a homesick feeling for an unknown world.

When I was about eight years old, I began to see my immediate past life in the same way I had seen the "movie" images of the events before my birth with the same vivid details. My past life was lovely. Seeing it made me happy. My vision always began in a green field surrounded by majestic, snow-capped mountains that were much taller than any mountains in Japan. I was usually walking in open fields near a blue lake, though sometimes I was riding in a horse-drawn wagon. My father was holding me, and we were going to a small, white church. I don't remember having sisters or brothers in that life, so it is very likely that I was an only child. I looked like I was in good health. Curiously, in these visions, I had a better recollection of my father than my mother. My mother was there, but only infrequently, and it seemed like my emotional attachment was to my father. He showed great love by hugging and kissing me. The people I saw in my visions were not Japanese. My father had blue eyes. That is the strongest image that stuck in my mind.

I started to miss this place. I was born in my present life with an optimistic and happy nature. My family was above the typical, and we lacked for nothing. If I had not had these past-life memories, I would have had no reason to feel unhappy living in this family. But seeing my lovely past life created an emotional dilemma. Japanese people, and especially men, do not show much affection. This is how we live, and my parents were very normal. Also the majestic nature I saw captured my heart. *Why was I not living there?*

Soon, I had another problem with my family. I started to talk about my past life, but when I did, I was not in a normal state of mind; I was almost in a trance. Every time I talked about my past life, it felt like I was experiencing that moment right now. From my descriptions, it became clear to my family that I was not talking about Japan.

I also talked about my cousins, boys I grew up with in my past life. I talked about the castle they lived in, a castle that was perched on the side of a mountain. I talked about how I loved the lake by their house.

Then, I heard Mother's voice. "Kayoko," she said, "stop talking nonsense."

I heard my name, but it was not a name befitting the splendid scenery I was seeing in my mind.

"My name is Belvedere," I said, without thinking.

The memories were so vivid that they actually superimposed themselves over my present life. I was a little girl in Japan in the 1950s, yet at the same time I saw myself as a child in some other place at some other time. One me had short, straight, black hair, but the other me had long, curly, light brown hair. There were two different worlds in my eight-year-old head.

I was not imagining all this. I was seeing another life, a real life, the life that I had once lived. Most Asian people, including my parents, believe in reincarnation, but almost no one knows their past life. But somehow, I knew too much about my past life, and that scared my parents.

My family was always telling me to be realistic. "Put your feet on the ground," they said. "Don't think about something that does not exist." I spent my childhood with these words echoing in my ears.

It was true. I had been dealing with the things that do not exist for most people. My eccentricities were slowly recognized by my neighbors, who heard my curious stories about another world and other beings. And now I was talking about my past life that wasn't in Japan. Rumors spread fast in a small village like ours. After my parents heard the gossip the neighbors were telling about me, they were embarrassed that they might be raising such an eccentric child. They always told me not to indulge my overactive imagination, especially not in front of the neighbors, even though the neighbors didn't take me seriously. Except for my strange stories, I was completely normal in every sense of the word, both at school and at home. In spite of the various maladies I suffered, I was a cheerful extrovert. I have never been diagnosed as having mental problems.

But when I was about ten years old, I began to feel that something must have happened to me to bring back such memories. I began to wonder about the machinery room on the ship I had visited.

Years later, I came to understand that hypnosis can work on the subconscious level of our minds to bring out unknown, dormant memories. I also learned about the past-life regressions of the famous psychic, Edgar Cayce. Some people can remember past lives in meditations or dreams, and some have remembered past lives after surviving an accident or a trauma. This means people remember past lives when they are in difficult circumstances. I think this indicates that some part of the brain holds such memories. If there are no past-life memories existing in us, people would never remember them. I firmly believe that we all have memories of past lives and the time before our birth. These memories are stored in some area of our brain.

In my case, I believe that a specific part of my brain was activated. This activation can be either natural or come through some external force. I might have been born with it. I believe this because I had some idea that I came from another world when

I was very young. However, following my first exposure to the machinery of *the others*, the ancient memory came back. And then other memories of the past kept coming back, one after the other, even things I didn't want to remember. That is the reason I think my brain might have been activated by their force. I knew that something had happened to me in that room while I was asleep. After I woke up in the room filled with machines, I felt different. When I faced *the others* after waking up, I did not feel like a child anymore. I had grown-up feelings. This had something to do with the huge number of memories that came to me. Because of these memories, I felt I had known *the others* somewhere long ago. I am convinced that my brain was stimulated by them.

It was some years later when I realized the place I was seeing in the "movie" images of my childhood was Bavaria. When I was a child, even though I had no knowledge of Europe or southern Germany, I could describe places in detail. My family had never traveled outside of Japan, and I didn't even know Japan very well, so talking about another country and being obsessed by it was unacceptable to my parents. But I persisted. And I eventually proved that I had once lived in Germany.

CHAPTER 4

The Heavenly World

THE GIRL SPIRIT FROM THE GOLDEN WORLD

When I was eleven years old, we moved to Kobe, a city about 400 miles southwest of Tokyo. Father had been promoted to district manager at his bank, Sumitomo. All my parents' relatives lived in this part of Japan, so they were happy. Kobe, which is not too far from Kyoto and known to be one of the most prestigious areas in Japan, is a beautiful scenic area, nestled between the Setonaikai Sea and Rokkou Mountain. Because it is a seaport, it has also been home to many foreigners, making the atmosphere very cosmopolitan.

My childhood ended when we left our old village. I knew that my encounters with *the others* were also ending because I no longer lived near their forest. I had wanted to bring *the others* to my home so I could prove to my family that what I said was true. I had also told to my playmates about meeting children on another world. They had asked me if I made friends with them, but what could I say? They still kept teasing me. Unfortunately, my hopes and wishes went unfulfilled, and so I resolved not to share my alien experiences with anyone unless they had adventures similar to mine. I also wanted to ask my teacher about *the others* and the golden city, but I soon came to understand that adults cannot explain everything. They are human, but *the others* are truly alien. I decided to keep everything I knew about aliens and other worlds inside me until I found the right person to talk to.

Our two-story house in Kobe was a big, typical Japanese house made of wood with a black-tiled roof. The rooms were separated by doors made of rice paper framed in wood, and there were straw mattresses on the floor in every room. One room was a Zen room that we used for the tea ceremony and meditation. Our backyard was a Zen garden with bonsai trees and stepping stones across a stream running into a small pond. Near the fence were maple trees and large rocks. Our Zen garden was a work of art, and for the first time, I began to appreciate Japan's beautiful culture. We had not had this kind of Zen space in our previous house. When Mother visited her relatives in Kyoto, we also went sightseeing and visited many famous temples, where we sat on the floor and learned how to make our minds quiet. This is Zen meditation.

It was after we moved to Kobe that I became more aware of an odd duality in my life. Sometimes, I felt like I was a foreigner in Japan, observing this unfamiliar Japanese culture even though I was obviously a Japanese child. Sitting on the floor was unfamiliar to me. Even though we had no chairs in our home in the village, I had always tried to sit on something high. I was the only one in my family who did such a thing, which annoyed Mother. Also, it is customary in Japan for people to remove their shoes when they enter a house, but when I was very young, I often forgot to take off my shoes. If I wasn't paying attention, I had a tendency to walk into the house with my shoes still on, which made Mother scream.

One evening, Mother took us to a classical music concert in a big, modern hall in Kobe. During the intermission, when we went to the bathroom, we discovered Western toilets, which were entirely new in those days in Japan. Asian toilets have no seats to sit on. When I saw the sign, *Western Toilet*, on the stall, I immediately went in, but my sisters refused to use it, even they had to wait in line for the Japanese toilets. When Mother asked me if I knew how to use the western toilet, I said, "Yes. I like it much better." This was the first time I had ever seen a Western toilet, yet it felt natural to me to use it.

According to Buddhist teachings, reincarnation normally occurs in cycles of three or four hundred years, though some people come back sooner. In the Dalai Lama's case, it is said to have been only forty-nine days, but that is very rare. I seem to have always felt that I came back fairly soon. Adapting to my new life in Kobe and seeing Western people immediately brought me a greater awareness of the European culture I had once lived in.

Chizu and I attended a school that was not close to our home but was said to be a better school than the closer one. That was Mother's choice. A good education for her children was a high priority for her. Our walk to Motoyama Elementary School was over thirty minutes, but the long walk made me happy because mountain scenery was beautiful. There were no mountains in Tokyo.

Ms. Itou, our teacher, was a stickler for learning from books. Almost immediately and even though I had done nothing wrong, I felt like she already disapproved of me. I did not like this school. I always felt cold there and had a problem making friends. I had no friends in our neighborhood because I attended a different school. I also wanted to make friends with boys, but no boys liked me. Without boys as friends, I felt like a part of me was missing. My new life in Kobe was not a happy one.

Soon after we moved, my heart problem became worse and I was prohibited from playing any sports, and then all the outdoor activities that I loved were prohibited too. This made me very sad. When I learned I needed to have surgery, my fear grew.

One day, when I was sitting in the Zen garden and missing my happy days in the old village, I noticed a beautiful girl standing among the trees. I saw her for a moment, and then I didn't see her anymore. When I had lived in the old village, I had sometimes seen spirits standing next to people. It is said that if our third eye, which is located between our two physical eyes, is opened, we can see spirits. Maybe that's what happened to me after I met the visitors from another world. I started to see many things I had never seen before, not only my past life and before my birth, but also spirits. They came and went too quickly that I hardly paid attention to them. There was nothing to suggest they were angels. In fact, they looked just like people, except they did not look whole. We hear about guardian spirits that protect us, and so I decided that maybe I was seeing guardian spirits. It was easy to adjust to seeing what other people didn't see because there was no harm to me, and so I got used to seeing them. Since I was obsessed by *the others* and the celestial beings and other worlds, nothing else mattered to me. This has been true practically all my life.

But what I was seeing now was so different, it stuck in my mind.

It was autumn. The ginko trees were becoming a deep, golden yellow. One afternoon, I was on my way home from school and decided to hike up to the mountains. It was an extra twenty-minute walk along the river to my favorite place on the mountain. My adventurous nature always brought good things into my life. I had found this place while I was strolling around by myself. My favorite place had a river view and a lot of cosmos flowers in soft lavenders. No one else came to this blessed place. I needed to be alone in nature because I was not happy. I often had problems with my teacher, Ms. Itou. She seemed to think I was an odd student and was always pointing out my shortcomings. A week earlier, she had summoned my mother to the school and told her that I was very different from any other students. She had been a schoolteacher for over ten years, she said, and she had never seen anybody like me. Well, it wasn't my choice to be different. I didn't want to be different. But I knew if anyone else had met aliens, they would be different too. Indeed, I did not feel the same as my classmates after I visited the other world where I gained so much knowledge. Yes, I started to look at life differently and to think differently.

On this day, Ms. Itou had again pointed out my odd character. I was not in a good mood, but being in this splendid natural setting really helped counterbalance my resentment. I began to forget my problems. I was overwhelmed by my feelings of how wonderful God's creation is! Majestic nature reminded me to appreciate God. However, formal religion was something that I could never really get into. Even though I was brought up Christian, it wasn't easy for me to just accept the Christian teachings because I had never been an easy believer nor very good at praying, even when I was not happy. I didn't pray and ask God for help. I have never easily asked anyone for help. That is my nature. I had always thought asking for help was a sign of a weak mind. I also did not appreciate God very much. There was nothing very wonderful going on in my life. My health became worse, I had few friends at my new school, my new teacher didn't like me, and I had to practice my violin for longer hours as I got older. And now, being in Kobe, I had lost my alien friends. I had good reason to be unhappy.

But whenever I was in nature, that's when my thankfulness to a blessed God overtook me, and my heart filled with joy again. That day on the mountain was one of those days.

I came to help you.

The voice shocked me out of my meditation. A girl I saw in the Zen garden was standing about ten feet away from me. It was hard to see her because the most of the trees were golden yellow, and she blended in with them.

She is not human, I immediately thought. Not even a human spirit. She reminded me of the celestial beings of the golden world and looked the same age as I was. I had never expected an alien child to come to see me on earth, especially not in such a spontaneous way. The images I had of my playmates on the golden world were of boys, but the being I was seeing now was a beautiful girl. She looked angelic, with long, wavy hair that ran over her shoulders. She wore a very simple, loose robe that ended just below her knees, and the fabric of the robe looked as soft as she did.

People do not understand you, she told me. *Do not be concerned with that. Trust the experiences that you are having. And do not talk about your experiences to other people until the right time comes.*

I knew immediately what she meant. She was talking about my peculiar experiences on the other world and with other beings.

And then, she dissolved into the golden trees.

What had I seen? I felt she might be a being from the golden world. Or was she an angel? But angels looked white, didn't they? And she didn't have wings.

As soon as I heard her words, I felt a difference in me. I was revitalized. My heart was filled with joy. The discontent I had felt just minutes before was gone. She had to have extraordinary powers to bring such a change so quickly.

She had said I could trust my experiences and I did not have to worry. I had been struggling with my experiences since I met *the others* and had never understood them. I had no doubts about my personal experiences, but people's reactions made me shaky. I needed to ask people to confirm my otherworldly experience. But her words wiped all my anxiety away, and I instantly gained a new, firm confidence. I was no longer intimidated.

I could only guess where she came from—the golden world. Her looks and her words made me believe this. I had been told I would get help, and now I felt that the help had finally arrived. Three times, three different nonhuman beings had said they would help me.

After school the next day, I rushed back to the same place. Truthfully, I did not expect to see the girl spirit again so soon, but whether she came or not, I had to be there. I hadn't been so excited in a long time. As soon as I got to my favorite place, I lay down on the yellow leaves on the ground to rest my body and looked up at the sky, which was azure blue. The deep, golden leaves captured my attention again. The colors took me far away—back to the golden world.

I have come from another world. I want to show you something.

Her voice made me jump up. I never expected her to come so soon. But those two sentences were all I heard. I did not see her again. I had prepared questions to ask her and I was disappointed that she went away so fast, but at least she had come back. I felt she was trustworthy.

Another world, she had said. Now I was convinced she was from the golden world. And I had connected with that world again! My excitement was so great that nothing else mattered to me.

I continued my after-school visits to the mountain as often as I could. Now I was obsessed with the angelic girl. I felt just like I had when I had met the aliens for the first time. *The others* are physical beings though, and she was a spirit. It seemed strange to be obsessed by a spirit girl, but I felt she was real. I also knew that she would have an important key in my life, just like *the others* had.

I saw her only those two times that autumn, and then I had a terrible winter. I was ill and could not go to the mountain.

Then things changed. One cold, windy February day, I had to stay an hour longer at school to finish the homework I hadn't done the previous day. All my friends left before I did, and the lonely, thirty-minute walk on that bitterly cold day was torture for me. If I had had company, I could at least have enjoyed a giggle. I did not like to be alone, especially on a cold day like this. I was eager to get home and get warm, so I started to run, and then I slipped on the ice. My legs flew out from under me and I landed hard. I almost started to cry, but when I stood up, out of the blue (or rather, out of the gray), I heard a voice behind me.

I came to help you.

I turned around and saw her. It was the angelic girl! She was exactly as tall as I was, and she was smiling. Everything brightened up. My smile returned. I didn't even feel cold anymore. But that was all she said, and I didn't see her anymore.

Since that day, however, even when I haven't actually seen her, I have always felt her near me. I have seen her again from time to time, usually when I am alone, always to my right. I had been seeing other people's guardian spirits, but I had never seen my spirit before. From that day on, I felt that she was my guardian spirit. Once I had wanted to meet children my age on the other world, but now, I thought she could be the childhood friend sent to me by *the others*. I felt that, finally, my wish had come true. I had something to thank God for besides his majestic nature.

After that cold February day, walking alone and being alone didn't bother me anymore. Not only that, I enjoyed being alone. I didn't need to have many friends to be happy any more. The angelic girl seemed to be with me nearly all the time, invisible but present. And soon, my grades went up and my personality changed dramatically. I became bold and more self-confident. After we moved to Kobe, I had been a quiet student, afraid to talk in class because I felt like I didn't fit in at the school. I became cowardly in many ways, but after I met the angelic girl, that changed entirely. I even confronted Ms. Itou. I thought she was insulting many students who did not earn high grades. I understood that she was trying to make sure her students excelled, but I knew many of her students were in pain. I was strongly opposed to her educational style.

No one was on my side, but I didn't care. I was alone, but I stood up for my belief and for other people who wouldn't speak up. Not long ago, I had been unable to stick up for myself, but now if I saw something unfair, I couldn't keep quiet. Now I was a different person altogether. Something I didn't understand was that when I spoke up, my words came out fluently. Several times after I finished talking, I amazed even myself by what I had said. This was a mystery to me.

One day, Mr. Matsui, our principal, called me to his office. Ms. Itou obviously felt I needed to be punished by the highest authority. But even when I faced the school principal, I was fearless and empowered. I ended up having a great conversation with him. Mr. Matsui was a Buddhist and also a follower of Mahatma Gandhi. He was the truly respectable educator and he supported me all the way to my graduation. He even spoke favorably about me to Mother and Ms. Itou, which surprised them.

Thus, the angelic girl caused many positive things to happen in my life. I started to spend more time alone so I could tune into the angelic girl. This was because I could hardly hear her when I was with other people and they were talking. It was a very natural feeling having her with me. Now I understood the work of guardian spirits and realized how important it is to listen to them.

It felt like my connection with her made me whole. Soon, I couldn't even imagine life without her. I assumed she would stay with me forever.

Years later, when I lived in the Himalayas, I learned about guardian spirits from the higher realm that belongs in another world. These are not human spirits. Buddhism also addresses this topic.

VIOLIN INSTRUCTION IN THE HEAVENLY WORLD

Now I was learning a little piece by Mozart called a rondo. When I practiced at home, Mother acted like a music teacher and told me when I was not playing right. Although she had never played the violin, she had studied the piano and knew music well. She used a metronome to correct my tempo when I was not playing a steady rhythm, but I always got a headache from the incessant clicking. Another time, when I was playing a serenade by Schubert, Mother said my sounds had no sweetness. "This is a serenade," she said. "A love song. Can't you add a little more feeling to it?"

Love song? What did she expect from me? I handed the violin to her and said, "Could you please play it and show me how it should be done?"

She walked out of the room without a word. I could never please her or my violin tutor.

Music has been a big part of my family for many generations. Mother always felt an obligation to pass the musical talent to her daughters because of her mother, Aiko who was once a famous pianist in Japan. My mother had two younger sisters, but neither of them were passionate about music. Mother's sisters had no children, which made Mother feel even more responsible about passing along the family's musical legacy. After the Second World War, when reconstruction was underway and things started to become normal again in most of Japan, parents were encouraged to give music lessons to their daughters. When Chizu and I each reached the age of three, we started piano lessons. When I was five years old, Mother added the violin to my repertoire. Kiyo was thirteen years old at the time and didn't have to learn to play the violin because thirteen was considered too late to start, though she practiced the piano. Chizu and I both were awful when it came to practice. Mother finally had to create a piggy bank for us. We were rewarded with a few coins after music practice, depending on the amount of time we devoted to practice. We were practicing solely for the money. In spite of Mother's devotion to her mother, neither Chizu nor I inherited any musical talent or desire.

When my violin tutor, Ishida, set up a recital for his pupils, everyone in our family attended. Mother put beautiful dresses on Chizu and me for our first stage performance, but Chizu got so nervous she forgot the notes in the middle of her performance. When she started crying, the audience sympathized with her and applauded to encourage her. Mother even took the sheet music on stage, but Chizu could not go on. This embarrassed Mother. I played Schubert's Serenade, but having seen Chizu's failure, I became so nervous that I was trembling. My shaking created uneven, funny sounds, and the famous love song turned into a comic performance that made the audience laugh. That was the longest three minutes I had ever experienced, even though I, too, got big applause. It wasn't because I played well or anything. The audience wanted to make up for their impolite laughter. Kiyo was lucky she wasn't part of this embarrassment. That evening, Mother made a special dinner for us, but Chizu didn't eat much. Father felt sorry for us and suggested to Mother that we stop violin lessons.

"Never again," I said to myself after my failure at the recital. "Who needs this?" The violin was bringing me nothing but problems. The violin is a most difficult instrument to master, I was told, so why had Mother insisted I learn to play it?

By now, it was June, the miserable, hot, and humid rainy season in Japan. I caught tuberculosis. Because of my weak immune system, I was always the first one to catch almost any sickness going around. I was isolated in my room and bedridden for nearly a month.

Lying in bed, I realized that I had not seen the girl spirit lately. I began to worry. Was she still with me? I lost my cheerfulness and confidence. I lost the feelings of contentment I'd had. I decided these changes were caused by her absence. Maybe, I decided, she didn't like being at my bedside. Indeed, who does want to stay with a sick person? She belonged to that fabulous golden world. These thoughts made me more miserable.

One day when Mother went to Kyoto to take care of some business, I was left alone at home. I took advantage of my temporary freedom and got out of bed. It was early in the afternoon, and the rain had stopped. I decided to go out to the garden. I did not know what kind of medicine the doctor was giving me. My stomach did not feel good and I had no energy. I felt cursed to have so many ailments. As soon as I reached the Zen garden, the direct sunlight hit my eyes and made me dizzy. I shielded my eyes with one hand and tried to sit under the trees.

I will show you something.

I saw the angelic girl standing to my right. That was the last thing I saw.

I don't know how it happened or how fast, but I was in a very bright, natural setting where the light did not blind me or even bother me. I felt neither heat nor humidity, only an incredibly fresh and amazingly comfortable air.

Next I began to see angelic beings, gathering in an open field. They were suspended in the air, their gowns swaying slightly in a gentle breeze. Some of the angels were hovering above a lake and looked as translucent as their reflections in the clear water below them. The light reflecting through their gowns made me think I was seeing an illusion.

This must be heaven, I said to myself. *I must have died and been carried to heaven.* I didn't know how I had died, but it must have been an instant death. My sickness must have caused my death, or maybe it was my heart problem. It didn't matter. My afterlife was all that mattered now.

Being born into a Buddhist and Christian family, I heard a lot about heaven, and I was always being told to do the right thing in God's eyes. Now, knowing I had finally entered his kingdom, I was delighted. Well, yes, I had a few doubts because I was such a naughty girl that I wasn't sure if I deserved admittance to heaven. But I was there! Perhaps, I thought, I had been overly critical of my actions because of my strict and righteous upbringing. I had learned in Sunday school that most children went to heaven. Though I was no longer a little child, I assured myself, I was still an innocent child. All the little crazy things I had done would surely be dismissed.

God had accepted me. I felt triumphant.

Yes, indeed, I was pleased with being dead. I had suffered enough on earth. All my illnesses had been insufferable. Violin practice had been insufferable. Being rejected by people for speaking the truth had been insufferable. But all my agonies had come to an end. Finally, I could rest. How did I feel? My body was in perfect health. I was rejuvenated. There was a complete absence of any physical problem I had suffered. Now I would never have to go through any more of the scary operations I had been told I needed.

In my great contentment, I just stood under the big trees and observed my surroundings. What I saw was the vibrant nature. It looked just like the golden palace. But that golden palace was a super-advanced, modern city, whereas the place I was looking at now was a splendid and exceedingly peaceful natural setting. The sky was so bright it was as if a dozen suns were shining, though I never saw even one sun. *Maybe heaven doesn't need a sun*, I thought. After all, the sun can be too strong for people's eyes and make the summer weather too hot. The sun also causes problem in our bodies. But here, I didn't have to worry about any physical problems. I relaxed in the bright light and felt exceedingly comfortable without the sun. When I looked around, the trees caught my attention. They looked very much like trees I had seen on earth. Why, I asked myself, were these trees here? It was almost as if they didn't belong here. I had no interest in seeing trees that I could see every day on earth.

As I switched my focus back to the unbelievable scene before me, I spotted one tall being wearing a soft golden gown and standing in front of me. He must have just flown in, I thought. At first, he had nothing in his hands, but suddenly, he was holding a violin. It appeared like magic. *Where had this violin come from?* It looked just like any violin found in a music store on earth. It was brown wood, just like my violin. I felt as if his violin was manifested from the tree. Seeing this violin in heaven made me wonder where I was. Until this moment, I had thought I'd died and gone to heaven. But now, suddenly, I felt that something strange was going on. Violin lessons in heaven? But I could not be tortured in heaven.

Maybe I wasn't dead.

Suddenly, the trees got my attention again. Their colors were one-dimensional earth colors. When I looked at myself, I, too, was the same color I always was on earth. Everything else here was filled with shining, translucent colors. The trees and I seemed like we didn't belong in this heaven. This made me nervous. I looked down at my feet. I was standing on the ground. The angels were up in the air. I was all alone, standing under the earthly trees while all other living beings seemed to be floating in the wonderful, clear air.

I had not died. I had not entered into the kingdom of heaven. Deep in my heart, I knew it was impossible for me to be in heaven.

Then I had a new thought—this was a waiting room, the place we wait for our next life after we die. Buddhism teaches us about this peaceful and joyous place where we see our family, ancestors, and friends. I had seen paintings of this resting place in Buddhist children's books that described beautiful fields and rivers. It is a bright place, and gods and goddesses are present. I thought I had been carried to that resting place. I looked around. There were no human beings anywhere.

I finally realized that I had been transported to another world again. I looked up into the sky, hoping to see the aliens' vehicle hovering above me. No, it wasn't there.

Now I remembered the angelic girl. She must have brought me here! She had said she was going to show me something. I looked around, but she was nowhere to be seen. There was no one here who resembled a child. All the angelic beings were adults.

While all this was going through my mind, the being holding the violin began to play. But I was not especially excited by that. My mother was always making me listen to violin concerts that nearly bored me into a coma. Classical music is not for the ears of children, unless they are gifted children, and I was certainly not one of those gifted children. Of all the imaginable things the angelic beings could expose me to, show me, or teach me, I thought, why did I have to listen to violin music?

He played.

With his first note, I was struck by the amazing sounds his instrument was making. What I heard was not a violin sound I knew. The violin is a small wooden instrument, and its sounds do not carry very far, but the music this being was playing carried like an echo on a high mountain; it sounded as if it were amplified by a dozen speakers, like the super high-technology sound systems used today in huge auditoriums. Although microphones existed in Japan in the 1940s and 50s, they were used for speech, not music, because of the terrible quality of their sound. But the magical sound of his violin vibrated in my body.

As he played, I noticed his floating or flying style, as if he were playing "flying music." This, I thought, must be how angels perform. It seemed as if the music he was playing made him so happy he levitated and danced with it. As he flew and spun, his long gown made golden sparks in the air. He was in the middle of the clouds, which looked like rainbows because of the soft lights above they were reflecting. I couldn't take my eyes off him. It was an amazing show. *This* was entertainment. My belief that violin music was boring was swept away. I had never imagined that music could be so fascinating, that it could be played in such a way. Uplifting joy filled my heart.

Next, the angelic violinist began to play slow music with tremendous deep emotion. The expression of his heart went directly into the violin. He and his violin seemed to merge into one musical being. I felt an electric current running through my body as the incredible, heart-shaking sound of the violin infiltrated my soul. I hung on to his every note. It sounded like he was expressing the human emotions and sentimental feelings that I identified as *human* feelings. But how, I asked myself, could he play with human emotion yet not be human? I thought there must be no sadness in this heavenly place, yet I felt sadness in his music. I was still a child, and at that young age, I did not quite understand love songs, even though I had been told, for example, that Schubert's Serenade is a love song. I was listening to music that had such sweetness intertwined with the sadness.

And then, another question came into my mind. This heavenly place was a highly spiritual world. Why was he not playing heavenly music? Or highly spiritual music, such as Bach, Mozart, or Beethoven, music that lasts for centuries. My mother had told me that those composers were inspired by God and the heavenly powers. Why was I hearing the music from earth? This feeling was new to me, yet I felt his music was not altogether unfamiliar.

Then I heard a voice. *These techniques can help your career*, the violinist said. *You must apply yourself more to practicing because in the future, you will be a violin performer and travel around the world, so it is very important for you to work harder.*

Me? A violin performer? Traveling around the world? I was thrilled to hear this, but how did he know that I hated to practice? I had, in fact, quit playing the violin and was very happy not practicing any more. But that day, on that heavenly world, a major change took place in me. Though I was still far from being a music lover, the idea of traveling the world was so attractive to me that I went back to my violin practice with a new attitude. This sudden change surprised the people around me.

My parents had made great efforts and spent a lot of money for a private violin tutor for me, but I was just never inspired. On this one day, however, seeing that heavenly violinist and hearing his music and his words changed me altogether. Back at home, my violin teacher soon suggested to my parents that I should declare playing the violin as my major in school. Mother couldn't have been happier. She had almost given up hope on me. Because my family lineage was filled with musicians, it was of monumental importance to her that I had the potential to become a violinist. Soon, I was sent to an advanced violin tutor. For Chizu, it was the right time to quit playing music. I am the only person in two generations of my family who became a musician.

Since the day the heavenly violinist told me I would be traveling around the world, leaving home became an obsession. My past-life memories were still haunting me. I needed to find the place where I had lived in my past life. I had to travel. But in those days, no one thought about world travel, and even though such a thing was beyond my imagination, the celestial violinist's words settled deep in my core and motivated me to cultivate my skills. I was eventually drawn to a serious musical path, and I have made a career as a solo violinist. I had never before imagined that the violin could be anything but a classical instrument, but entertainment became my direction.

PART 2

CHAPTER 5

Paranormal Awakenings

MIRACULOUS HEALINGS OF MY AILMENTS

My heavenly experience led to another change in my life. I experienced a true miracle. I felt different almost immediately. All my ailments were cured. But even though I felt fantastic, it never occurred to me to connect my healing to my otherworldly adventures. It was too good to believe, so I didn't even ask the doctors to test me right away when I returned. I just left things alone. I knew the tuberculosis was cured right away, and I tested myself to see if I could run without a problem. My heart felt fine. Heart valve disease is an especially serious problem, but suddenly, there was no trace of the disease. I had suffered from many other ailments for a long time, including hernia, tonsillitis, and sinusitis, just to name few. I had no idea what a healthy body was. I needed constant medical care. But now, my ailments felt like they were all gone.

It's important to understand that there were no advanced surgical techniques when I was a child, and I kept hearing about terrible outcomes of surgery in our old village. This made me paranoid. My agony was enormous because I needed to have many procedures, but I was afraid of the doctors in our old village. I had no idea in what kind of situation I would end up. Even today, just thinking about this makes me tremble.

I finally went in for a regular checkup; even though no problems were found, I could not change my life right away. The doctors had no way of knowing if my healing was permanent.

Gradually I stopped visiting the doctors. Ten years of bad health came to an end. Once I had been the first person to catch a cold or any other transmittable disease. Bad food had always made me sick. But now, my immune system was changed. I learned this a year later when there was an episode of food poisoning at my school. All the other students who ate lunch there became seriously ill, and the next day, only a few people appeared in school, and these were people who had been absent the day before. This kind of episode, which had hardly ever occurred in the history of Japan, became news, and I was interviewed. Why was I the only person who didn't get sick? Since then, I have always been the healthiest person I know.

The doctors overseeing my care could offer no explanation for my unprecedented healing. Even if I knew what the cause of my healing, since I could not prove it, I did not offer any explanation.

Mother was greatly confused by my healings, but she could not take the time to do any research. Kiyo also contracted tuberculosis and was hospitalized. Chizu had been struggling with diabetes for years. There was more. Mother's youngest sister, Kimi, who had been struggling with complications of pneumonia, died in her mid-thirties. Mother commuted to her sister's home near Kyoto for many months until she passed away. Kimi's death devastated her so much that all of Mother's attention went to her and my sisters. I was suddenly left alone.

Another activity that made Mother even busier was looking for a new house. The house we were living in belonged to Father's company. Since both of my parents were from this area, they wanted to settle there permanently. Father left the search for a new house to Mother. She spent nearly every day searching for a house.

This is another reason why she did not take time to research what was really happening with my health, but just gladly accepted my miraculous healing and thanked God.

While I believe God had a lot to do with my healings because Mother always prayed for my health, I really did not mind the idea of dying at an early age. The longer I lived, the worse my health got, so I was not optimistic about my future. I was not interested in living a long life in this troubled body. My oldest sister, Yuko, had died at the age of three. I thought she was lucky. I assumed she was now living in a fantastic new body in some other glorious place. I envied her. This was another reason I did not pray to God for my healings. After I visited that heavenly world, I found that death was not something to fear. It was something to look forward to. But suddenly I got healthy. Though I was still not sure what to think of my total recovery, since I had avoided all the scary surgeries, I could not ask for more.

I saw many miraculous things on the other world. I think it must have some kind of essence that cures illness. This is the only explanation I can think of, and I know it is not logical. But after my visit to that miraculous world, my healing felt natural to me.

Though I grew up with strong, spiritual teaching from my parents, I never wanted to follow what I was just told to follow, unless I was truly moved by their teachings. That is who I am, not only spiritually but for every area in my life. I am a free-thinking person. I do not like to be bound by any traditional doctrines. But when I visited the golden world, immediately I wanted to be cultivated by the spiritual path, because I wanted to live in there. The alien's path became my path. And now seeing this miraculous healing and amazing violin teaching, I am no longer interested in conventional religion on earth.

My junior high school was located next door to my elementary school, and my new teacher was another woman. Though I had no positive expectations, it wasn't long before I discovered I liked her. After I returned from the heavenly world, I started to see other positive changes in school. I was accepted more and more by the intelligent students. I was surrounded by good friends. Boys in my elementary schools in Kobe had never liked me, but now, I met a boy who interested me romantically. My life was moving in a positive direction.

Sadly, the angelic girl never came back to me. The last time I saw her was in the Zen garden. If I had known she would be there as my secret companion for such a short time, I could have made myself available to her as much as possible. I had never seen *the others* again either. I began to realize that *the others* and the angelic girl came to me for some special purpose, and once that purpose was fulfilled, they had to leave me. They were not there to stay with me forever.

I thought that the celestial beings were like angels and lived somewhere up high and did not come down to me. I could not call them my friends. But knowing she came down to me and stayed with me changed my concept of angelic beings. I felt they were my true friends; even though they lived in the celestial world, I started to have very special feelings about them.

Once I thought that adaptation by aliens happened to everybody. Sooner or later we all meet *the others* who guide us in our lives. When I met *the others*, I thought it was just my turn. I got in line, so to speak, at an early age. I assumed that an experience on another world was another kind of education, different from what we receive in our schools. After meeting *the others* and visiting the other world, I began to think that if we only know life on earth, we have no basis for comparison with anything else, and if we cannot compare, how are we supposed to know the difference? To set a high goal and purpose in life, we need to know the other world. We need to be inspired by the difference. We also need to be guided by someone higher than us. Of course, we should be guided by God, but I think one God for everybody is too much work for him. Even if God controls things overall, we still need *others* who show us things in personal ways. Parents are our first and immediate teachers. Then comes private tutors and school teachers. But they all belong to the earth. We also need someone from another world. *The others* are the private tutors who guide us to the higher level beyond the earth. As each person has his or her own parents and we can all get our own special way of training, we also get different aliens for our further education, depending on our purpose in our life. This is what I believed.

I often wondered how other people dealt with their experiences of being visited by *the others* or visiting another world. I wondered how other people kept their experiences to themselves. Because I had never heard anyone tell stories like mine, I became confused. What I thought that meant was that either they were told not to speak of their own encounters or their first encounters had not happened yet. The angelic girl told me not to speak. Since she affirmed my peculiar experiences, I ignored people's reactions and trusted her words. I also tried not to be caught up too much in the thoughts of the nonhumans and the other world I visited. I knew that my mind was often in some other place, but I did not want to give people a strange impression of me anymore.

There was another reason I ignored people's reactions and their thought. That was the help I received from nonhuman beings. I have always had an independent mind. The help from *them* was not, therefore, something I expected or was eager to receive. But if their words were true, I might run up against such awful problems that earthly people might not be able to help me with. I would then need the help of *the others*. These are the reasons why I have relied almost totally on myself for my entire life. That's how my feelings of independence grew, as well as my belief in the strength of my own counsel.

Sometimes, we cannot give logical explanations for things that happen. Sometimes, we cannot provide evidence or find a witness. I know I can never prove what happened to me, but this lack of so-called proof should not make anyone conclude that my experiences are false. I had my own evidence, solid evidence, not only of being healed, but also of my renewed interest in the violin. My view of life changed. I no longer believed that our life belongs only on earth. I gained an idea of higher realms. I also realized I had lived before this life, but not only as a human being. All of these changes were caused by nonhuman beings. These undeniable facts are my evidence.

I lived in two different worlds, this one and that other world. They were somehow mixed together.

Peculiar experiences had been a normal part of my life but I was about thirteen years old when I finally realized that something very extraordinary had happened to me. Although I stopped talking about *the others* and the golden world, I still believed that someone else on earth had had similar experiences and time would prove me correct. I remained alert to find these other people because I knew the aliens had not come only for me. They came to contact people on earth. *The others* told me so.

THE POLTERGEIST IN OUR NEW HOUSE

One night Mother had special news for us. "We are making an excursion next Sunday," she said. "We are going to see a house I found."

Mother had been searching for an ideal home for nearly a year and had found our new home in Nigawa in Nishinomiya, on the mountain side of Kobe. Nigawa was a popular area for picnics and was known to be a high-class residential area. Though Nigawa was nicer than where we had been living, I was not too excited about moving there. I did not want to change my school. But when we arrived at the train station in Nigawa, I saw the cherry trees in full bloom along both sides of the river that flowed down from Rokkou Mountain. The scenery was so beautiful that even though I would have to change schools again, I felt eager to see what Mother had found. The house was not the typical dark, Japanese house that made me happy. As soon as we entered the gate, the roses in the garden welcomed us. There were trees and flowers, but the owner had not taken care of the garden well, so it was mostly barren. The house had only two bedrooms and two living rooms, but there was a big backyard. This was where our parents were going to add three bedrooms for us girls.

I couldn't help but feel there was something strange about this house. Maybe I was still harboring a bit of resentment that I had to leave my school, but I felt like the house was not welcoming me. Because the rest of my family was happy, however, I tried to ignore my feelings.

After we viewed the house, we strolled around the area. Across the street from our house stood a famous Christian university, Kansai Gakuin. It was one of the most beautiful universities in Japan. On the hillside, there were perhaps twenty big, old, two-story European houses with brick walls and dark, orange-tiled roofs. These were the homes of the American and European professors who taught at the university. Looking at them, I had a sudden feeling of nostalgia that came from my memory of my past life. I just stood still for a moment. The university campus looked like a huge park. As we walked, we saw a pond and a white chapel. I was transfixed. A white church was one of the strongest images I had from my past life.

"I saw so many places," Mother was saying, "but there was nothing better than this. This place is truly a blessing."

I also had to admit that the area the house was located in was beautiful. I thought I should be happy.

I was thirteen years old when we moved. This house became our permanent residence, and to this day, my mother still lives there and I still keep my stuff in my room.

I spent a lot of time strolling around the university campus. I also watched student activities. I loved the free atmosphere and couldn't wait to attend the university.

Except for a few Americans and Europeans who were professors and missionaries in the university, there were scarcely any people in Japan at that time (the 1950s) who were not Japanese. But this house had belonged to a Chinese couple. Later, I overheard a strange story about them. He was a successful businessman, but they had isolated themselves from their neighbors. People assumed they had done this because they were foreigners, but the truth was that the man's wife had succumbed to mental illness and had a nervous breakdown, which lasted a long time. The man wanted to go back to China, regardless of the decreased market value of his house.

When my mother had visited this house for the first time, though she was not sensitive to spiritual matters, she also felt something strange about the house.

She was encouraged to look at other houses, and she did, but nothing else impressed her as much as this house. Besides, it was too big a bargain to resist.

Before we moved in, Mother performed a Buddhist ritual of purification. Even though she had embraced the Christian faith, she still did the ritual, which is a common thing people in Japan do when they buy a house or move into a new place. She had not blessed the house we had moved into three years earlier, but something here had made her feel afraid. After the purification ritual for the new house, my parents built three additional bedrooms, one downstairs for Kiyo and two smaller upstairs rooms for Chizu and me. We had a small, Western-style living room, which became a guest room and my music room, plus a second Japanese living room that became our family room. Probably because Mother did the purification in our house, I thought everything would be fine. In time, I forgot my strange feelings.

As much as I missed my old school, I liked my new school in Nigawa. Getting used to my good health, I had too much energy, and in an effort to release it, I became a bit of a prankster again and found a number of girls who loved to play practical jokes. Teachers scolded me often, but they never held bad feelings toward me. I cannot think of anyone who did not like me. The more trouble I got into, the more popular I became. Once I thought girls were not fun, but at this school, I had more fun with girls. I had finally gotten my childhood life of fun back, at least for a while.

ALIENS ON EARTH

A Mormon church was being built near our new house. It was a typical American style that was new to us. When the church was completed, I thought it was okay to go inside to take a peek. I was not aware that people had already moved in. I looked in through windows, shielding my eyes from the glare with my hands.

"*Konnichiwa*?" said a voice. (That means "hello" in Japanese.)

I jumped. Then I saw two foreigners smiling at me. I lost my voice.

"Sorry. Surprise you?" one of them said in broken Japanese. "My name is Elder Moon." To me, he looked like a movie star.

"I am Elder Cater," the other man said. He was over six feet tall, slim, and handsome. While I was gazing at them, I saw other foreigners; five of them near me. These foreigners were in their early twenties, all tall, all nice looking. Suddenly I was invited inside their church.

"I am Elder Smith," said a man with blond hair and blue eyes.

"We just moved here. We're doing missionary work. We came from America."

Elder Smith spoke Japanese reasonably well.

"I have already lived in Japan for two years," he added, "but they are new. These people are studying Japanese. Do you want to study English?"

"Yes," I said. I had never liked English class in school, but all of a sudden, I wanted to study.

"Would you like to see a slideshow about our church?"

"Yes."

"That's great. You are our first student. I am glad you stopped by."

"Stopping by" was not exactly what I had done, but what fun this would be! When we are adventurous, exciting things can happen.

They showed me their slideshow. There was American history in the slideshow. It was wonderful to learn something new about a faraway land. I had an appointment next day to learn more about their beliefs. I couldn't wait to tell my family that I had just become friends with these handsome aliens who came from the other side of the world.

Meeting these missionaries was very similar to the experience I had with *the others* on their ship. The Mormons came from a faraway place and looked different from us. They were all adult men and tall. I hardly said anything, but they spoke to me in Japanese and were quiet and kind and treated me like an adult. They were temporarily residing near my house. I wanted to become friends with them, and they also wanted me to be their friend. They could teach me new things of their world. In their church, I was the only girl in the room. I was surrounded by aliens. Their devotion to their mission inspired me. I looked at them with respect.

Indeed, it was very similar, but these aliens were much nicer looking than the aliens I had met on the ship. When we came to their religion, I couldn't believe what I heard. But that wasn't my concern. I only wanted to know about a different world and different people.

I had special feelings for Elder Moon. My special feeling was sort of a similar feeling I had for the alien I had met in the forest. Elder Moon's younger beautiful sister, Rachel, who lived in Salt Lake City, became pen pals with me. She was the same age as me, and I still remembered the day when I wanted to become friends with the alien child my age. In her letters, she said that some day I should visit her home. She lived on a huge farm with acres and acres of land. That fascinated me. All these activities brought back my old memories.

In 2014, I learned that Mormonism has something to do with aliens and believes in reincarnation. This information came to me a surprise and makes me think I met those missioners for a good reason.

BUTTERFLIES' INSTRUCTION

One day, as I started to practice my violin, a yellow butterfly came fluttering into the room. That had never happened before. I tried to make the butterfly go back out the window by gently flapping my bow to scare her away, but she wouldn't leave. So I left her alone and resumed my practicing. The butterfly seemed to react to the music. When I sped up, her wings moved more quickly, and when I played slower, her movements got slower. When I stopped, she stopped. It was fun to watch. After practice, I went outside and forgot about the butterfly.

The next day, as soon as I started to practice, the butterfly came in again.

"Go outside," I said.

She flew out the window right away and stayed there, hovering in the area as if awaiting further orders. I called for her to come back inside, and she came in. I repeated these commands a few times, and she obeyed them. Yesterday, when I made her go away with the bow, she didn't go, but today, she reacted to my words.

"Hello, beautiful butterfly," I said. "Do you understand me?"

Her wings moved slowly a few times, as if fanning the air. She was responding! I liked it. I thought about the disk creatures that once responded to my voice. As I played my violin, she began dancing in the air to the music.

After I finished practicing, I said to her, "Now you can go home. Come back tomorrow." She left immediately, and the next day, she flew right in again. As before, I played my violin and she danced to the music. When I finished, I tried to trick her for the fun of it.

"You don't have to come back tomorrow," I said, and, sure enough, the next day I didn't see her. She wasn't even in the garden.

The day after that, she came in again. It was weird. Did this small insect really understand my words? *It must be a coincidence*, I said to myself. On this day, while I was playing, she came near me and flew around my head. My eyes on her, I continued to play. Then I started to spin. Normally, I could not spin, but I was spinning now. Not only that, I found myself able to play while spinning. Whoa! Suddenly, the spinning and flying technique I had seen in the other world flashed through my mind. This was it! Although I could not play well yet, I thought it was fun.

After practice, the butterfly still stayed with me in the room. I began to wonder if my communication with insects was limited to just her. I decided to make a test. "You can go home now," I said to her, "but tomorrow, bring a friend."

Sure enough, the next day, I found two identical butterflies waiting in the practice room. I was astounded.

When practice was over, I told them to go home. As they began to leave, however, I quickly said, "Stay." They fluttered back and landed on my music stand.

"Tomorrow," I said, "bring more friends." *If she really brought more butterflies*, I thought, *that would scare me.*

The next day, five butterflies arrived. I was stupefied. They seemed to be waiting for me to play my violin, and when I started, they all started fluttering about the room. I was dancing and spinning and playing. I wished I could take a picture of us. This was something I could see in a children's book. Since I played terribly, making a lot of squeaking sounds, Mother suddenly walked in.

"What are you playing?" She saw the butterflies flying all over the room. "Oh my God! What is this?"

The butterflies all stopped flying.

"Go outside," I quickly ordered them.

They flew obediently out the window. Mother just looked around the empty room and left without saying anything. I looked outside. They were waiting on the flowers.

I said, "Go home and do not come back anymore." This was not because I didn't want them to come back, but because I was kind of afraid. It was uncanny.

That was the last day I saw the dancing butterflies, but the spinning technique I acquired would be used in the future in my musical show. When I saw the angelic being spinning and playing violin, I never thought it was humanly possible or that I could do it, but I got a lot of jobs because I can spin while I play the violin. My show was often called *Dancing Violin*.

COMMUNICATING WITH GUARDIAN SPIRITS

After my contact with aliens, I started to see the spirits. I had been seeing guardian spirits for many years, but except for the angelic girl, I had never heard spirits talk. Now I began to realize that spirits were eager to communicate with me. It was sort of like the butterfly that had flown into the practice room and wanted to communicate. Sometimes, I saw as many as three spirits around one person, but it was mostly just one or two. They were always quiet. But one day, a woman spirit started to scream at the top of her lungs.

No, no, no. He should not do that!

It happened when a friend of Father's started to talk about the business he wanted to start. Father had invited him for dinner, and our family was having tea in our living room with him. I was the only one who saw the woman spirit. As loud as she screamed, no one else heard her, so I had to interrupt the guest and repeated her words. Mother knew I had been seeing spirits, but she never had heard me saying something like this. I was harshly reprimanded and sent back to my room.

Many months later, I learned that the man had pursued his business endeavors, but the business failed and he had lost all his properties. My parents asked me how I knew he would fail. What else could I say? I had just heard it from his guardian woman spirit. This was the beginning of my communications with spirits. I know spirits were talking to people. I also knew the spirits want me to hear them, though I didn't know why. Was it to help people, or for some other reason? I soon realized that I was getting into trouble with my family again.

One afternoon, when Chizu and I were sitting in guest room, I saw two spirits standing next to Chizu. The female was talking about Chizu's marriage. I wondered if Chizu was aware of their existence, so I asked her.

"Do you know how many people are in this room? Do you know what the person next to you is saying?"

Chizu was the only person I felt comfortable enough asking such questions. If I asked Kiyo, things would become serious. My elder sister was going to become a psychologist and was already interested in any abnormal condition that she could study and diagnose. Since I had been talking about strange things for so long, I was the first person she evaluated. She gave me a Rorschach test, which interprets one's personality by noting what a patient says as they interpret what they see in inkblots on the cards. Kiyo never found anything abnormal about me, but she always reported her tests to our mother. That was why I was reluctant to talk to her, whereas talking to Chizu was easy. But she was no longer a little girl who shared secrets with me. I think I made a mistake when I asked about the spirits with her. Without saying a word, she got up and left the room. I knew where she was heading.

A minute later, Mother was yelling at me from the kitchen. "Stop talking nonsense to your sister. It's time to practice your violin."

If only my sister could have kept this between us, I could have advised her. But now if I said something, I knew I would be in trouble with Mother. So I decided not to say anything. I thought that what I heard was not necessary for Chizu to know right now because she just entered junior high school. And then I wondered why, if this wasn't important now, why was I hearing it now? It took ten years for the things I heard that day to come to pass.

Chizu's spirit person also mentioned marital problem we three sisters would face in the future. About this time, our parents began preparing Kiyo for marriage and looking for a suitable husband. That was how it was done in Japan. After dinner one night, Mother brought out a picture of a man a friend of hers had introduced to her. It was a happy occasion, but when I looked at that picture, blackness appeared in front of my eyes and a fear filled my mind. I saw a spirit standing next to Kiyo. It was her guardian, a woman wearing a navy blue kimono. This spirit was almost crying.

Not this man. Not this man, she said. *She should* marry the *neighbor.*

I repeated the spirit woman's words and tried to persuade Kiyo to wait until a neighbor would come along. But our parents said I was too young to influence such a serious decision.

A few days later, Kiyo and the man in the photo met. At the same time, a neighbor brought a man who lived just a few blocks away to our house to meet Kiyo. This man was worth many millions. As soon as I saw him, I shouted to Kiyo to marry him. But she was not interested. Father, of course, wanted her to marry this wealthy man so she could still live nearby. The final choice was Kiyo's. After she met this second man, her spirit appeared again looking very sad.

Then the spirit woman started to move away from Kiyo. She backed away, never turning her back on Kiyo. But she wasn't walking backward. It looked as if she was being pulled back by some force. It was interesting to see something like this. In a moment, the spirit woman was far away, and I saw a dark space between her and Kiyo, and although I could still see her, I couldn't hear her anymore. Then she dissolved in the darkness. I never saw her again. I have learned that guardian spirits can sometimes change. Perhaps that's what was happening here. Kiyo married the man in the photo, and because of his business they moved to Kamakura, a scenic, historical city about forty miles from Tokyo. Soon Kiyo's life took a very bad turn, and she continues to be miserable to this day. Many years later, I learned that the root of her calamity had something to do with our family background. This was what Chizu's spirit had spoken to me about.

I soon realized that people seldom heed the warnings and end up in different directions from warnings. I know that most people do not hear the voices I heard, and my repeating the words has never seemed to help them either. So what purpose did these warnings serve? If a bad situation was destined for an individual, why did their spirit guardians so passionately try to warn them? Wouldn't the spirit know they could not change their fate? About this time, I began to think about the idea of fate.

THE VOICE

This event happened just before Kiyo married. Every day, there were reports of professional burglars successfully breaking into homes in our area. This was very alarming to the residents of our neighborhood, as this area was not known to have problems with crime.

One night after dinner, Mother and Father were in the family room, and my sisters and I were studying in our own rooms. All of a sudden, from nowhere, I heard a man's voice saying very clearly, *Burglars are here.*

The voice came from above me. I looked up, and at that moment, I saw a vision like a movie, and it was terrifying. I saw two men wearing black T-shirts and trousers and holding big kitchen knives in their hands. They were studying our house, looking for the best place to get in. They already passed our gate and entered into our front garden.

Fear swept through my body like a tsunami. I jumped up and ran down the stairs, screaming to my parents, "Call the police! Burglars are here!" I wanted the burglars to hear my voice. I thought that would scare them into leaving. Hearing my loud scream, Kiyo came into the family room, followed by Chizu.

"We must call the police. *Now*," I shouted.

In spite of my pleading, however, no one moved to call the police.

"How do you know this?" Father asked.

"Did you see them?" Mother asked.

"No time," I screamed. "Check all the doors and windows. Hurry! Everybody! Do it before it's too late! They have big knives. Two men are here!" I was crazed with panic.

I have had a phobia about knives since I was little. Now my family became alert and checked every door and window. I ordered Chizu to go upstairs and make sure the windows were locked. We never locked the windows upstairs, but tonight, I suddenly knew how vulnerable our home was.

"Let's call the police!"

Mother made Father call. With the recent reports of burglaries, it was enough for them to call. Two officers came and looked all around our garden and house. They found nothing suspicious. It was near midnight, and our neighbors came out to see what was happening.

"How did you know burglars were here?" one of the police officers asked me.

Now I knew I was in trouble.

"Why did you say burglars were in the garden?" Mother asked me.

It was impossible to see the front garden from my room. Everybody's eyes were suddenly on me, but what could I say? I remained silent. The policemen and our neighbors left. No one said another word. I went upstairs. I felt as small as an insect.

It was after midnight, and I knew Chizu was asleep as on any other night, but I definitely knew the burglars were still on our property. Then I saw another vision: *people in the garden shed*. We had checked the shed, but that's what I saw. I urged Mother and Father to call the police again, but they refused.

"The burglars are hiding in the tool shed," I insisted. "They're wearing sneakers and black clothes. Their faces and heads are covered by their black caps."

I couldn't sleep. By now, it was nearly three o'clock in the morning. Kiyo was still studying, but when she finally went to bed, I did too. I was exhausted.

My father got up at six o'clock every morning. That morning, when he went into the kitchen, he was stopped in his tracks. He yelled loud enough to wake up the whole family. The kitchen door leading outside was wide open and the kitchen was in total disarray. The mess had nothing to do with burglary. The burglars had made breakfast for themselves. The shells of a dozen eggs were strewn on the counter. They must have made fried eggs. There was bread by the toaster, plus the leftover meatloaf from yesterday and glasses with traces of orange juice in them. They even made coffee. Since Kiyo had stayed up so late, the burglars must have been starving. When I heard the mysterious voice, it was ten o'clock. They had only two hours to work before six o'clock yet they still had enough spare time for breakfast. That shows how professional those burglars were.

My parents and Kiyo slept downstairs, so the burglars went through every room except their bedrooms. We saw all the drawers in the living room and other rooms standing wide open. Our belongings were all over the place, and the burgled rooms had sneaker footprints everywhere. They just stole a little money and a few other items. Mother kept a secret cache of money to be used for food and our education, but the burglars had missed that. They had to be angry when they left, having put in such great effort for so little reward. I think that's what made them eat breakfast in our kitchen.

The same policemen came back. We found where the burglars had been hiding. It was in the tool shed. They had been hiding way in the back and covered themselves with a loose tarp when we looked in the shed. The police were amazed that burglars had cut the lock on the thick kitchen door without making a big noise.

I was again questioned by the police officers. How had I known there were burglars on our property?

All I said was, "Intuition." That was the right answer.

Those two burglars were finally caught after more break-ins. The television reports said that they were wearing black clothes and caps and carrying big kitchen knives. All the information I gave was correct. Not one detail was wrong. I was vindicated.

It was at this time that my family began to realize that I had supernatural abilities. When I think back on this event with the burglars, I realize that no matter how hard I tried, I could not prevent this incident. It was fate. But if we had worked harder, it might not have happened. This made me think how difficult it is to change fate. Even when our guardian spirits are screaming at us, awful things can happen.

But the information about the burglars didn't come from my guardian spirit. After the angelic girl left, I didn't even know who my guardian was. So *who was talking to me?*

It was the same voice that had said, *Competition is not for you,* many years earlier. That voice also came from above. That voice belonged to one of *the others.*

The others had never come back to me. I began to wonder if this would be their new way of communicating with me.

Ghosts

My three years of junior high were the most enjoyable time of my life. I was just like any other teenage girl, my life was simple, and there was no drama. I had every reason to look forward to my life at Takarazuka High School which was located near the top of Rokkou Mountain. There were no houses for miles around. This was a school truly set in nature. Takarazuka, which is the next city over from Nishinomiya, is famous for its hot springs and is a well-known tourist attraction with beautiful scenery. The city is also famous for its entertainment venues, which are similar to Broadway. I liked everything Takarazuka offered.

There was another reason I choose this school. I missed *the others*. I thought that if I would make myself available in nature, *the others* might visit me again. The angelic girl had come to me in the mountains when I was alone. I needed to be in nature. In junior high, I had been so involved with my classmates that I was rarely alone. Although I enjoyed my interactions with my friends, mere human interactions never quite satisfied me. Elder Moon left Japan after two and half years at the mission. I saw him off at the Osaka railway station, and after he left, I stopped going to the church. After I heard the mysterious voice in my house, my heart turned to aliens again.

Walking in the mountain along the river was so refreshing it made me glad I had come to Takarazuka. But a few months later, my plan to be alone and available in case *the others* wanted to visit me was interrupted when I met my new best friend, Torii, who was extremely spiritual. She began walking with me. Because there was no guarantee that the aliens would come when I strolled alone on the mountain, it was agreeable to be with her. While most of our classmates were enjoying their youth and dating and having fun, Torii and I were discussing our spiritual paths.

One day, she said, "Yesterday, I was in a funeral. My grandfather died at the age of eighty. During his last month, he was very confused about his life. I wonder what his spirit is doing now." Then she said, "My eldest sister just had her first baby. I think about life and death."

We also started visiting temples and churches and attending lectures on spiritual topics. I had a few other close girl friends who were also serious, and so I made a radical change in myself. The idea of practical jokes was now out of the question with these friends. I missed the fun times, but I was getting older, and so this transition felt acceptable. After I visited the golden world, high spiritual quality became my concern. It was a time for me to get educated on a spiritual path. I became an obedient student and didn't give Mother any problems. I was contented with my life now.

Then strange things started happening in our new house.

THE GROWING SPIRIT OF MY DECEASED SISTER

It was August, my father's birthday. We had just finished dinner and were enjoying Father's birthday cake.

"Eat some more," Mother said to me.

"No, that's enough," I said as I watched her put another slice on my plate.

We were enjoying a program on television, laughing, and having a good time. And then, I suddenly felt someone turning my neck almost ninety degrees. I had to look at a corner of the room, and there I saw a girl sitting on the floor, just like we were. My heart skipped a beat. She looked a little older than me. And then, my eyes went to the framed picture on the wall above her. It was the picture of my deceased sister, Yuko. She was the sick girl I saw in the "movie" before my birth. Everywhere we lived, that picture always hung in our living room as if she were still a part of the family. That's who this girl on the floor was, though Yuko was now many years older than the girl in the picture, which had been taken when she was three. In the picture, she looked cute, but this older version of her was very skinny. More than anything else, the sight of her sad face pierced my heart.

My body froze. Yuko and I locked eyes for the longest time, and then she looked down. I noticed a small table in front of her, a dark brown table with very short legs. On it I saw a small rice cup, an apple, and a glass of water. Yuko wore a simple, dark blue dress like all Japanese students wear, but her clothes looked poor in quality. People say ghosts do not have feet. I was not sure if she did or not because her legs were covered by the skirt. But I noticed that she was not sitting on a cushion as we were. My heart sank.

The first idea that came to me was the contrast between us. Our family was having fun, eating lots of food. We laughed a lot. But my deceased sister was sitting all by herself, as if not part of our family. Was she a lost soul? Up until this time, the spirits I had seen next to people were their guardians. They all wore decent clothing and were pleasant to look at. They all had some dignity and displayed a willingness to help. But this spirit was very different.

Everybody noticed my sudden silence.

"What's wrong?" Mother asked.

I was reluctant to speak. I didn't want to dampen my father's birthday. Finally, I said, "Oh, I just thought I saw some girl sitting in the corner." I shrugged, as if it was no big deal. I was the peculiar daughter, so no one commented.

I had heard that Yuko loved Father very much. She climbed up on his lap whenever she could. It probably had something to do with the war. They had so little time to spend with each other. Yuko was also Mother's beloved daughter. I had heard that even when Yuko was sick, she never complained. She died in her sleep one morning. Hearing all those stories about Yuko, we never doubted she had gone straight to heaven. But now, I didn't think so. She looked like she was in a trouble. But so was I if I dared to say anything.

I guessed that she came to us because it was Father's birthday. While Yuko and I sat in forlorn silence, Father and the rest of our family continued to celebrate.

Because my father was a Buddhist, we had a family shrine where we put flowers and incense. Occasionally, like most Japanese families, we also placed offerings of food and water for the deceased on the altar. Now it dawned on me that the small, dark brown table inside the shrine in our house was identical to the one I saw Yuko sitting by.

The next day, I secretly took more food to the shrine. I wanted Yuko to know that I had received her message and that I cared about her. I didn't tell my parents because I didn't want to stir up any trouble.

After that first visit, Yuko often appeared at dinnertime and always sat in the same spot beneath her picture. Sometimes, I sat next to her and tried to hear what she wanted to say, but I could never hear her because either the television was on or everyone else was talking. I also looked for her during the day when no one was around, but she never appeared.

There were many things I didn't understand about Yuko's appearance, but the thing that scared me most was her age. Do ghosts continue to grow? It had been fourteen years since her death. If she had lived, she would be about seventeen now. She certainly looked seventeen. But where, actually, was she living? Had she been living here with us all these years and we had never seen her? If so, how frustrated she must have been.

Ghosts appear for a variety of reasons, usually signaling negative situations. They disturb us because they're trying to let us know they exist and are asking us for help. But once their needs have been met, they leave.

Yuko's visits remained a mystery, but I secretly promised her that some day I would learn the reason of her appearance and help her. I was her replacement in the family. I felt some obligation.

Later, I learned that Yuko and I shared the same destiny, which I had never shared with Chizu and Kiyo. We had a special bond before my birth. I believe my visit to the bunker was for the purpose of seeing her. When little children die, they normally do not stay on earth, although under different circumstances this kind of thing can happen. I was about to enter the most difficult time of my life. Since no one else in my family could go through my experiences with me, Yuko's great concern for me as a sister must have kept her alive on earth.

THE ANNOYING MAN GHOST IN OUR HOUSE

Around this same time, a man ghost appeared. I had no idea who he was, and his appearance made me more aware of the strangeness of our house. The first night I saw him I was in the kitchen and he was in the backyard looking in the kitchen window. I thought he was a thief. As we made eye contact, I jumped and let out a loud scream. He should have run away, but he didn't react at all. I could only see his chubby, round face because the window was so high, which made me think he must have been standing on his toes or hovering in the air. He was nearly bald, perhaps fifty years old, and did not look scary. Though his face was totally without expression, he looked pretty normal.

Everybody rushed into the kitchen when they heard my scream.

"There's a man outside," I said, not taking my eyes off the window.

"What? Where?"

My family looked alarmed, thinking this might be a second burglary attempt. But when the man dissolved into the darkness, all I could think was, *Oh, no! It was a ghost.*

This was upsetting to me. When we were burglarized, I never saw the intruders in the yard, but they were real. This time I definitely saw a man, but he was not real. My only reason for believing that he was a ghost was his disappearing act.

This proved not to be an isolated incident. This man ghost kept coming back as did Yuko's. Both kept appearing where I first saw them. The man ghost's face didn't show any sadness, so I knew that he wasn't coming for help, but soon, he started appearing in the bathroom window too. I never thought that would happen because I had heard that most ghosts appear in same spot. The bathroom and the kitchen were next to each other and both facing the backyard. Japanese bathrooms did not have toilets, just a shower area and a soaking tub. The toilet is located in another part of the house.

One night while I was relaxing in the tub, I saw his face, looking at me through the window. I jumped up. I loved luxuriating in the tub, but now I couldn't relax. After I had seen him at the window a few times, I asked Chizu to help me hang a bath towel over the window. Sometimes, I left my bath so quickly I forgot to take down the towel. Mother didn't like towels left in the bathroom, so after I had put my pajamas on, I ran back in and grabbed the towel, but I did not look at the window. When he appeared in the kitchen window, I simply ignored him. But I felt violated and angry, seeing him at the bathroom window. I could hardly report this appearance to the police. Except for spying on me in the bath, he never bothered me. As far as I knew, ghosts could pass through walls, but he never came inside of our house. And his expression never changed. Was he the ghost of someone who had died in this house?

Soon, Mother started asking me what was going on in the bathroom. I finally told her about the man ghost in bathroom window. Then I told her about seeing Yuko too. And then I started talking about the strangeness I felt in this house. Mother asked her pastor to do a blessing to our house and placed a flower and a candle in our shrine. But both ghosts continued to appear for the better part of a year. *Something in this house was very amiss*, I thought. I wondered if the former owner of our house, a Chinese housewife, might have seen him in the bathroom too. If so, I understood her reported mental disorders. I only saw him in the dark. I could see Yuko under the bright lights in the living room, but I never saw her during daylight hours. I saw guardian spirits during the day or under bright lights, which led me to decide that negative ghosts only appeared in the dark. I saw the guardian spirits always beside the people, but the ghosts were by themselves.

Soon, I found myself focused on the negative side of paranormal situations. I would be forced to deal with unknown concepts.

THE WOMAN GHOST WHO ASKED FOR HELP

One year had passed since I first started seeing Yuko's ghost. Luckily, I hardly ever saw her or the man ghost any more. My life seemed to return to normal, and I enjoyed spending time with my friends. Torii and I were both interested in going to the university and often discussed our future.

One hot evening, unusual for the month of September, Mother prepared an exceptional sukiyaki dinner. The simmering pot of mixed vegetables and thinly sliced beef was a family favorite during the Obon festival. Kiyo had come home to join the celebration.

Around nine o'clock, while we were all chatting after dinner, I felt a strong urge to excuse myself from our festivities. We start dinner at eight o'clock and we girls were allowed to stay in the living room and watch television until 9:30, and I was the one who normally tried to linger a little longer and watch another show on television. That night, I had nothing pressing to do, and there was still a lot of food on the table, but I told my family I had a lot of homework. I went upstairs to my room, which was never completely dark because of the light from the staircase. I could see in my room without turning on the light. As I was about to step into my room, I felt a strange drop in the temperature. It was as if I had entered an air-conditioned room. But the air conditioning was not yet on in the upstairs.

I knew something was about to happen and not something good. I almost turned back to go downstairs, but in the next second, I felt an extreme chill and my blood turned to ice. Standing in front of my desk was a nice-looking, middle-aged woman. She was dressed for a formal occasion in a traditional Japanese kimono, with her hair done up in a neat bun, secured with pins in the traditional geisha style. At first, I thought this was a stranger who had entered our house and had quietly made her way to my room.

She just stood there in the shadows, her head tilted slightly as she looked at me. Her face was so devoid of color, she looked like she was wearing kabuki makeup. I couldn't scream. My voice had been snatched from me. She made no threatening moves, no sudden actions, but just stared at me, looking wan and sullen. I couldn't move. My eyes were fixed on her.

She raised her head and turned to face me. Then I saw it. The right side of her face was almost destroyed and her hair was a knotted mess. The rest of her body was likewise mangled. Her left arm wore a sleeve, but her right arm was bare. Fear ran through my body. Then I noticed that she had no feet! The bottom part of her legs did not touch the ground.

Between quivering lips, I squeaked out the word, "Ghost!" I couldn't scream. We both just stood there. My feet seemed to be fastened to the floor by invisible spikes. She looked at me with imploring eyes, and after what had to be the longest minute of my life, I managed to squeeze some sound through my clenched teeth.

"What do you want?" I asked.

Help me. I am suffering immensely.

How could I help her? Could anyone help this ghost? Her left side indicated that she was a woman of class. It was hard to believe that she could have been tormented in such a grotesque way. She said no other words, but just kept staring at me. The pain showing on her face was too much for me. It hurt just to look at her, yet my eyes were fixed on her left side. If I look at her right side, I might have fainted, but it was too dark to see clearly. Her left side had light, but her right side was covered by very dark shadows.

I offered no words, nor did I ask how I could help. Maybe I was too slow to process what I was thinking. But it did not matter. In a moment, she began fading away. I could see through her, see my window behind her as she dissolved into nothingness. The last thing I saw was her left eye staring at me, forlorn and despondent. I could still see that eye in my mind long after she was gone.

I had two choices: either go downstairs and tell everyone what had just happened or stay in up my room and think it over. My brain wasn't functioning. I couldn't move. I was still standing in my doorway. Finally, when I was able to move, I stepped in and turned on the light. Then I walked very slowly around my bedroom. I couldn't go near my desk because I was hesitant to pass through the air where the ghost had hovered. The air still felt cold. So I just sat on my bed, across the room. I looked at the clock. It was 9:15. The ghost had been in my room for near fifteen minutes.

Now I was sure there was something wrong with our house, though I had never before felt anything wrong in my room.

Before, all the ghosts had appeared downstairs. It is said that ghosts appear in old houses, but my bedroom was newly built. Yuko had never told me what she needed, but this strange ghost had asked me to help her.

At 9:30, Chizu came upstairs, singing cheerfully. I wanted to talk to her, but I couldn't. If I said anything, she would tell our parents, and I was afraid that I already had too many problems with ghosts. What would my family think? I decided to remain silent for the time being. *Well*, I said to myself, *at least I wasn't all alone upstairs now.* I went to my desk and tried to study, but how could anyone ever study after seeing a ghost in such pain?

I finally went to bed with the lights on. I didn't dare turn them off. It wasn't until after two a.m. that exhaustion finally took over and I fell into a shallow sleep.

The next morning, everyone in the family noticed that something was wrong with me, though I didn't say anything and stayed downstairs all day. The gruesome image of the woman ghost was still very vivid in my mind.

Evening finally came. We would have dinner, and then it would be time to go to my room again. My fear grew by the minute. I decided I would try to stay downstairs as long as I could. And yet, as the hands on the clock approached nine, I found myself looking up the stairs. I began to feel compelled to go up.

MYSTERIOUS PHENOMENA WITH OTHER BEINGS

As I left the living room, I took a deep breath, trying to prepare myself to see the woman ghost again. I had no way of knowing that from this night on, very mysterious things would start happening to me. But as soon as I set foot on the first step, I felt a shock. It's hard to describe, but my normal small, light steps became big and heavy. I felt as though something had come inside me. The change was immediate. My eyes were fixed on the air right in front of me. As I approached my room, I was no longer a frail, frightened, sixteen-year-old girl.

Just like the night before, the woman ghost was hovering in front of my desk. A split-second chill went through my body, but tonight, fear did not take me over. Instead of being fearful, as I had been the night before, I felt a masculine power surge through me and somehow took control. I was completely awake and sober, yet for the next thirty minutes, I had no control over myself. It must have been this masculine spirit that had compelled me to go up to my room at precisely nine o'clock. I was still somehow present, but he was in control. It was an eerie sensation of duality.

I stepped closer to her. I don't know what happened in the next moment, but I felt words leaving my mouth. It was not me speaking, however. It had to be the masculine force, and I was merely his vessel. Soon words were flowing as if spoken by a professor or a minister. I had not uttered a word the night before, but tonight, a voice was coming from my mouth.

This was not a two-way conversation. The ghost barely spoke. I noticed that she was listening intently, but her eyes were cast downward the entire time.

I still couldn't move, I couldn't summon my own thoughts. I could see her and hear the words, but my consciousness was blurred. I tried to listen to what "I" was saying, but the subject matter was far beyond my comprehension. I could remember some of what the masculine spirit said through me, though my memory was spotty. From what I remember, I came to understand that this woman ghost was my mother's relative and that she had descended into the Realm of the Hungry Ghosts because she had committed suicide. The Realm of the Hungry Ghosts is one of many Buddhist hells, but by no means the worst one. She was in torment there, and I understood that her unfulfilled desire had something to do with her suicide.

Julliena Okah

I never saw this masculine being, but I felt him right behind me. Then I heard, *I'll be back.*

The very moment the masculine spirit spoke those words, the woman ghost dissolved into darkness, as slowly as she had the night before.

My fear did not return for a good five minutes. I just stood there in front of my desk, feeling as strong as an eagle. Then I felt *him* leave my body. It was not the same, strong sensation as when he had entered, but felt rather like a spigot inside me had opened and his spirit simply drained out. I slowly returned to my normal state.

Then I panicked.

I turned on all the lights and I fell on my bed. What was this all about? Last night, a ghost I did not know had appeared before me and asked for help. That was scary enough, but nothing like tonight. This was much more than just ghosts coming to visit me. Someone else, probably a man the woman ghost knew, had come through me to speak to her.

Was I possessed? Is "possessed" even the right word for what happened to me? My body had been used, taken over. And not only had the masculine used my body, but these two had also used my room. I had nothing to do with the woman ghost's problems. What was going on? Who was the masculine spirit? I knew he had come to guide the woman ghost, but neither he nor she was living on the earth at that moment. Why did they meet in my room of all places? I had some serious questions that required answers.

Finally, it dawned on me—it was Obon. Obon is a Buddhist ritual of deliverance for spirits who have fallen into the lower realms. It begins in July and ends when the full moon rises in September. Our ancestors who are suffering come back during this festival. There is a fire ritual conducted by monks. Many temples have professionals on hand to assist lay people who need help.

Yes, I decided, it was Obon that had brought the woman ghost to my bedroom because I was related to her. I could understand why she appeared.

But the masculine spirit was still a mystery to me. I was puzzled until I began to think about the aliens. They had all said they would help me. This spirit must have come because he knew I couldn't help the woman ghost on my own. He must have had something to do with *the others*. *The others* said *We will be back.* This mystery man said *I'll be back.* Maybe he was someone who was sent to help me. Because the ghost was a spirit, a spiritual being was sent to me. That made sense.

Then I began to wonder if he and the woman ghost have a predetermined agreement to meet in my room? By now, my head was spinning. Was it really my mother this woman ghost wanted to contact? She was my mother's relative and seemed to be about the same age as my mother. I wondered why the woman ghost appeared to me rather to Mother.

Then it came to me—Mother could not handle this. She had no experience with extraterrestrial beings. Ghosts are not earthly. The woman ghost's needs were so great that she needed someone who had more power than most human beings. Since I communicated with beings from other worlds, she came to me. She knew one of *the others* would come to help her.

Obviously, the woman ghost and the masculine spirit resided in different places. Two different worlds. Only this time, it was his world and her world, good and evil, and not my simple division of the real world I could touch. This situation was more complex. My two visitors did not belong in my world, yet these two could communicate. Somehow, a third or fourth dimension had been created in my bedroom.

There were just too many nonhumans populating my life, but now I was beginning to understand that interactions between various forms of existence were taking place in all these different worlds. Why was this happening? I could only think of one reason. To give help. It became crystal clear in my mind.

A SECRET IS REVEALED

The ghost woman appeared every night for a week. Every time she appeared, the mysterious man was also present. By the seventh night of her visits, however, I had had enough. Now I was angry. Why was this happening to me? I was just a high school student. I was also facing exams, and it was impossible to study with ghosts and spirits coming every night. Feeling desperate, I decided to tell my mother. This woman ghost was her relative. She should know about these visits. Maybe she could somehow take over for me.

Mother was in the kitchen when I decided to speak to her.

"Mother, did you once know a woman who was beautiful and tall, with an old-fashioned Japanese hairdo? She has a long, oval face. She was your relative and committed suicide."

Mother stopped what she was doing and looked at me. Right away, I knew she knew the ghost woman. "I want to know about her," I said.

"You do not know her." Mother's voice was harsh. "How do you know she committed suicide? She died before you were born."

"I know that. But she fell into the Hungry Ghost Realm and she's suffering. She keeps appearing in my room. It's been seven nights already."

Mother became very quiet. I could feel her reluctance, but finally, she spoke. "She was my aunt, Takako. She was known as a woman of great beauty. She married a prestigious English millionaire."

"A millionaire? Then why did she fall into such a horrible place?"

"How am I supposed to know such a thing? All I know is she committed suicide."

"Why?"

Mother could not answer.

"We have to do something to ease her suffering," I said.

Still, Mother did not reply. This upset me, but I could tell she was even more upset than I was. She had never talked about her aunt Takako, in fact she hardly spoke at all about her family. There was no way I could know about Takako, but I had just described her.

"You will never talk about this again!" Mother finally exclaimed. "Go practice your violin!"

Something bad had happened in Mother's family, for otherwise she would not have reacted so strongly. There must be some hidden secret. I knew she avoided discussing any kind of paranormal topics since I was little. I had gotten a little bit of information from her, but no offer of help. I was left on my own again.

Thank God! Takako stopped appearing in my bedroom. I assumed that being known to my mother caused the woman not to appear again. Perhaps it was meant for my mother to know. Everything seemed to return to normal until a few weeks later, when I learned who Takako was.

It was after lunch one Sunday afternoon. My family was gathered in our family room, each of us tending to our own tasks. Chizu and I were doing an art project, and Mother was cleaning out some drawers of the chest.

When the doorbell rang, Mother went to answer the door. As soon as she left, I felt drawn to look at what she was doing. There were pictures all over the floor. One of Father's hobbies was photography. He loved making albums, and occasionally, he showed them to us, but Mother had never shown us any pictures. She did not have albums. Now her photos were strewn all over the floor.

I picked one up. It was a formal family portrait of eight people, four of them women. My eyes were drawn to the men. One of them, a handsome foreigner, suddenly stood out from the rest.

I froze. Seated right in front of him was the ghost woman! I recognized her right away. The woman in the picture wore the same kimono and had the exact same hairstyle as the ghost woman. Of all the photos Mother had, I had picked the one I needed to see. This was no coincidence!

When Mother returned to the room, I pointed to the woman in the photo and said, "This is the woman I was talking about." I showed it to my father and sisters. "This woman appeared to me for one whole week."

Nobody knew about the ghost except Mother. I could immediately see their reactions. I knew exactly what they were thinking. *Her. Again. What is wrong with her?*

I didn't want to hear anything. I went outside to take a walk.

As I was walking in the residential area of the university campus where the foreign professors lived, I kept thinking about that photo. If Takako had shown me only her damaged right side, I would have never recognized her. The more I thought about her distorted side, the more curious I became. How did she hide her right side in a very dark shadow?

The residential area for Japanese professors was next to the foreign residential area. Sanae, one of my junior high school classmates, lived here. We had often shared long walks around the campus. She was home, and when I asked, she agreed to walk with me. Our conversation drifted toward music.

"My parents said your violin sounded nice at the concert the other night," she said. "They also liked your expression."

We had had school concert and I had played my violin. Our parents had come to see us. I never thought I would confide my secrets about aliens to anyone, but today, especially today, I needed to redirect our conversation.

"Sanae," I said, "this is between you and me. Please don't tell anyone, not even your family. I have never told this to anyone, but I am telling you because we are best friends."

"Of course, I won't tell. What is it?"

"An alien taught me how to play the violin. On another world."

"What? An alien? Another world?"

"Yes," I said. "I know it's a strange story, but that's what happened to me."

"How did you go to another world?"

"I wish I could give you a good explanation, but I can't. I think maybe it was an out-of-body experience or maybe I flew or maybe I entered some kind of tunnel that just took me to another world. I don't really know"

Sanae just stood still and looked at me. "What?"

"A lot of strange things have been happening to me since I was little," I began. "But every time I try to talk about these things, I get into trouble. So I stopped talking about them. But when I arrived on that world, I saw angel-like beings. Then I heard one of the angelic being playing a violin. I'll never forget the sound or the fascinating technique I saw. The violinist also told me that someday I would travel around the world performing as a violinist. Before that happened, I used to hate the violin. After hearing him, I started to practice seriously. This is not a dream or my imagination," I said. "It happened when I was twelve years old, so I remember it well."

"I don't know what to say!"

"I know. Me neither. But please don't tell anyone. I don't need any more problems."

"Your secret is safe with me," she said. "I promise I won't say anything. If I did, I would probably get in trouble too, so I just won't talk about it."

"Sanae, a lot of good things have happened to me since I met the aliens, but I'm facing a very difficult situation right now. I think there's something wrong in my house. Strange things keep happening. And now, ghosts are appearing in my bedroom. Not only ghosts, but something else too. I don't understand what's happening. Your father is a science professor. He might know. Could you ask him if other worlds exist and if we might visit them and how we would get there? Maybe someone from another world comes to help us. I want to know because that's what happened to me."

She thought this over. "I've heard some of his students talk about other worlds," she said, "but nothing like you're describing. Those students normally come to our house on Saturdays. Why don't you come and ask them yourself? I'll arrange it."

I was delighted to have this opportunity.

When I went home a couple hours later, I saw that Mother's photos were still in the living room, though they had been pushed to one side. She told me to clean up the art project materials before dinner. As Chizu and I started picking things up, another photo caught our attention. It was a photo of an enormous mansion, as big as a hotel. The park-like property was located on a hilly landscape and had a river, complete with waterfalls, running through it. Chizu asked Mother where this place was.

"That was my grandfather's house," Mother said.

"Was it a private house?" Chizu asked.

"Of course. I was born there."

During dinner, I couldn't help but think of what I had learned today. I now understood that my mother's family was privileged. But why hadn't we known about this all these years? As soon as we had finished eating, Mother went to watch her favorite music program on TV. I looked at more of the pictures. There were many family portraits. I could not believe the quality of the photos. They must have been taken by professional photographers while she was growing up. Unlike my father's amateur snapshots, many of Mother's photos were eight-by-tens and framed in gold leaf.

Then I came to one of a huge European house. "Whose house is this?" I called out to Mother.

"It's Takako's house."

My heart skipped a beat. "Takako's house?"

"Yes. It was my uncle's house." She stopped watching her music program and said, "Takako married the owner of this house. I was going to tell you. Next Saturday, my sister Miyo and all of us are going to Kobe to visit this house. It has become a museum and is open to the public, but we will be the only ones visiting on that day."

"Why are we the only ones?" I asked.

"Because this mansion that is now a museum once belonged to my family, and I received an invitation. It's called the Hunter Museum."

When Chizu asked who Takako was, Mother said, "She was my father's elder sister and the oldest daughter of my grandfather, Zentaro. Takako married the owner of this house, an English millionaire named Ryutaro Hunter."

Mother's background was a surprise to us. I thought we were normal people.

The Hunter Museum was located halfway up the mountain in the center of Kobe. This museum was Takako's house. Was this a coincidence? Did she know we would be visiting her house and talking about her? Perhaps that was why she appeared to me.

Two guards in green uniforms stood outside, holding their batons in front of their chests. As they opened the heavy metal gates for us, I thought someone would act as our guide. But there was no one inside the house. Mother just walked right on in, as though it were her own house. She and her sister Miyo became nostalgic as they led us through the garden and into the house. Mother told us she had stayed in the west wing many times when she was a child.

Edward Hunter, an English millionaire, had come to Japan and built the mansion using materials imported from England. He was one of the first foreign businessmen in Japan and also one of the wealthiest. He was also Mother's grandfather's friend. After Edward died, his son, Ryutaro, inherited the mansion and married Takako. After Takako and Ryutaro Hunter died, the mansion was left vacant. Eventually, the government took possession of it, and then it was designated as a national treasure.

Around 1960, the Hunter Mansion was featured on a postage stamp and a prepaid telephone card.

After a while, we went out into the garden again and sat beside the pool. Miyo began talking about Takako.

"Takako was like a second mother to me," she said.

"How I wish Kimi were here with us today," Mother said with great emotion. Kimi, their youngest sister, had recently died.

I spoke up, "Takako must have been happy living in such a fabulous mansion."

"Well, her marriage to Hunter had been arranged by the government," Miyo said.

"Arrangement by the government? Why?" I asked.

"The government needed our family to prosper," Miyo replied.

I wanted details. I felt that Takako held some key to our family secret, but Mother said there was nothing for me to be concerned about and her family matters were all in the past. Mother just wanted me to concentrate on my studies. Entrance exams for the university were coming up, and the competition was stiff. She felt it was crucial that I gain admittance to a good university.

One Saturday a few weeks later, Sanae invited me to her home. Five male university students were sitting in her living room. One of them brought up the subject of the Pacific Bermuda Triangle, which is a huge area south of Japan in the Pacific Ocean. It is about the same size as the Bermuda Triangle and is located on the same latitude. Both triangles are in the deepest parts of the ocean. People were curious about it because it had been featured on a TV program. The Pacific Bermuda Triangle is also known as the Dragon's Triangle. The Dragon's Triangle, though it sounds Chinese, has nothing to do with China or dragons. It was only named that because "dragon" sounds Asian to Westerners. There have been mysterious beings appearing in the Dragon's Triangle for many years. One being, which was floating on the ocean, was witnessed quite a few times. UFOs have also been spotted in these parts of the ocean many times, and many disappearances occurred there—ships, airplanes, and people have vanished without a trace, and there have also been many sightings of ghost ships with no people aboard. The ancient Japanese were aware of these unexplainable disappearances and referred to them as *Kamikakushi*, which means "hidden by God." Discoveries seemed to confirm ancient beliefs. *Kamikakushi* is something we all know about. It was mentioned in one of Japan's oldest scholastic books, *Nihonshoki*. These mysterious happenings had recently been discussed in reference to the existence of other dimensions and other worlds.

The students also talked about Urashima. The utopia he visited is referred to as the Dragon Sea God's Palace. Another mystery connected to Urashima's story is time dilation. He came back to earth hundreds of years later, and now time dilation is called the Urashima effect.

Sanae's father, the professor, began to give a scientific explanation and spoke of Albert Einstein and relativity. Unfortunately, science and math were my weakest subjects in school, so I did not understand very much, but when the professor mentioned time dilation, he had my full attention. I never could figure out what happened to time during my experiences in the other world.

"Einstein explained time dilation with speed and gravity." the professor said. "Where time flows faster or slower, depending on speed and gravity, time dilation occurs. The discovery of the speed of light explained this dilemma." He also used Einstein's theory to explain the *Kamikakushi*. This is the theory of deformation of embedded spaces. It is gravitational physics. Then he spoke about a tunnel through space that might exist. I thought that the aliens' vehicle might have used either this tunnel or deformation as a shortcut when they visited me or took me to other worlds.

Our conversation continued during tea time.

"Do you know," one of the students said, "that some of our ancient stories speak of Japan being created over ten thousand years ago through the intervention of aliens?"

"As you know," the professor said, "the origin of Japan goes back to the Jomon civilization, perhaps nearly 15,000 years ago. Scholars say that our ancient clay figures, the *dogu*, could be the oldest things found on earth so far. The origin of Japan is indeed mysterious. Nobody knows for sure, but it's all mixed with the worlds of the many gods and goddesses who live in heaven. The *dogu* are seen by some researchers as astronauts from other worlds who came from the sky in ancient times. The *dogu* do not look like Japanese. Their clothes aren't Japanese clothes either. This makes us think that some other beings might have existed in Japan in that long-ago time."

"So is it possible that aliens helped to create our civilization?" someone asked.

"It is true that many unexplainable things had happened and are still happening in the Dragon's Triangle. There are many mysteries in the world. We have not solved these mysteries. The *dogu* and the Dragon's Triangle were often connected with unidentified flying objects. There is some possibility that extraterrestrials visited ancient Japan. They might have influenced ancient people."

From Sanae's father's lecture, I understood that other dimensions and other worlds that we cannot see with our physical eyes might exist in this universe. I wondered if my bedroom might be a venue for ghosts and spirits and poltergeists and the events they create. Was I living near a gateway into another dimension?

When I brought up the subject of another dimension and ghosts, we discussed what happens after death. We all die, yet we know very little about our state of being after death. It was, and still is, a huge scientific challenge.

But who would have thought that I was about to experience that world after death myself?

CHAPTER 7

Hell

MY FIRST NIGHT IN HELL

As her marital problems grew, my sister Kiyo visited us more frequently. During one of her visits, Mother took us to Kyoto to visit the grave of Taro, her father. The cemetery was located on the grounds of the famous Buddhist temple of the Chiyo Inn, and his grave was among the largest there. His father, Zentaro, had built it as the family gravesite, meant to include many generations, but the family name, which had endured for thousands of years, ended with my mother's generation. I had seen Zentaro's enormous house in one of Mother's photos. It was rare to own such a large piece of property in Japan. Mother said that after World War II, the government had confiscated much of the land, but the main part of this house exists to this day and is one of the biggest houses in Kyoto. I knew Mother respected her grandfather, not because of his social standing or his wealth, but because of his spiritual devotion after his conversion to Buddhism.

After we placed flowers on his grave, Mother took us to visit the last house she lived in before her marriage. I noticed the workers were respectfully addressing Mother as though she were the owner. I knew that she periodically visited the house to tend to legal matters, but we had never been told that the property was hers. Mother hardly spoke about family history to us.

Soon, Kiyo's curiosity got the better of her, and she started researching Mother's family background. The reason for her curiosity was that being the eldest in our family, she would be the inheritor of Mother's name and property. Kiyo was wondering why Mother did not bring up the importance of her family when she was looking for a husband for her eldest daughter. She was already having financial problems in her marriage. My interest in Mother's family was different from Kiyo's, but we shared our curiosity about Mother's background.

There were many more surprises in her background.

Mother's ancestors had worked with the emperor for over five hundred years and held the titles of governor and chief samurai. Throughout the generations, the family had gained increasing power and also produced some of Japan's most prominent scholars.

Mother was born as the first child of one of the most prestigious families in Japan. When she was young, she lived an extravagant life, having her own maid. They were one of the first families to own a car, in which Mother was chauffeured to school, unlike her contemporaries, who were transported by rickshaw.

But sadly, the majority of her relatives either committed suicide or died unexpectedly from a variety of tragic accidents. Mother's mother, Aiko, had died during the bombing in the war, and her father, Taro, committed hara-kiri. Taro's elder sister Takako and Taro's younger brother Shigeo also committed suicide. Taro had one more sister, Suga. Although she did not commit suicide, her three children did. Taro's younger brother, Shigeo, had four children of whom three committed suicide.

I learned that Takako had died five years before I was born, which means she had been living in the suffering realm for about twenty years. Twenty years seemed to be a long time to me. Takako had not returned, and I felt somewhat relieved, yet I still felt her near me. Home was supposed to be a place where I could feel safe, but it was hard to stay in my room. My thoughts were murky. I was painfully aware that Takako had asked for help with indescribable agony. I wondered what happened to our other ancestors.

Soon, I got the answer.

I found myself standing somewhere. I was not in my room anymore. I do not know how I left my room. I was just suddenly somewhere else, just like I had been transported to the forest and to the heavenly world in my childhood. But this time I remembered the jet black area I passed through. It felt like I blacked out for some short period. Later in my life I would have many experiences about this jet black space.

The first thing I noticed was an absence of color, which made me think it had to be nighttime. I could see mountains in the distance, but they were separated only by shades of black and gray and looked like giant pieces of obsidian sprouting from the ground. Overhead, the sky was empty. No stars. No moonlight. I saw smoke coming up. Maybe, I thought, the smoke was so thick it blotted out the moon.

Then, I smelled a stench I had never smelled before. I began to hear screaming. I carefully made my way to the edge and looked down to see where the screaming came from. Below me was a gorge. It was only then that I saw I was standing on a plateau. I heard a second scream, then another. As I neared the precipice, I heard a chorus of voices crying out. The sounds made the hairs on the back of my neck stand on end.

Down below, I saw a burning fire like a river of lava, fire erupting from the ground like a volcano. Then I saw the people, hundreds and hundreds of them, wading through the fire, fighting and climbing over each other in their desperate attempts to get away from the fire. Their shrieking pierced my ears. My legs gave way and I collapsed on the ground. I crawled to the edge of the plateau and looked down again. One man caught my attention as he crawled up the side of the plateau. His skin was red and his clothes were smoking, but he did not seem to be a victim of the sweeping fire. When he looked up, we made eye contact. For a brief second, I got the feeling that he recognized me. It seemed that I was important to him. He reached up, imploring me to take his hand, but the distance between us was too far to reach.

Then his head caught fire. I saw him tumble down into the fires. Though I was sickened to watch this, I made a point of keeping my eyes on him. The flames engulfed him, and his screams started to taper off. Soon, I thought, he would know blissful death. Thank God! Death was infinitely preferable to what had to be the worse way imaginable for someone to die. In another few seconds, he stopped moving, and the flames started to subside.

His suffering was over. I stared at that human briquette.

But then, that bundle of human firewood moved. He wasn't dead! Or was he? I strained to make out what was happening. The body appeared to be swelling. No. It wasn't swelling. It was regenerating. The body was healing itself. Soon, I saw hair growing again on the top of the head. With the body intact, skin reappeared, growing like mold, and his clothes returned, knitting themselves over the man. I was dismayed to see such a scene. In an instant, the burned man looked as if he had not been touched by fire at all.

His eyes blinked, and I could imagine the horror of that memory in his mind. He was conscious of where he was and what was happening around him. He screamed and bolted upright. He did not look around, but suddenly took off in no particular direction. I lost sight of him in the chaos below me. All this happened within a few minutes.

Had I just witnessed the death to birth process? But no, this man was not an infant. He had regenerated into middle age. Did he start his life anew in middle age?

Soon, I saw another body reanimate itself, then another. People were dying and coming back middle-age, only to experience the same terrible suffering and death, time and time again. I was not sure what I was looking at, yet I knew I was witnessing incredible regenerations. All the people below me were destined to relive this holocaust. Life here was brief.

I suddenly understood. "This is hell!" I had been so caught up with all the commotion that I had not even considered where I was. I felt my body turning to ice, even above those awful flames. "Oh, God! What's going on?"

Am I dead? I asked myself. *No, I am perfectly alive. Then what am I doing here? What happened to me? I should not be here. Hell is a place for those who have committed heinous crimes. Only evil people end up in hell. I must get out of here!* I looked for an exit, but there was no exit.

And there was nowhere to hide. If I was stuck on this plateau, I thought, I would not have to suffer this unholy demise, but I would find myself alone on an island in a sea of death and I was doomed to witness this hell.

What, I began asking myself, *could I possibly have done to deserve being here?* What evil must a person do to warrant such a wicked punishment? I was as desperate to understand as I was to escape, but I was ignorant. The wailing and screaming below me went on. Maybe I was not here to experience the physical torture of the people below, but my mental anguish was unbearable.

This must be a dream, I tried to tell myself. *It is the worst nightmare I have ever had.* I tried to wake myself up. *Yes, it will be only a matter of time before I would wake up in my bed.* I struggled to wake up. No bed. Then I thought, *If I fall down, I will surely wake up.* I remembered a dream I had once in which I had been frightened of something and fallen. In the dream, when I hit the ground, I woke up. Cautiously, I got up on my feet, walked to the edge, and stood with my toes over the side. I closed my eyes and tried to prepare myself to fall. My balance was tentative. *A little more. Keep going. Almost there.*

Someone cried out. It sounded like my name. Opening my eyes, I saw the land of fire filled with the damned, all of them ready to receive me.

I fell back on my rump, my legs dangling over the edge. A man standing between two burning corpses below was pointing at me and screaming at the top of his lungs. Did he know me? He started to make his way to me, pushing people aside. I felt as though I knew him. He must have just come back from the dead. Then another man saw me, and I saw a look of recognition on his face too. But how could they know me? Yet there was something familiar. They were fighting to get to the base of the plateau.

More and more people started to take notice of me. I tried to recall where or how I might have known these men.

Family? That was it! They were family, ancestors in my bloodline. Mother's ancestors. I did not know how many of them were part of my family, but I saw a mass of them coming at me. I guess they had to grab anything or anyone they could to get out.

They started to climb up the side of the plateau, but the way was steep. The first man fell, taking two men with him. Others kept climbing. If something bad didn't happen soon to the next man, his hand would soon be grabbing hold of the ledge I stood on.

Should I help him? I did not know what to do. My vision drifted from the men scaling the plateau to the mass hysteria unfolding below. I saw arms clawing at the fissures, the closest man to me, maybe five or six feet below, reaching to grab my dangling legs like a shark going for bait. Panic swept over me.

I pulled my legs up. I wanted to help them, help all of them. But how could I? The men trying to reach me were mad with pain, screaming and shrieking incoherently. If they reached me, took hold of me, I would catch fire like them.

I had never been so scared. I screamed. Death was taking hold of me. I ran as fast as I could.

Something hit me. I fell.

Then…*life*.

Another scream forced itself out of my lungs as I fell back and hit my head on my desk. The jolt knocked the desk lamp over, casting weird shadows on my wall. I was back in my room!

I sat up. I knew what had happened, yet I had no idea what had happened. Had I gone to hell? *That was insane.* How could it possibly be? I stood and picked up my desk lamp. A quick scan of my room told me everything else was in place. Why shouldn't it be? I looked at my body. I was fine. The clock by my bed read 9:30 p.m. Could I have mentally crashed and lost consciousness? That nightmare had felt so real, but I was back in my room now. Awake. That's what mattered. After meeting the man ghost and the woman ghost night after night, I must have been due for a nightmare.

As I walked toward my bedroom door, I could hear Chizu talking in the living room. I heard her unmistakable laugh. No one had heard me scream. Good! I wouldn't have to account for it, but I wouldn't have anyone to talk to about it either. One more story I had to keep bottled up inside. My isolation was starting to take its toll.

I went back and sat on the foot of my bed, all the time telling myself, *It was just a dream, it was just a dream.* The night was cool, but I was soaking in sweat. I still felt heat on my skin. That was weird. I changed into my sleepwear, went back to my desk, and opened my geometry book. I would immerse myself in my studies in an effort to rid myself of the fear and dread. I had a major exam at the end of the week.

But the thoughts of hell stayed in my mind. I had seen pictures of hell in a children's book about Buddhism. One hell I saw in that book was, in fact, very similar to the hell I had just seen for myself. There were many hells, the book said, such as walking on a needle mountain with bare feet or being in a cold, lonely place without God's love. In Asia, we are taught about the afterlife in accordance with Buddhist beliefs, and maybe we are more conscious of hell than Westerners, though the Bible also mentions a fiery hell.

I also thought about the men trying to climb up to the plateau, the man who was reborn. Were they really my ancestors? Had he been enduring the fires of this inferno for centuries?

For hours, I sat at my desk, not reading a single page, dark thoughts hanging over me. Eventually, I made my way to my bed and crawled beneath the covers. How glad I was to be in my room.

The inhabitants of hell were running and struggling all the time, but here in my bedroom, I could rest. Lying down felt like heaven. Overwhelming happiness filled my heart. Since I was born, I had slept every night in comfort. But tonight was different. Sleeping was blissful.

MY SECOND NIGHT IN HELL

The next day in school was awful. All day, I did not know where my head was. Since my terrible experiences with the ghosts, I was no longer the optimistic child I used to be. I had never imagined I would have to deal with a ghost appearing seven nights in a row. Yet she did, and I wished from the bottom of my heart that I would never have this kind of dreadful nightmare again. I needed to turn my mind away from these images.

Today was Saturday, and we attended school only half the day. After school, I decided to go to see the Takarazuka musical show, which was the most colorful and delightful show I could think of seeing. My classmate Misaki had been studying musical shows because her dream was to become an entertainer. Her parents were choreographers in Takarazuka and could get free tickets. She had been inviting me to catch one of the shows, but I hadn't had the chance yet. Today was the perfect day to go.

The two-hour show, called *Roses of Versailles*, was fascinating. It was a story of Marie Antoinette, her life, her romances in Vienna and Paris. The costumes were colorful and fabulous, the stage lighting was bright and sparkling. I almost forgot my troubles. Beautiful colors always do that for me. The show was breathtaking.

After the show, Misaki and I strolled along the river. The sunset was brilliant, the bright orange sun reflecting in the river and adding dashes of gold to the water. How glad I felt that I could live in such a blessed place on earth! I felt how important color was in contrast to the blackness of hell. I wished I could work with something involving beautiful colors and bringing happiness to others.

It was time to think of my future. Misaki had been taking singing and dancing lessons since she was four years old. Her wishes and her parents' wishes were the same. I envied her and began to wish I shared her passion for music. I had been practicing my violin since I had visited the heavenly world because I wanted travel around the world, but I had yet to find something I felt passionate about.

Now I began hearing a lot about my grandmother, Aiko. Mother told me about her mother's lineage, so I would understand the importance of the musical path I should be taking. As Mother talked, I learned there were still more surprises in her family tree. I did not know Aiko had been one of the very first persons in Japan to play the piano. Aiko's family imported a piano for her from England. This was big news in Japan as no private citizen before then had done such a bold and costly thing. Aiko contributed to the development of European music in Japan, which was the reason music was a big part of my family's history.

And there were more surprises. Aiko was also the first, or one of the first women, to wear Western clothing. At that time, all Japanese men and women wore kimonos. The reason for Aiko's Western dress had a lot to do with the piano. The piano came from Europe, so her family decided she should wear European dresses to go along with the piano and imported Western clothing from England.

A piano concert with musicians dressed in Western clothes was reported in all the major newspapers and magazines. More people started to wear Western clothing and became interested in the Western style of living. Aiko's pictures were often in magazines as well as newspapers. Photographs of Mother's family appeared on the front page. The newspaper headline read, "Royal Family with Western Clothes." Mother did not remember the name of the newspaper because she was too young, but she told me it was comparable in circulation to the *New York Times*. After Mother showed me these pictures, I felt a familial responsibility to carry on the musical tradition.

I decided that it was not Mother's maternal ancestors who were the tormented souls in hell. Those souls must have come from her paternal lineage.

A few months passed, and then one day when I was finishing dinner, I was drawn to go to my room at nine o'clock again. As before, when I reached the foot of the stairs, I felt a strange vibration around me. I sensed the masculine presence again. The same thing that had happened before happened again. I was rapidly pulled up to my room.

Then something really unexplainable happened. As soon as I walked in, I walked into hell. Instead of passing through the door of my room, I passed through a great portal and stepped into another world. As before, I found myself on the scorched, rocky plateau with a panoramic view of the pandemonium all around me.

I *knew* I had walked into my room. It felt like I had stepped into a different dimension and was sucked into another world. This strange incident happened when this action was still taking place. It did not resemble the common out-of-body experience, but rather a real and physical experience. I was not lost. I had not even sat down at my desk. There was no way I could have fallen asleep while I was walking. I made a conscious effort to test myself to see if I was awake or asleep. I punched my arm, pinched my wrist, and rubbed my eyes. I had to know for sure that I was not having a nightmare.

After several of these tests, I was convinced I was awake. But, I thought, if this is not a dream, then what could it be? If this was real, then what was I doing here? The first night, I had been in such a desperate panic that I had not examined my experience carefully. This time, I had to pay close attention to see what was going on and find out why I was there. The last time it happened, I focused my attention on a few struggling men. This time, I would broaden my focus. I noticed that I had control over both my mind and my actions. Unbelievably, I felt very calm and objective. It must be the masculine presence.

I carefully looked around. Black smoke came up from burning bodies and filled the air. My eyes followed the smoke. Now far up in the sky, I saw a dim light. Since it was so dark, I believed it was night, but now, I thought maybe it wasn't night. Then I noticed the strangeness of the dark gray part of the sky. It was contained in a very small circular section. Other than that, it was all black. It looked as if we were trapped down in a hole, a deep, inescapable hole.

This is difficult to explain, but think of a sandbag. If the sand in the bag fills about ten percent of a bag in a standing position, the bottom part of bag stretches to the all sides and is held down by the weight of the sand. The top of the bag is closed with a string and pointed at the sky. If ants were trapped in the sand at the bottom of this bag, they would see only darkness around them, but if someone untied the string and opened the top the bag a little bit, light would shine inside. The ants could then see the sky through the opening above them. But the sky did not exist inside of the bag. It seemed like I was standing halfway up from the bottom of the bag and was able to see both below and above.

I thought about the light and gazed at it for a while. This opening and the light might be salvation for the people in the fires below. I did not know if that was true, but I hoped so. If the burning people were able to hang on to something positive, this should be it. I wondered if the inhabitants of hell could see the light. Probably not. They were so tormented and caught up in their plight, they did not have the strength or fortitude to look up. Somehow, I felt there was salvation, even in hell.

"Look up, look up!" I shouted down at the burning people.

As I tried to get their attention, my eyes were caught again in the hell before me. I noticed the mountains were filled with thorny bushes. People who were trying to run to the mountains were constantly getting caught in the thorns. The mountains were so steep that it was impossible for them to climb. People trying to climb were falling, yet they kept trying again, desperately attempting to avoid the flames. Even if they climbed up a mountain, they would not escape. There was no place to go. They would be trapped. They would suffocate in the thick black smoke. They ran in every direction until fire consumed them. I could see they were almost naked.

Thousands of dead bodies lay in the chasm below me where everything was scorched and burning. The thirst of the burning people was so great they tried to do anything to get water, yet hardly any existed. I saw they were eating. Was there food? When I realized they were eating dead bodies and picking out the guts, I almost threw up.

My eyes were drawn farther down into the bottomless pit. There was a huge basin at the bottom of the mountain, and the torture there was so severe that people were seeking higher ground, but most of them were dragged back down to die. Big black animals were attacking people and dragging them down. They were hiding all over the place. They looked as ferocious as wolves, but they were not wolves. Such scary-looking animals do not exist on earth.

The beings tormenting the people were also scary. They were giants, three times bigger than the people. Some of the giants were crushing the people, causing their internal organs to pop out of their bodies. Some of the giants were piercing the bodies of people with sharp spears until they died. No matter how hard they tried to run away, once they were in the basin, there was no way out. There were many giants engaged in all manner of torture. Strangely, they seemed not to be affected by the fire. Were they good beings or bad ones? I still do not know. I could not see their faces, since I was far away and they did not look up, but I thought they must be angry because their actions were so powerful and swift. Screams pierced my ears, my heart. This was certainly a much worse hell than I had seen in any book before. The torment was more than I could bear.

Even though I tried to observe these details, soon I couldn't take any more. I had to get out of there. I started to run.

Then I saw my ancestors again. They were right beneath me.

In the next moment, I felt *his* existence again. I now knew I was not alone. I remembered how he, the man who professed to be a scholar, the man who spoke with the conviction of a minister, had taken me over entirely. I suddenly felt like a lion. I saw myself standing firmly on the rock. I experienced a strange duality and knew his sermon would start shortly. I made myself focus on this mystical phenomenon. In my experiences with the ghosts, I have somehow lost myself and, to this day, have very few memories. Did he possess me? I thought that if I refused to allow it, I might be able to keep my memory for, as far as I knew, a possessed person does not have memory.

But I did not know how to keep from being possessed. It seemed like it was all happening automatically and spontaneously.

He started to lecture them, just as he had lectured the woman ghost. I wanted to find immediate help for these people, but I realized that he was not going to rescue them as I wished. His subject was causation and karmic law as Buddha expounds. He spoke about the purpose of life. His point was that life was something that needed to be exceeded. Spiritual progress is the purpose of life, he said. Our focus should not be on the activity of the world. He explained how reincarnation takes place. His words reminded me of the things I had heard from the celestial beings so many years ago. As I listened to him, I could feel myself, and I could even think. That had not happened before. Now I was feeling a dual existence and was able to assess my situation more calmly.

Then, while I was looking at the people below, a "movie" appeared, just like when I saw my past lives and before of my birth. I was no longer looking at my ancestors but at their past lives, their history. I saw a brutal war in Japan, I do not know when it occurred, but by the people's clothing, I assumed it was many hundreds of years ago. Houses were burning, children and women were being killed by men with swords, their screams were terrifying. Horses were running wild and crushing people. It was nighttime, and huge fires were spreading through the city. These people I was now facing were part of this scene. I was so caught up in this "movie" that I was no longer listening to what the man was saying. Then things got worse. I did not see myself in this war, but I felt that I had something to do with it. Maybe because of my family.

And then I heard, *We will be back.*

That brought me back from this past-life journey.

I jumped up. "No," I said aloud.

And at that very moment, I found myself standing in my room again. My eyes were wide open, but I could hardly see anything. I always turned on the light before I entered my room, so the room was bright, yet I was still surrounded by darkness in the middle of my room. It was an awful moment. I stood in the darkness for a few minutes, and then gradually it dissolved.

It was 9:30 exactly. I clearly recalled the scene and all the events. I had gone to hell where I had had to face my ancestors.

We had several horrendous wars around five hundred years ago. This period was, in fact, called the Age of Civil Wars, and many people were killed. This is Japan's Dark Age. Being the head of the samurai and working with emperors, our ancestors had a lot to do with the civil wars. But I had nothing to do with that war, any war and if I had, I would be with them in hell. What was the reason for a young, innocent girl like me to be involved in such an ominous matter? Experiencing such horror made me very angry. I decided it was better not to think about it.

My visits to hell continued after that night from time to time, but I stopped counting them. They were not regular visits. I also encountered the lecturing man, and I was exhausted every time. Until now, I thought the lecturing man had something to do with Takako, but obviously, he was more than that. This was entirely different from Takako's apparition. She appeared in my room as a ghost. These tormented men I was seeing in hell were not ghosts, and these events were not happening in my room. They were living in hell. They were suffering unbearable pain, *now*. And I was with them.

Tonight, however, I experienced something unbelievable. I learned how I went to hell. When I entered into my room, I saw that my right leg was stepping into another world. It was absolutely inconceivable and insane, but, as I watched, half of my leg vanished. I panicked, and in that moment, my entire body was sucked into the other world. It happened in the blink of an eye. It was not an illusion. After a few times, I paid close attention to what was happening to me. I did not want to go to hell. When I saw my leg disappearing, I tried to pull it back, but

I never succeeded. I tried many times, but once my leg started to disappear, it was too late. I went into the jet black area where I could see nothing at all. And then, I found myself standing on a plateau in hell.

I came to realize that there was one spot in my room that seemed to be the entrance to the other dimension. It seemed like there was a small gate that opened occasionally and sucked me in. It's a mystery for me to this day, but that's how I went to hell.

MY LAST NIGHT IN HELL

I guess that kind of violent hell is for men, for I never saw any women there. I wondered why I had never seen human beings in the golden world, and there were so many humans in hell. I had to prepare for the university entrance exams, but it was impossible for me to switch my mind from my journeys to hell to my ordinary studies. My room was no longer the normal room where I could study and rest. My grades were suffering. It was hard to pretend to be happy when my mind was so preoccupied with disturbing images. In school, I tried hard to mask my troubled thoughts and pretended to be cheerful, but at home, I was lost. I no longer participated in our after-dinner chat. I had no interest in watching television. As soon as dinner was over, I would excuse myself and go to my room. My parents never objected. They preferred for me to go to my room rather than watch television.

I had no idea when the visitation to hell would end. But I knew that everything must eventually come to an end.

My last visit to hell was the worst. Before I was on the plateau, there had been some distance between me and the tormented people, which gave me some relief, but on this night, I found myself standing right in front of them. That was the last thing I wanted. When I was facing these terrifying beings, even though I was not afraid, I had to turn my head away. I no longer remembered what had happened before.

I won't come back anymore.

These words struck my ears as I regained consciousness. Had the final day come?

I heard the man still speaking. *You will train and enlighten yourselves with the instructions I have given you. But someday, I will come back to help you.*

What? Come back again some day? I panicked. "Not me!" I screamed.

But the tormented people were all around me, and at that moment, their hands, their cold and bony hands were on me, touching me, grabbing, and holding on. Desperate fingers like a hundred vices were clamping down on my arms and hands. I screamed and tried to run away, but there were so many of them around me, so many fighting to get to me, actually to him, as if by sheer touch they could alleviate their own suffering. Their bloodcurdling touch made me nearly faint.

They were screaming, *Don't leave us!* They pulled me down.

I screamed as loud as I could.

And I was standing in the middle of my room, alone, drenched in sweat, my heart racing, still feeling their hands on me. I looked at my arms. Thank God I did not see any hands clinging to me. My breath was labored, my entire body was shaking and cold. The man had been with me, but now, I was back to being the fragile girl.

I sat at my desk, my head buried in my hands. The lecturing man had said he would go back to save them someday. I know he had only spoken to them this time. To give a lecture and to actually offer salvation are two different things.

According to him, they should be training themselves for their enlightenment, and then he would come back to help them. But when? Would their suffering continue until he came back? I had been there briefly, not even feeling their pain, except for the mental torment, yet I could not take this. How could they suffer every single day, and who knows for how long? I hoped he would go soon to help them, but without me or after I died.

I do not know how long I will live, but if I live for a long time, does that mean they will suffer until I die?

No. This whole thing is very wrong.

Even as I went through these events, even after they ended, my mind was still tormented, and now that weight was getting even heavier. When that male being was with me, he took my fear away, but now, I was all alone. This was not a dream or an out-of-body experience. I experienced these things in my body. Now I knew that hell exists just as the fantastic world exists. It is not merely a story used to scare people. Both worlds are real.

I had visited fantastic worlds as a child, and at the age of sixteen, I went to hell. That was something I never wanted to know about. I could keep my fantastic experiences of other worlds secret, but I could not keep this utmost scary thing inside. I am an extroverted person. I needed to release the negativity from my system. But I already knew that talking about my paranormal experiences created nothing but problems. I decided it would be better for me to be quiet.

I could never prove what happened regarding the encounters with nonhumans in my childhood, I know now that without the help I received from otherworldly beings, I could never have managed. For the first time, I began to recognize my difficult fate. I had never thought the problems in my life had anything to do with other worlds, especially with hell. No wonder I was told by the otherworldly beings (*the others*, the celestial being, and the angelic being) that they would help me. I was very thankful for their help. But I was also very angry. These problems were not things a teenage girl should have to deal with. These were issues for more spiritual people like Buddhist monks. I just hoped I would be exempt from going with the lecturing man. I could not take this anymore. This was not something I could accept.

I was aware that the hell situation might happen again. But it did not matter. He had said I would not go back to hell any more. That was good news. Very good news! The worst was over. Thank God! I should celebrate.

The field near the Shakujii River and forbidden forest behind. This is the field my alien encounter took place. *Left:* Chizu. *Right:* Me.

From left: Me, Mother, Chizu, and Kiyo around the time of the alien encounter in Shakujii, the village near Tokyo where I grew up.

The field by the Shak jii River and forbidden forest behind
it. Photographed m any years later. I thought this place
was heaven until I saw the golden world.

浦島太郎像　（詫間町　メモリアルパーク）

Statue of Urashir a in Kagawa district of Japan.
He is riding the turtle to the sea god's palace.
The turtle is often connected to UFO.

Father and deceased sister Yuko during the
war. Yuko appeared as a ghost for a year.

This is picture where I noticed the ghost woman Takako.
From left, standing: Taro (Mother's father), Zentaro
(Mother's grandfather), Ryutaro Hunter (Takako's
English husband), and Ziro(Taro's younger brother).
From left, seated: Chikako (Zentaro's wife),
Shizu (Zentaro's mother), Takako (Taro's elder
sister), Sugako (Taro's younger sister).
Takako appeared similar to this picture, but right side
of her face was covered with much darker shadow.

The postage stamp showing the Hunter mansion that was built by Edward-Haslette Hunter, 1843. It became Takako's house.

The newspaper headline read, "Royal
Family with Western Clothes."
From left: My grandmother Aiko, grandfather Taro,
Kimi (being held by a maid wearing a kimono),
Mother, Miyo, Mother's maid

Dogu is nearly thirteen thousand years old. Found in Japan, it is the oldest recorded artwork on earth so far.

The NHK TV show *Music Around the World*. We are playing an Argentinean tango music. I (nineteen years old) am second from the right in the second row and the only female in this band.

Sato, me, Professor Kimura, and the two music students on the Ringstrasse. The University of Vienna is behind us on the right.

Neuschwanstein Castle in South Germany. It is this alley where I experienced the time machine.

Gold colored kimono was the image of the celestial violinist I met in the golden world. Photo was taken in 1999

The photos of me performing on Royal Caribbean Cruise Lines cruise ship show room in 2004. It was Liberace who encouraged me to create my own violin show. Dancing violin show was introduced to me by the celestial violinist in the golden world.

Dancing and playing gypsy music.

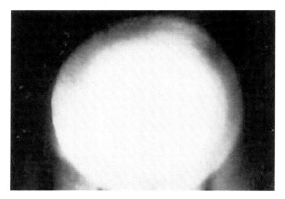

The photo of Masahisa Goi that was buried in the ground of my apartment in Tokyo. This light appeared instead of Goi's face when his picture was taken.

Left: Masahiro Goi (1916–1980). He appeared as a
spirit in my room in Tokyo 1975 and chanted,
"May peace prevail on Earth."
Right : Friedrich Nietzsche, German
existential philosopher (1844–1900)

Seiyū Kiriyama, founder of Agon-sh,
Buddhist association in Japan.

The article appeared in *Waikiki Beach Press*, 1981. I was a gypsy strolling violinist in Pacific Beach Hotel in Waikiki.

The article appeared in the major newspaper *Bild*. My name was Kyoko in 1988. I was one of the acts of the international variety show at the Hansa Theater in Hamburg, Germany.

One-Woman Art Exhibition with 110 paintings accompanied by my musical show that was written up in the *Miami Herald* in Florida, 2004.

One-Woman Art Exhibition with over a hundred of my paintings, Florida, 2004.

Local artist an otherworldly talent

Julliena Okah, who recently settled in Southern California, draws inspiration from paranormal experiences.

BY BONDO WYSZPOLSKI
STAFF WRITER

Most artists are encouraged to pursue their craft, their dream, their vision, by family members or by teachers in school. As a child in post-World War II Tokyo, Julliena Okah was already practicing on the piano and violin, but her real encouragement came from "the others."

Okah currently has several pictures on view at 608 North in Redondo Beach. In the words of gallery owner Kevin Holladay, "Julliena is not only a very talented painter, she is also a violin virtuoso and was gracious enough to play at the opening of 'Another Summer with the Ladies.' This was probably the finest art exhibition opening that 608 North has had and possibly one of the finest in the South Bay, thanks in part to her performance."

Okah has followed an artistic path that has led her through most of the world's countries, and she has even

PHOTOS: COURTESY OF JULLIENA OKAH

"Tango," by Julliena Okah.   "Spiritual Wonderland," by Julliena Okah.

If you go ...
"Another Summer with the Ladies" remains on view through July 19 at 608 North, located at 608 N. Francisca Ave., Redondo Beach. 310-376-5777 or go to 608north.com.

It was an effortless purchase, almost as if it was meant to be. She's also lived in New York City, Florida and in India, where she studied Indian philosophy. In 2001, after five months in Peru, Okah returned to Nice. On the first day of September she was painting her room. As she did so, "my hand mysteriously started to move and began to paint something on the wall. My sudden desire to paint artistically was enormous, and I went immediately to buy materials. I painted nonstop with watercolors and oils for months."

Los Angeles Register in 2014. Newspaper article was written by Bondo Wyszpolski

While I was exhibiting my paintings and playing the violin in the art gallery, this newspaper articles was published. Photographed by Gloria Plascencia.

"May peace prevail on Earth" The image of
Goi's message, painted in 2004.

"Salvation" in the hellish world, painted in 2005

"Wonder World" The image of the nature I saw
in the golden world, painted in 2005.

In Las Vegas, May 1976 at 3 a.m. First night in America. The lights moved high above my head, zoomed back and forth, then totally disappeared in one second.

In Waikiki Beach, March 1977 at 2 a.m. It appeared suddenly and stayed for about ten minutes. The most amazing and beautiful sighting I had ever seen.

On the way to Mt. Charleston from Las Vegas, 1983.
My friend and I saw.

In Nice, France, October 1988. Three vehicles appeared
at 3:00 a.m. Each ship was shooting a laser beam directly
at me. Appearance lasted for about fifteen minutes.

Nice, France, November 1992. Many small disks came down from the center of the big vehicle. Some of them went back to the big vehicle. Many of them disappeared when I tried to catch them. Mother ship stayed for about ten minutes.

Southern California, December 2007 at 2:00 a.m. This appeared out from nowhere and disappeared after about twenty minutes.

CHAPTER 8

My Own Death

Sometimes, the truth can set you free, but sometimes it can take you prisoner. My prison was about to get bigger, with me still as its only resident. One's teenage years should be filled with promise and expectation, with dating and dreaming about the future. All my peers seemed to be living that normal teenage life. But my life was totally the opposite. Although I felt some relief in thinking that possibly the worst was over, I suddenly found my life heading in a different direction. At the age of seventeen, I experienced the most horrific death imaginable—my own. But miraculously, I am alive today to tell about that death and about the ultimate despair and then the saving grace that I experienced on the other side.

After I had "stumbled into" the most frightening hell, I was no longer in any shape for ordinary life. How could I forget the ghost-woman Takako and her imploring eyes? How could I ever forget my ancestors' desperate entreaties? I could still feel their cold, bloodcurdling touch on my skin. Soon, I found that my mind was solely focused on those lost souls who needed help. Going to school became extremely difficult. Anything written in a textbook had no relevance to the life or realities I was living. The teenage chatting with my classmates that I had once enjoyed now annoyed and disturbed me.

I began isolating myself and spending my time in the school library. I needed to learn about the world beyond and find some path to salvation for my ancestors. At home, I spent a lot of time alone in the attic where my parents couldn't disturb me. This attic wasn't a real room, but merely the space between the ceiling of my room and the roof of the house. No one else in the family even knew it existed. It was accessible only from the walk-in closet in my bedroom. The way I discovered it was quite bizarre. The same alien voice that had warned me about the burglars guided me to this place.

I was told to go through the closet, where I would find the way to the attic. I used a small ladder and climbed up above the top shelf and saw a square of wood that looked like a little door in the ceiling. I pushed the "door" up and discovered a space big enough for me to walk around in. The place had enough sunlight streaming in between the planks of the roof that I could read during the day. It was a perfect hideaway. I brought up the cushion, the lamp and few more things I needed. I made it as comfortable as possible so that I could stay there for hours on end.

Most Japanese houses do not have locks on their doors. Chizu's room was not accessible except by passing through my room. When she passed through, she usually spoke to me or came near me. At this point in my life, however, it was crucial for me to have my own private space. My parents knew where I was hiding, but it was not easy for an adult to climb up into my little attic. So I was left all alone.

What would happen to me if I talked to my family about my hidden life? I was afraid to bring up the subject even to my closest friend, Torii. I had overwhelming feelings of shame around my experiences of ghosts and hell, and if I told anyone I had "gone to hell," they would certainly have questioned my sanity. What if someone asked me how I got to hell? What would I tell them? The answer, of course, was "I walked in." But who would believe that? I shut myself down and stayed away from the outside world because I thought no one would ever understand what I was going through.

Soon, I discovered that doing research at the school library was not enough, so I began going to the public library instead of school. Mother was angry about this, but I ignored her. I spent my days in the library and left my schoolwork far behind. For months, I sat in the library, researching everything I could find related to other worlds. My world now consisted of the public library and my private attic sanctuary.

I found few books of Dante's Inferno. I identified the things I saw. There is a lot about hell in the Bible, but that hell seemed to be a place of eternal damnation with no possibility of salvation. But when I read about the Buddhist conception of the various hell-worlds, I thought there seemed to be more possibilities. Buddhism teaches us that nothing is eternal except nirvana.

Delivering one's ancestor from the lower realms is a common practice in Japan. Ancestors who fell into the lower realms rely on their descendants for their salvation. That's why we offer water and the food at the temple and family shrines. Because salvation is still possible, the monks still perform the ritual. We all know this, even children, but hardly anyone actually goes to hell to do something for his or her ancestors

Though I came upon a description of how to release fallen spirits from their torment, there was nothing I could use because it required rituals that could be performed only with a lifetime of intensive training and ascetic practice. I learned that those rituals were commonly performing in India and Tibet. It seemed impossible that I could find someone who could help me, let alone anyone who could or would perform such a ritual for me around my area.

I also tried to research the subject of aliens and the help we get from the other worlds, but there were no books on these subjects.

After eight months, my mother had become greatly disturbed that I wasn't attending school. Even our neighbors were aware that I was not attending classes. This placed my family in an uncomfortable situation. In addition to my absence from school, my mother was especially displeased that I had stopped practicing the violin. And she was now aware of what I had been reading instead of my assignments from school. She thought my choice of subject matter was not at all acceptable.

I had not yet told anyone the real reason of my absenteeism. At this point, however, I changed my mind and decided to open myself up. I thought, if I tried to explain what I was doing, my family might understand. After all, the problem with my ancestors belonged to the entire family. They should know what I had gone through. One day, I carefully brought up the subject.

My parents were at their wits' end when I told them the truth of my life. I was not surprised when they took me to a mental hospital.

When the test results came in, they showed I was perfectly fine, though the doctor prescribed tranquilizers to help me relax. I was back where I started. None of my problems had been solved. My sister Kiyo was a psychologist now and was constantly testing me, but she too found no definite signs that I was abnormal.

This was a crucial time in my life. *The angelic girl* had told me that no one would understand me, but that I shouldn't worry. Well, I decided, she was wrong. *The others* had said they were watching me, but if they were, then they should have known what was happening to me and helped me. I was greatly confused and very angry. In my seventeen years of my life, I had not done any evil things to deserve these horrific experiences. I had never asked to meet aliens. I had never wanted to communicate with spirits, but now, my life was destroyed. What had I done to deserve such suffering?

I started to think that if I had never met any aliens, my life would have been much simpler. When I think back, in fact, all my problems began the day I encountered *the others*. Because of them, I was different from everyone I knew. I was leading a peculiar life because I had knowledge of another world. And now I was involved with the worst world possible! I wondered. *Is this part of the package?* I know we cannot only have good things. Life does not work that way. If this was part of the package, I was not so sure I wanted to have aliens in my life. No matter how fascinating were the experiences I had with the aliens and the girl spirit, my life at this point was out of control. I needed to understand so many things about the other worlds, but at this point, I did not care anymore. I just wanted to be a normal seventeen-year-old girl.

It was also clear to me that the spirits of my ancestors were the cause of this calamity in my life. My life was being destroyed because of them. I had put all my heart and energy into trying to help them find salvation, but what did I get for my efforts? How many people have tried to rescue their ancestors from hell? My good intentions turned into bitterness.

My parents now began sending me to various experts for help. They sought advice and treatment from a myriad of psychological authorities, teachers, school principals, counselors, and doctors. One by one, these experts came and tested me and talked to me and advised me—and all to no avail. At the end of the day, I was always alone and back where I started. Not one expert came up with one helpful solution to my problems. How could they even begin to understand me? I was dealing with things that do not belong to this earth. I needed an expert who knew about the other worlds, but I never met any such person. I was sure books were more helpful than any person I ever met. Books had never interested me before, but now I did nothing but devour books that described life after death and other worlds.

There is a limit to the number of absentee days a student is permitted to have and still be allowed to graduate from high school. I had certainly moved past that limit. I wanted to graduate, of course, and even had dreams of attending a university. In addition, it was truly painful to me to see how my actions were causing extreme anxiety for my parents. Like me, they were under extraordinary pressure, though their concerns were different from mine. I could sense Mother's pain and see the sorrow in her face. As I watched my family's hopes for me being crushed, the weight of my guilt became unbearable.

It was more than I could handle. There was no joy in my life. I was the cause of unnecessary pain in the lives of those I loved. So I made a decision. I would put an end to all the suffering and all the misery.

I knew I was not mentally ill, so I only pretended that I was taking the prescribed medications. I took only a few of the tranquilizers. At first, I'd throw the pills away, but now, I started keeping them. It had not yet occurred to me to wonder why I was saving the pills.

MY "FINAL" DAY

It was a Sunday morning at the end of October, a beautiful day. The air was crisp, the ginkgo trees were still banana-yellow, and the Japanese maples were apple-red. Even though my heart was wounded, I wanted to see the colors of the mountain for the last time. These bright colors healed my pain for a little while and made me happy. Even in this critical moment, beautiful colors helped me more than the words of the experts who came to talk to me. I had been obsessed with color ever since I saw the beautiful garden in the golden world. To this day, I've always been amazed at the power that colors hold.

So I spent that Sunday morning sitting in the field, admiring God's work in the universe, and thinking how happy God must be with his creation. I wondered what it would be like to be a true artist and paint the majesty of God's design and heal people's pain. But then, a feeling of melancholy took hold as I came to realize that I could not create anything. All I could do now was absorb the beauty of nature for the last time. That is how I saw myself on that last day.

I wondered how God saw me.

It was time to return home. I had plans for the afternoon. It was nearly lunchtime, and the family would be around the table.

Up to this point, everyone in my family had expressed concern for me in one way or another, but I had been avoiding them most of the time and only joined them at dinner and sometimes for lunch on the weekend. On weekdays, I got constant pressure from Mother because I was the only one at home when I was not in the library, so I usually hid in my attic, and when she called me to come out, I refused to reply. Sunday was a good day because I got less attention.

Today's meal would be different. I would be present at the meal. And then I would go forward with my plan for the afternoon— without interruption. No one was aware that I was planning to end my life that day. I acted as if it were an ordinary Sunday. Even if this was to be my last time for family conversation, I was not interested in talking to anyone. My heart was cold. I did not feel sad or happy to be ending my life. I was numb.

After I finished eating, I said, "Thank you for lunch. It was good." Those were my last words.

It was two o'clock when I climbed up to my loft in the hidden attic. I could still hear my sister's happy laughter downstairs. I remember thinking that I used to laugh. But that was all in the past. I would not be expected or missed by anyone until dinnertime. They were used to the fact that I spent my afternoons alone in the attic. The few times I had allowed Chizu to visit my hiding place had ended several weeks earlier, so I knew on this Sunday that I would not be disturbed until dinnertime.

My drinking water and my collection of pills were waiting for me. Everything was on schedule.

I sat down and absorbed the last moments of my life. I figured it was necessary to contemplate one final moment—to say a prayer, maybe, or silently apologize to my family, perhaps to express a moment of relief that all the torment and pain would soon be finished. But my heart was too wounded to do any praying or reflecting. I figured if I started with a few pills their effect would ease my suffering. They did. My body relaxed. My sorrow dissolved. Now I could think more clearly.

And happy memories came to me. I thought about the incredible worlds I had seen. The fleeting images of those worlds almost made me smile, but the happy memories only accentuated the current pain in my life. It was regrettable that my life had to end in such misery. Thoughts of my unfulfilled life caused tears to stream down my face.

There were so many instructions I had received from the nonhuman beings. But what was the purpose of everything they had shown me? What was the reason the alien had shown me the special violin technique? Everything he had taught me would now be unfulfilled. All the education my parents gave me to train for my future, all the money they had spent on me—everything was wasted. I was a total failure. My feelings of resentment were surfacing again.

I knew it was time to take the remaining pills. I had forty-two pills in all. I separated them into piles of seven, so I would know how many I was taking at a time. One by one, I swallowed them. By the fourteenth pill, I was feeling no pain. My sadness was greatly reduced. I felt better—even euphoric. I wanted to stay awake for a little longer to absorb that comfortable feeling, so I put the pills down. In my semiconscious state, I was delighted by the thought that there was no need to rush to end my life.

An ancient memory that my alien friend in the forest had brought to me appeared in my mind even in my semiconscious state. *The others* wanted me to come back to their world. They had come to earth to tell me so. Well, I had certainly failed at that too. Why didn't I get any help from the others? I was back in my negative thought pattern again. Everything was unfair, but I didn't have time to dwell on that. I put another seven pills in my mouth. My mind wasn't shutting down as fast as my body. My thoughts again turned to blaming those who ruined my life. Certainly at the head of the list were my ancestors. *My death is all their fault!*

I was melting, slipping away; all physical feeling was starting to leave my body. I was numb. If this was dying, I still felt a bit afraid. There was one tiny second where I thought, *I can still save myself.* It wasn't too late to call for help. What was I thinking? If I changed my mind, I would have to explain my actions, and that would do nothing but create more problems. *No.* I would not put myself or my family through this anymore.

I swallowed another seven pills. I should take them all in order to avoid just falling asleep. I did not want to wake up after a long sleep, and I certainly did not want to be saved at the last minute. *No waking up to a future in a mental ward! No living death!*

Seven more pills went down my throat. My thoughts were no longer coherent. All I could do was swallow more pills. My hand could barely reach my mouth, but I managed to take all the rest of the forty-two tranquilizers.

Up to this point, my consciousness was more or less intact. Now I felt my body getting cold. I couldn't breathe well. My body hit the floor. My eyes closed.

My system was shutting down.

It was time to leave the body. Forever.

THE GRAY SPACE BETWEEN LIFE AND DEATH

I don't know how long I lay there in my attic, teetering between life and death, but suddenly, my consciousness came back. I was totally calm. I did not feel sadness or any negative feeling. There was no pain, either physical or emotional. My body held no sensation. It seemed like my eyes were open. Well, yes, I could see, but I was not ready to look at anything. There was absolutely not the slightest sound around me. I normally love silence, but this silence was alarming. *This place was dead silent.* Or perhaps I was deaf? I tested myself.

"What's going on?" I said aloud.

No, my hearing was fine.

My body was floating. I was as light as a feather tossed on a gentle breeze. I was still lying down.

This is confusing, I thought. *I'm lying in my bed.* There was no weight to my body. *I'm as light as a leaf. Why do I feel so light?* These were my very first thoughts when I regained a vague consciousness. I turned my head. My body swayed right and left calmly. I felt no gravity. What place in the universe existed that had no laws of physics? I was getting curious. *Where am I? I can still think.* I lay still for a while longer, just floating, thinking of nothing specific. Though my head was still groggy, my curiosity was growing. I was becoming aware of my being, becoming myself again. I looked for something to identify, something familiar that would tell me where I was.

I saw nothing I recognized.

Gray. I was in a gray space. The light side of gray. This vacant space had no distinctions of shading. *It's all empty. I'm in the middle of it.*

Maybe my eyes needed time to adjust. I was aware that I was making a conscious effort to stare at one point and not look away. Within a moment or two, I began to make out tiny silver fragments of something shining against the canopy of gray.

I saw more shiny fragments, and then sometimes, I saw no fragments at all. When I could not see them, I became fearful. These tiny fragments were the only source of any light in this gray place. The denser the fragments were, the less gray there was.

This "scenery" of fragments was shifting slightly. I'm moving! But ever so slowly.

With my consciousness returning, I was becoming more perceptive. Now I was noticing subtle shades in the gray. It was as if I were looking at a wall. I could see in three dimensions.

Suddenly, I became aware that my movement was not only in one direction. I felt myself turning. I was sliding through a maze in slow motion. Strange as it seems, I got the distinct feeling of being brought into a room, staying there a little while, then being taken to another room. This feeling went on for some time. Then I felt I came to a vast vacant space again. This emptiness seemed not to have an end in sight. *How long am I going to be floating in here?*

I finally experienced my first mental sensation—nervousness.

Then, a sudden realization. *Death. I have died.* Yes! That was the logical explanation for that mysterious space. *That's why I'm floating like this.* I didn't panic, but neither was I elated. This was curious, this lack of feeling or sensation. *Well,* I told myself, *Nothing will be what I was accustomed to before I died. This is how death feels.*

My body kept moving. *Maybe I haven't completely died yet? Maybe I'm still in the process of dying? Do we stay in space before being transferred to the next realm?*

There was no one here to answer my questions. So far I hadn't even met any other dead people like me traveling through this area. On earth, it is a fact that people are dying every moment of the day. *Wouldn't you think I would find at least one person to talk to?*

How long have I been here? I don't believe time existed where I was, but I was feeling like I had been there for a very long time. It was frustrating. Nothingness was starting to get on my nerves. This void was very difficult to handle. *I need to talk to someone! I need to do something!*

The sharper my thoughts became, the more impatient I became. Feeling desperate now, I tried to move my legs. I needed to walk. Nothing. I willed myself to stop moving, but that achieved nothing either. Everything was happening automatically.

Great. I'll just continue floating and doing nothing. I'll go crazy! There has to be something more than this! I was getting extremely irritated. *Just wait,* I told myself. *Be calm. This transition from life to death will not last forever. Eventually, I will make the crossover.* My mental stress was at its peak.

Maybe my restlessness had somehow registered in this void. I started to notice that I was moving faster, still not by my own volition. My consciousness was as alert as it had been when I was alive. This realization only reinforced my perception that I was about to leave purgatory and finally move on to my destination. I no longer thought I was in an expanse of nothingness. I felt the space around me becoming narrower. Now I seemed to be traveling through a tunnel. The tunnel was getting smaller and smaller. The silver fragments were disappearing, the gray was disappearing.

I must be nearing the end. Now I was so afraid that I even wanted to go back to the empty gray space. But there was no way I could turn around. My body was now moving forward at full speed. I held my breath and mentally prepared myself to finish dying. It was then I noticed I was breathing heavily. *If I'm dying, why am I breathing?*

Oh, God—what's going on?

I came to what looked like a chute. There was barely enough room for me to squeeze through. I could not bear to see what was coming. In a panic, I shut my eyes tight. The end was inevitable. *Don't let there be any pain!*

And then, the end finally came. I blacked out.

THE WORLD OF DEATH

To this day, I don't know what happened after my tunnel experience or how much time had passed. Now, I was no longer floating and moving forward. I was stationary. I could feel gravity and the weight of my body. Soon, I found myself sitting in the same position in which I usually sat in my attic room, except now I was leaning against a rock. My head was down, my chin nearly touching my chest. My mind was numb. I had no strength. I felt like I had just gone through enormous physical labor. Slowly, I raised my head and looked at my surroundings. *Nothing looks familiar.* It was silent, but not like the dead silence in the gray place. I was no longer in that space of nothingness. This new place was gloomy, but there were colors. The sky was red, yellow, blue, and black, all mixed together, hanging low, as if somehow weighted down. Yellow and blue were the colors I loved, but now these colors frightened me. *Is this a sky?*

No, this place was not on earth! I could see some dark knolls here and there, their tops like black shards stabbing the multicolored sky. The ground was little more than dust and rocks. *It's weird. Intimidating.* I had never seen such scenery before, not in pictures, not in the movies. I could not make out one tree or anything green. In fact, there was no sign of life, neither animal nor plant. The absence of any scary animals that I might have to run away from brought a whisper of relief.

A slight breeze started up, disturbing the dust around me.

I felt disoriented, but I could still think. I remembered the vacant space, the endless floating. In fact, I felt like my mind was still in that vacant space. I couldn't adjust to this new space—this new world. My numbness must have been caused by the shock as I passed through the narrow tunnel.

It was chilly. This place was cold. And suddenly, I was attacked by an unbearable sadness. Where before I had known the tranquility of feeling nothing, now I was feeling my emotions welling up again. All the misery I felt in those final moments of my life was beginning to plague me all over again.

My heart was consumed by grief. I was suffering devastation all over again. My mind was thinking exactly the same forlorn thoughts I'd been thinking as I took the forty-two pills. I wrapped my arms around my knees, bowed my head, and began to cry. After what seemed like ten or twenty minutes of unrelieved sobbing, I lifted my head again and stared at oblivion. *What's happening to me? Where am I? What is this place?*

The memory of my suicide, the shock of it all, was haunting me. I remembered taking the pills. *Yes, I have died. I am now looking at death. This is death. This is what happens when we die.* My blood froze. *Or did it happen to just me?* Terror hit me hard, almost knocking me over.

Coming to the realization of my death was the hardest thing I have ever experienced. I could not accept this reality. There were two reasons why. The first was the place I was in. If I had been in the golden world, I would have been delighted. If I had found myself among loved ones, perhaps getting to meet my deceased sister Yuko, that would have been acceptable. But this place was not anything I could take. No human could.

The second reason was that I did not *really* think I had died. I was confused. I was still very much alive. *Nobody,* I told myself, *could think they were dead if they felt this much life.*

I was convinced that I had not died. I had entered other worlds before; perhaps this was just another one to add to the list. In the past, I had visited a heavenly world and had wished to stay there, but I was brought back to earth. I had also been in the hell in which my ancestors were trapped and came back from there too. Perhaps, I thought, I'd simply fallen into a deep sleep after taking all those tranquilizers. Once this was over, I'd be back in my room. *What a horrible nightmare! I have to wake up!*

Is this hell? Am I visiting another hell? Compared to the fiery hell I'd been to before, this was much better. If this was hell, it was the opposite of the hell I saw before. It was cold, not hot. It was abandoned and desolate, whereas the other hell had many tortured beings. But it also was the complete opposite of the golden city I had visited. *That golden city was heaven. This is hell.*

My thoughts suddenly became exceedingly clear. *I am not visiting* hell. *I have been* delivered *to hell. I really died. I will not wake up.*

The logical conclusion I reached brought me nothing but terror. There were no words to express the shock I felt. This dreadful fear was far greater than the fear I had felt in the fiery hell. This time, I was not observing someone else's death. *This is my own death, and it is irreversible.* I had taken my own life. It was over. Now I knew that I could not go back home anymore. I felt like my head was being smashed to pieces.

"Help me! Help me!" I screamed aloud. I prayed to God in earnest as I had never prayed before. I prayed to the same God who may well have placed me here.

No reply.

I had never felt so abandoned, so all alone. I started to cry. I wanted to die again to get away from this awful, ugly place. *But how do you die again? The idea's absurd.* How could I kill death? *Here, I have no choice in death but to live.*

The last state of our mind before death affects the next life. These words, which I suddenly remembered from a book on Buddhism, flashed into my mind. My last state of mind was devastation and desolation. I had received exactly what was in my mind. I had wanted to be alone. I was now alone. Dead alone.

Even after I recognized my death, this was a confusing moment. I did not see death. I could not see any difference between life and death. I had not even lost my body. I could see myself exactly the way I was. I was feeling the same hurt I had felt before I swallowed the forty-two tranquilizers.

My reason for ending my life was to end my suffering. But nothing had ended. I was alive here. Because of my heightened awareness, the sharp pain in my heart was more intense than before. My perceptions and brain functions were more acute. All of this made my suffering worse. I had all my memories with me, even memories of things I had forgotten in my life. Death cannot

195

terminate anything, not suffering, not memories. Death cannot even terminate existence. *How ironic! Death brings more life than before. I am more alive in hell.* That realization terrified me to the point where I almost lost consciousness again.

I fell on the ground. I was attacked by all sorts of fears. For a long time—how long, I don't know—I just lay there, but eventually, I felt able to rise. I thought I had to do something. Otherwise, I would go insane. *Anything is better than just lying here.* I tried to stand up.

I started to walk, and then I noticed I wasn't wearing shoes. It was painful to walk without shoes. The ground was sharp and hard. The approaching wind brought with it an eerie sound. Soon, the dust on the ground was stirring as the wind shrilled and circled around me. This world was unwelcoming, inhospitable. Looking up, I saw the colors in the sky swirling together to form new colors, orange and purple and green. The colors seemed to be accusing me. I turned away. I was beyond terrified at this point.

"Hello! Is anyone there?" I screamed over and over. *Am I the only being on this dead planet? It cannot be.* Somewhere deep inside, I held some faint hope that I would be discovered by someone. It seemed like a good idea to wait until the storm had passed before searching for help. I headed for a giant boulder I saw nearby. I sat against the boulder and screamed.

Why? Why? What have I done wrong? Hell is for people who committed serious crimes on earth. What crimes did I commit? I was trying to help my ancestors. What kind of cruel god would banish me to such a place? I could find no reason for me to deserve this much affliction. If someone had ever told me what the cause of this suffering was, then I would accept it.

Now I remembered the words of the Buddha. *Nothing comes by accident. Everything has a cause. Being delivered here*, I thought, *should have a cause.* As I sat there shivering, I began to reflect on my life. Every little thing I had ever done started to parade through my mind. I was now totally on my own and going through it all alone, I pondered each passing thought, memory by memory, only this time there was no movie screen. As this life-review process concluded, my blood suddenly froze. I had come to a major realization.

I had made a huge mistake! I had committed suicide.

The face of the ghost woman, Takako, came into my mind. She had committed suicide. She had told me that she lived in a realm of suffering. I started thinking. *She must be somewhere like this.* In human law, murder in the first degree is punishable by death, but suicide cannot be punished because the perpetrator is already dead. We can escape the punishment of human judgment, but probably not the punishment of God. Murdering oneself is still murder. In God's eyes, suicide might be the same as murder. An uncontrollable shaking swept over me.

I was starting to regret what I had done. I had thought I was helping the people around me by ending my existence.

Obviously, being in this world was not the result of good intentions.

Until this time, I had never considered suicide to be a transgression. When the Japanese lost World War II, my grandfather committed suicide. The hara-kiri of a samurai is well respected in Japan. It shows strong will power to end one's life rather than surrender to an opponent. And many of those who died by hara-kiri were honored. There is a small tropical island near Guam called Saipan. Later in my life, after I grew up, I worked there and heard the story of how hundreds and hundreds of Japanese people, including children, had taken their lives during World War II by jumping from the high cliffs instead of surrendering to Americans. Until this moment, I had no guilty feelings about suicide.

However, my situation was much different from war. In the end, I could not justify my action, no matter how hard I looked for a good reason. My action was based on my weakness. This was the truth I had to face. Later in my life, when I was in Thailand,

I learned that Buddhists believe that suicide is comparable to murder in sinfulness. The consequence of taking my life was much more than I ever imagined.

As my desperation reached its peak, I once again bitterly accused the ancestors who had pushed me to the edge. *My hell is their fault!* Then I started to blame myself for everything. After I saw hell, I tried to follow a spiritual path, but where did I end up? I was drowning in self-condemnation. I could not stop crying. I had needed help desperately, but the depth of my shame prevented my asking for help. After a long thought, I finally decided I would accept responsibility for everything I had done in my life. *No more blame. The spiritual level determines the next life.* I remembered the world of the aliens and clung to this memory. Now I would go on from this point of acceptance and continue with whatever life I have here.

If this was a test, I told myself, then I needed to pass it. Now it was up to me to prove I was worthy of graduating to a better life. Proving myself seemed to me my only chance to move on. There was no way I could stay in this dead place alone. Also there was no way I could save myself from this hell. I had to depend on someone. *God* must approve me for the next, better life. God was my last and only hope, the only thing I could hang on to. Just yelling for help or doing nothing while consumed by self-accusation had been no help at all. They certainly were not relevant at this moment to get me out of this hell.

What I had learned in the library back on earth led me now to a shamanic path. I was no longer a spoiled girl. With a firm determination, I took the first step of my new life in this death world. As disoriented as I was, bit by bit, I was digesting the knowledge I acquired from the books I read. Here it was no longer mere academic or theoretical knowledge. With all my heart, I began to put the knowledge I had acquired into practice.

First, I told myself, I would spend what time I had in this death world immersed in reading and study—not at first thinking of where I would find books here. I would pursue knowledge and find the path of enlightenment. *Certainly*, I said to myself, *that is an effort worthy of some sort of existence.* I would combat this world by achieving some inner peace. These thoughts brought me a little hope. Since there were no other living beings here, there was nothing I could do for others, nor could I learn from them. *If I am the only living being here,* I thought, *then self-study and self-enlightenment are the only things left for me.* Through this fervent effort, I thought that God might approve me. But what would I read? The sacred books of Buddhism? The Bible? If only I had any of those books here, I would be contented. But where could I get books? *No libraries here—nothing but rocks.* Even my last hope was taken away. *What else is left for me? What is there to do now?* All the energy I'd summoned up minutes ago vanished. *How much more of this torment can I endure—and for how long?*

I was not sure I could survive. There was no food or water here. Without food and water, I would probably really die and very soon. Well, what purpose did it serve to try to prolong my existence here? If the weather and lack of food resulted in death, I could not ask for more.

*My body...*my body felt like it did on earth—yet I was dead! My physical body was in the attic. My blood turned to ice at the thought of this.

Another thought came to me. Takako must have kept on "living" without food for many years. The body after death may not need food, water, or oxygen. *It is possible that nothing will kill the body I have now.*

Would I end up like her if I remained here?

Was there *anything* I could do to reverse my tragic mistake? Was there any way I could go back to earth to resume my life? If I could ever go back to earth again, I promised, I would do anything to redeem myself.

I remembered the light in the inferno, that small, light opening in the gray sky. *Maybe there's salvation even in hell.* I looked up. All

I could see was the gray sky, void of stars or moon. Even the scary colors were all gone.

God does not care. Why should he? Isn't hell the last place one would expect to find God? With a trembling heart, I began to wish my alien friends would come for me. I felt that since they had taken me in their spaceship to another world, they might also come to this death world to rescue me. Were they watching me now? If they were, maybe they could hear me.

"Help me!" I screamed aloud, but all I heard was the echo of my voice.

God, aliens, even death had abandoned me. I was so exhausted, I could not even cry anymore. *Let the storm eat my body. I'll just wait till my next death arrives. Since I can't do anything bad here, then maybe my next life will be better.* That seemed to be my only hope. I wanted to sleep, but even sleep did not come. I lay down against the boulder and curled up in a fetal position. I would no longer ask for help. I would endure my fate without complaint or blame. I would die on this world when my creator decided I had had enough. The Buddha had said everything passes away. My heart needed to believe this.

A MYSTERIOUS MAN SPEAKS TO ME

As I lay there, my mind became filled with blurry memories of all the people my parents had enlisted to help me. I could hear them talking to me, lecturing, advising, offering useless answers. Their words were shrieking in my ears, louder and louder, filling my head. I sat up and leaned closer to the rock.

The storm was as intense as ever. The wind seemed to be screaming with laughter. I wanted to shut it out. I closed my eyes and held my hands over my ears, but I could still hear the voice. It was different from all the other voices in my head. Whoever was speaking had to be close by. It was a male voice. Suddenly, I realized that the storm had gone away. It was quiet. I could hear the man's words clearly, and little by little, what I heard began to penetrate to the core of my being. I was totally enveloped in that voice. No one I had ever known in my life had impressed me so much with their words. I was listening to a philosophical lecture—not a new one, but it seemed fresh. One word especially caught my attention.

Transcendence.

Something happened deep in my soul. That was the message I had once received from the celestial being.

This unknown man was talking about how to rise from the human level. Finally, I lifted my head and looked in the direction the voice was coming from.

Standing perhaps ten feet away, but directly in front of me, was a man. He looked human, but he was also unlike anyone I had ever seen in my life. I knew right away that he was not an inhabitant of this hell. He was wearing a white robe that barely fluttered in the horrendous wind, and he looked like a saint. Soft light surrounded him. Even though it was still dark, I could clearly see his face. He looked bigger than any man I'd ever seen and completely different from the aliens I had encountered on the ship. He was also unlike the ethereal beings in the golden world. He looked Caucasian. He was slim and had a mustache and a full head of short, dark hair. He was speaking to me in Japanese. This did not surprise me, as the aliens had also spoken Japanese. His gaze was steady, but he did not look directly at me. He seemed to be lecturing in a grand hall.

It was unbelievable! His words were like fresh air on a mountaintop. As he spoke of life and its purpose, I felt light entering my darkened soul. His lecture went on for what felt like hours.

Suddenly, I felt a need to ask questions that had been inside me for so long. I began asking this saintly man about everything—life, death, hell, other worlds, aliens, spirits, my past lives, my ancestors. I couldn't hold back. I needed to know everything. One after the other, I posed my questions. He answered all my questions. The more answers I got, the more my soul was revitalized.

I could not help but be amazed. This man's words echoed the words I had once heard spoken by ethereal beings in the golden world. I thought he must have something to do with them, even though he did not look like a celestial being. But he had appeared when I called to the aliens for help.

It did not matter who he was. What really mattered was that I was saved. His words brought me back to life. Like a thirsty flower that had been left unattended for too long, I was being watered. My thirst for knowledge was enormous. My tutors in the other worlds had left so many unanswered questions regarding life, and now I was finding what I had been looking for. This man in the white robe was teaching me a different way to see the transmigration of the soul. He was telling me about a path to another, higher spiritual world. It could lead to some place like the golden world I had visited, but it was not the heaven of the Bible, nor was it the Buddhist nirvana. It seemed to me that there were many different worlds existing in the universe, which is what the celestial being had also said.

My heart was completely filled. I took a deep breath. My tired body felt renewed. I was no longer cold. Enormous energy now boiled inside me. I knew I was getting my life back.

All of a sudden, the man in the white robe stopped talking. He looked at me. I will never forget his eyes. His deep, dark eyes pierced me to my heart. In that moment I saw a huge, bright disk. It seemed like the sun rising was behind him, though it looked enormously bigger than the sun. I was struck by its great white light. I couldn't keep my eyes open. I put my hands over my eyes to shield them from the intense light.

And then I heard him say, *Go to your own sky with your own wings. Fly high. I will be with you.*

The power of that sun struck me, and I was so overwhelmed by its warmth that I failed to notice the pulling force gathering behind me, an enormous vacuum that tugged at every fiber of my being.

I lost consciousness again.

MIRACLES AND REFLECTIONS ON MY DEATH

I opened my eyes. I was in the attic. The emergency doctor, who had climbed up into the attic, was shining his light in my eyes. The powerful sunlight that had pushed me back to earth was somehow linked to this doctor's light.

Bit by bit and in broken pieces, my brain function and senses came back. There was no pain or discomfort in my body. In fact, I felt peaceful and calm. But I knew what had happened.

I've come back!

No one knew exactly how long my heart had been stopped, though the doctor guessed it was only for a short time. I was blue when he began pushing on my chest, and this happened at the same time that I felt pushed by the power of the great white light. Since I had had a heart valve problem, the doctor arranged for a series of tests. All the results came back perfect. The doctor found not one thing wrong with me. Amazingly, no one ever found out about the pills I had taken. What I was most thankful for was that there was no brain damage.

How could this be explained? How could there have been no evidence of the overdose of forty-two pills? These were prescription tranquilizers; one pill a day was the dosage limit. With no evidence of what I had taken and no brain damage, I felt I had experienced a true rebirth—a true miracle.

As long as the doctor didn't know about the pills, there was no need to try to explain. When I could talk, I insisted that I did not know anything. Nevertheless, I was forbidden to go back up to my hideaway. That was just as well—I had no desire to go up there anymore. The air in the attic was moldy, and the ventilation was poor. The doctor concluded that the mold might have contributed to my heart failure.

I brought all the things I'd taken to the attic back down to my room. I also found a few pills and thought they might have fallen out of my hand in the last moment just before I lost consciousness. I stared at them for a minute, then threw them into the garbage can.

My incredible journey was now over. No one knew where I had gone. I had been given soul lessons, which I did not need to share with anyone or prove to anyone. The lessons I learned would not be applicable to anyone else. I decided to remain silent regarding alien interference in my death world until the right time came.

I spent one day in the hospital, and then, after being absent from school for nearly nine months, I went back to school. My parents were still in a state of shock, but I was now a different person, exceedingly bold, like a lion in the field. Nothing bothered me.

I had come back to school two days before final exams. Because of all my absentee days, I was not qualified to take any exams, but I asked the teacher if I could take them anyway. For nine months, I had never opened a textbook, yet I was relaxed and confident. I felt compelled to take the exams. This I couldn't understand. It was definitely not like me.

So I took the exams. Normally, I would check and recheck my answers, but not this time. The tests were less than challenging, and when I wrote the last answer, I left the room. I still remember the stunned look on my teacher's face.

When the results came back, I learned that I had earned the second highest overall score in my class. The top student was a boy who had done nothing but study all year. Math and science had always been my weakest subjects, yet I earned one of the top scores. I was a renewed person, but I had never expected this kind of incredible outcome. Everybody was puzzled by my achievement, and the teachers asked Mother for an explanation, which she did not have. Everyone had assumed I had had a private teacher and was studying all along. My mother totally denied this. But she did ask me if I had been secretly studying up in the attic. Of course not, I answered. No one had believed my words in the past, and now, I decided to let everybody think whatever they wanted to think. Needless to say, my parents were very happy with the new me and my good scores. They started to see me differently.

Finally, I felt I was doing something to make them happy.

This was when, for the first time, my parents begun to realize that there was something extraordinary about me. They knew my peculiar traits, like seeing spirits and knowing my past life or before my birth, but they had always disregarded what I'd said. They are logical people. But my test scores at school made them wonder. When Mother persisted in asking me what had happened, I just said, "Don't you remember *the others*? I told you about them a long time ago. How did I cure all my ailments? Do you know?"

I did not hear another word from her. She just stood there and stared at me. To this day, however, she still knows that I have had something to do with aliens.

In 1988, in Nice, France, Mother was one of the people who witnessed the appearance of the alien vehicle. She had come to see my violin performance at the famous Hansa Theater in Hamburg, Germany, and then we traveled for three weeks in Europe from north to south without any plan. It was supposed to be a simple vacation for us and Nice became our final destination.

On the third and last night in Nice, which was October 21, 1988 before we went to sleep, I told her not to close the window. "Aliens are coming to see me tonight," I said. That was the only night I ever said something like that to her. We always closed the windows before we slept. During that day, we had walked on the beach and enjoyed the golden sunset. There I felt the strange sensations. I received a message from *the others*. I knew they would come to see me that night.

At three o'clock in a morning, I was awakened by a tremendous white light in our room. Looking out the open window, I saw three of their vehicles—the same shape as the disk I had seen years previously—up in the sky. Each ship was shooting a laser beam directly at me. The narrow beams were white against the dark sky, and our room was ten times brighter than daylight. I was stuck on the bed and could not move. I was facing the window, but Mother was sleeping in the opposite direction. At first, she pulled the blankets over her head, but then the brightness woke her up too. Her body was not affected by the light. She could move. She knew what was happening.

I gazed at the alien vehicles for fifteen minutes as they beamed their laser lights on me. I knew why they had come and what they were telling me. Basically, it was again about my ancient memories. They also brought a warning.

The next day, Mother flew back to Japan. I was supposed to go to New York City, where I lived, to change my suitcase for my next engagement on one of the Caribbean cruise ships on which I performed my show every winter for the past twenty years. I had three free days in New York. I immediately changed my ticket so I could spend those three days in Nice. I found a perfect summer house across the street from the beach where I received the message from *the others*. This condominium was found by the first real estate agent I talked to and it was the first condominium he showed to me. It was in the heart of Nice, the best area. It is extremely hard to find inexpensive condos in such a fabulous area, but I found this one without any stress. This became my first condo I had ever owned. However, buying that condo was something I had never thought about. In those days, France did not allow for foreigners who did not have jobs or relatives in France to buy real estate. It was a miracle that I was allowed to buy. Indeed, who can shop for a house in five minutes, find the perfect place right away, and take care of all the legal work in a few days? Ordinarily, it would be impossible—but it was done supernaturally. I knew that if the aliens wanted something, a miracle always happened.

It took until that year—1988—for Mother to finally believe my childhood stories of aliens.

Knowing that beings from other worlds have been watching over me and guiding me has given me a sense of well-being and security. Since I left the forest near my village, I never saw *the others* again, but now I know they were helping me in different ways. I still do not understand all the strange phenomena that have been generated, but I know they are still coming to me to help me through crises in my life wherever I am. I now truly understand that human beings could never have helped me outside of earth. That is the reason I encountered aliens.

I had never thought that the aliens' prediction would come to pass so soon. I thought it would be much later in my life. But I concluded that this event was meant to happen sometime in my life. Help was already provided, possibly even before my birth. I was pre-informed. I was mentally prepared. If not, and not knowing what this was all about, I would have been in greater chaos. I might have gone insane. As I look back, I feel that the experiences of hell and death were assignments that I had to work through for some reason in my life.

These experiences made me feel like I was undergoing spiritual training. It seemed like I was being forced to learn about other worlds, about unseen worlds, both good and bad, whether I wanted to or not.

I truly feel that God never gives us things we cannot handle. If a problem cannot be solved by human beings, then God will send nonhumans to assist us. Nonhumans are also God's creations. We all coexist in the same universe under the same God.

After experiencing what I now think of as a ruined death planet, I know that this earth is beautiful. I can no longer take anything for granted. Here on earth, I have everything. I can see the blue sky. There are pretty flowers and lots of books to read. There is nothing for me to complain about. I am even happy while I am practicing the violin. How wonderful it now feels to be alive on earth!

PART 3

CHAPTER 9

Guidance and Miraculous Help

It was a cold afternoon with a wintry gray sky. The sun was hiding behind the clouds. I like this kind of sky because it calms my mind. I was in my room gazing out the window, when suddenly I heard a familiar voice.

Leave your hometown and go to Tokyo, then go all over the world. The hell experience is over for now, but it will come back again. At that time, you will have a helper. In the meantime, do whatever you want.

It was the same voice that had told me about the burglary. *The others* were giving me new instructions. I was happy to learn that the hell situation was over. And the voice had said I could do whatever I wanted. How exciting! But—

Go to Tokyo? I had never thought of going to Tokyo. No one I knew ever went to Tokyo to study. But why shouldn't I go? The words I had just heard were the same words I'd heard from my violin tutor in the other world. He had said, "*Go all over the world.*"

The place I was dying to explore, of course, was Europe. But there was no way I could do it at age of eighteen. For my first stab at independence, I thought Tokyo would be the logical place to start. Besides Tokyo was the place *the others* came to see me. I needed to be there again. I felt as if a dream that had been lost was coming back to me.

It was also a good time to leave this strange house. I was convinced that my room had to be an entrance to another dimension. The gate to the other dimension must have opened up in these few years. I had no idea what happened, but I just wanted to end this mystery.

The period between high school graduation and a student's entrance into a university is a very intense time for anyone who wants to continue his or her education. It was especially intense for me. The date for the university exams was right around the corner, but I wasn't ready.

Although Mother was still expecting me to study music in Osaka, the second largest city in Japan, which was not too far from our home, by now she had almost given up any hope for my future at the musical academy. With all the intense reading I did while I was absent from school, my interest had turned to literature and ethics. I had previously been fascinated by Buddhist teachings, but after I met the mystery man in my death world, my interest in Buddhism suddenly decreased. Besides, the voice I had just heard did not say go to Kyoto where there were many Buddhist universities.

I set a goal to leave home and bought a book that described all the universities in Japan.

While my mother was preparing tea, I was turning the pages of my book.

"I may need to take a few more entrance exams," I told her. "Everybody takes second and third exams if they don't pass the first time."

As I spoke, Mother noticed the page I was looking at and exclaimed, "I know that university! I know the founder. He was a friend of my mother's."

We were looking at the description of Tamagawa University near Tokyo. I could see beautiful scenery in the photographs that showed the huge campus and its mountain views. And what a coincidence! It was a Christian university with a proper music curriculum. This was probably the reason my grandmother had known the founder, who had lived in Tokyo, where she was a professor of music at a private Christian school named Seisin Jogakuinn. My parents would never allow me to go to the center of Tokyo alone, but—another coincidence—this university was located just outside the city. I did not look for any other university. After these few minutes my direction was set.

A week later, Mother and I went to Tokyo so I could take another set of entrance exams. This test was very easy. I had, in fact, purposely failed the exams at the musical academy in Osaka. It was the only way I could follow the directions I'd been given. At Tamagawa University, I chose European literature as my major subject and added music to my curriculum, which made my mother happy.

Even with all my absences, I was allowed to graduate from high school. Though the principal and the teachers were greatly confused, they were glad to let me go. My high school did not want to deal with me any more.

Arrangements were soon made for me to reside in a dormitory on campus near the founder's residence. It took very little time, however, for me to discover that dormitory life was not for me. I did not like the dormitory's strict rules. I was expected to live there for the entire four years, but three months was more than I could tolerate.

My new lodgings that I found behind the university were great. The landlords owned an entire mountain, which was their garden. I gained the freedom I needed and made lots of friends with the other students. This was the university life I had dreamed about. I was popular and was soon at the head of my class.

These miracles and positive changes were very similar to the time when the girl spirit came to me. She brought me the miraculous healings of all my ailments and violin guidance including academic help. But she left me when I entered junior high school. I did not feel the existence of the man in white robe any more, either. I guess he too had left like the girl spirit and *the others*. I guess he had been with me until I passed the crisis. I could not thank him enough for all the help he gave me.

And now, something else that was new entered my life. I started to date. My first boyfriend loved to read, so we visited bookstores together. We were both interested in spiritual paths. I discovered many books devoted to the subject of unidentified flying objects, a very popular subject at the time. Even though he was very much into UFOs, I chose not to discuss any of my mysterious experiences with him. In fact, I never brought the subject up with any of my new friends. I had good reasons for this. Nobody thought I was odd. I felt at peace with myself. I only wanted to discuss subjects my peers could relate to, so I kept my knowledge inside me. I was no longer interested in researching anything I had experienced and did not want to take any chances that I might be linked to another supernatural event that might interfere with my normal life.

I had lost so much time in the past that now I was determined to enjoy the sweet teenage life!

MY MUSICAL CAREER BEGINS IN TOKYO

Because it was important to my mother that I continue seriously studying the violin, I was sent to a private teacher. My university was expensive enough, but these private sessions were an extra expense for my parents. For my second year, therefore, I decided to attend a public musical academy. This was Geidai, the best musical academy in all of Japan. In Japan, the top universities are the public universities, and there are not too many of them, but if you meet the requirements and are deemed good enough, you can be granted a scholarship. My grandmother had graduated from Geidai, and now I became a part-time student of the violin there, though my major studies were still at Tamagawa University. Geidai was located beside a big park, a good ten minutes' walk from the Ueno train station in downtown Tokyo.

In our country, the new semester begins in the spring, which is cherry blossom season. On my way home from music academy one late afternoon, I sat on a bench near a fountain and let my thoughts return to my childhood. Though it was quite far away from the place I grew up, I was back in Tokyo. It had been another spring, also filled with cherry blossoms, when I had encountered *the others* for the first time. I felt overwhelmed just thinking of those far-off days. The cherry blossoms always took me back.

"Hi."

Standing in front of me was one of my classmates. We had nodded to each other before, but had never really spoken. Her name was Reiko. She was a petite, pretty girl. What began as a casual conversation that dreamy afternoon evolved into an animated, hour-long discussion. Even though we had just begun to talk, we both felt as if we had known each other for years. I didn't want our conversation to end, so I suggested that we might go for a cup of coffee.

"I'd love to," she said. Then she looked at her watch and said. "I have to go to work."

"Do you work? Where do you work? What kind of work do you do?" I could not contain my questions because none of my friends at the university worked. I admired her independence.

"I work in Sinjuku," she said. "Would you like to come with me?"

Sinjuku is one of the biggest districts in Tokyo, located thirty minutes from the park and on my way back home. I had been planning to visit there, but I had never gotten off the train at that station. This was an excellent opportunity for my adventure. I was excited. As we walked, I asked her again what sort of work she did.

"You'll see," was all she replied. She seemed pleased that I was accompanying her to her workplace. I had no way of knowing that this moment was leading to my day of destiny.

As she led me to the front door of a huge building, "I play music here," she whispered. I was in a dance hall filled with people dancing under the sparkling lights. Coming from such a conservative family, I had never been exposed to anything like this.

Reiko led me into the backstage area. There were no women here, only adult men, all musicians. Reiko and I were the only girls present.

Suddenly, it was show time. One of Reiko's coworkers led me to a spot on the second floor, the perfect place to see the band perform. Within minutes, the lights were changing, and the sounds of crisp, energetic, live music began. The curtains opened, and the band appeared in dazzling costumes, playing passionate music. I had never heard this kind of music before. The feelings it conjured in me took my breath away. I loved it. I counted four violins, a piano, a bass, and an instrument that I had never seen before, a bandoneon, which is similar to the accordion. Three musicians were playing this instrument. When the band finished its first thirty minutes and took a break, I joined them backstage and learned that the music they were playing was called the Argentine tango. Although the hour was getting late, there was no way that I was not going to stay for the second set. As the musicians were about to walk back on stage, the bandleader turned to me and asked a question I was totally unprepared for.

"Would you like to play with us? Just for fun? "

I was speechless. I had no idea if I could play tango music, which is very different from the classical music. Then Reiko simply opened my violin case, handed me my violin, and pushed me out on the stage.

I have no idea how well I played that night, but for the first time, I enjoyed being on stage. I had played in numerous student recitals, but I always hated to perform on stage. I was asked to join them for another set, which I enjoyed even more. Hours passed. I should have been at home. I wanted to tell the bandleader how much the evening had meant to me. As I was just about to speak to him, he surprised me with another unexpected question.

"Do you want to work here? You could start tomorrow night."

Reiko was standing nearby, looking at me with imploring eyes. What could I say? "Yes!"

The magnitude of what I had agreed to finally hit me on the ride home. The job would require me to be at work six nights a week. I would have classes during the day at the university and the music academy, then I would go straight to work from six to ten-thirty. I would arrive home near midnight. First, I eliminated my social life and my sleep time. I moved out of my favorite lodgings to a place closer to Tokyo. I ended up settling into a miserable place right across from the train station. I missed my lodging and friends but the sacrifices were worth it! I was establishing myself as an independent person. I had jumpstarted my musical career a step ahead of my classmates.

As I learned the techniques of tango music, my career as a musical performer began. Within six months, I received another job offer that nearly doubled my salary. I was now working at an exclusive private club in the most fabulous place in Japan, the Ginza.

All of this was happening only seven years after my alien violin tutor had told me about the life I would lead. Now finally I understood why it was crucially important for me to practice seriously at that age. The celestial beings had filled the spaces in my life that my parents couldn't. It is not easy to make money playing the classical violin as a profession. It is thanks to the entertainment business that I have been able to stay single all my life.

One Sunday, I played for a professional dance competition with the tango band. It was the most fantastic dancing I had ever seen. The women wore beautiful, sparkling, long dresses that glowed in the theater lights. In the billowing stage clouds formed by the smoke machines, the dance floor and the performers created a heavenly illusion. It brought back memories of seeing angelic violinist in the heavenly world. On my way home after the dance competition, I stared up at the star-filled sky and thought about celestial violinist. What I heard in the other worlds was now gradually coming to fruition.

Now I was sure that going to Tokyo had been the right thing for me to do. Kyoto is a traditional city, Osaka, an industrial city. I could never get the career I aspired in those cities. If I had not heard the voices of *the others*, the idea of Tokyo would never come to my mind and I would never have received an opportunity to leave home.

I wanted to have more guidance from *them*, but that was the last guidance I heard, their voices in Japan, though I was still hearing their reminder, *We are watching you.*

A NEARLY FATAL ACCIDENT, MIRACLES, AND QUESTIONS

In Tokyo, job offers came steadily, and I eagerly accepted one at a famous theatre called the Mikado. It was the biggest cabaret theater in Japan, seating upwards of a few thousand people. It was located in the Akasaka, another expensive area in the center of Tokyo where the finest geisha houses were also located.

Everything was going well until my adventurousness led me to a life-threatening calamity that brought enormous and inexplicable questions into my life.

Every night, two bands played on the stage, the ten-piece tango band in which I played the violin, and a twenty-piece jazz band. The two bands alternated, each playing thirty minutes at a time. When one band was playing, the musicians on the other bandstand left their places, and their stand was lowered into the deep pit under the stage.

The Mikado was a highly sophisticated theater, and I was curious about every part of it. One night during my thirty-minute break between performances, I decided to walk around the backstage of the theater. I hardly ever saw anyone there. As I strolled, I noticed the sign that said, *Prohibited*. It was in front of a big, roped-off area. This area was under the stage, where the electrical equipment and many other things were stored. Only the stagehands could go into this area. There were no lights except for a few small exit lights on the walls.

This, I said to myself, was a good opportunity to learn something new about how the stage worked. Even though it was clear that we were not supposed to go in there, I decided I would just take a quick peek.

I checked my watch. It was about twenty minutes to nine. There was just enough time before my next set for a little adventure. We had to be on stage five minutes before we started to play. The last number each band played was always a waltz, which signaled the other musicians to take their places.

My accident happened fifteen minutes before the waltz. There was no one there to stop me from stepping over the rope and entering the forbidden zone. It was dark. My eyes did not adjust to the dark. Since I was wearing high heels, I walked very carefully, but I must have stepped on a cable, for I started to fall, and it felt like I was falling forever. My body did not hit the floor. Instead, I landed somewhere in the pit, ten or twelve feet below. It was like I had fallen into a swimming pool with no water in it.

How long did it take to hit the bottom? Maybe it was a second? During that second, I saw most of the sins of my life. It was like a movie, the same way I had looked at my past lives. It still does not make sense, but that is what I saw.

I saw my sins in the order of the degree, the heavier sins first, then the less severe ones. Toward the end of that movie, my sins were childish antics. In my family, moral conduct was a serious matter. At the age of twenty, even though I was working in secular places, I hadn't really done anything too sinful. Except for my suicide attempt at age seventeen. However, that part was not shown in this imaginary movie. I guess I already learned about it. I saw all my other sins. Sometimes, my friends and I bought train tickets, but we passed through the stations without paying the fifty cents. Many people did that. The station officers knew it, but we were mostly immune because we were students. The rules were whoever got caught was the loser. It was thrilling, like we were gambling. Although I was probably the one of leaders of the pack and felt a little guilty, I still enjoyed it. There was also the cheating on my tithing in my childhood. There were times when I gave back nothing after I spent for myself. Yes, these were the images flying in front of my eyes as sins. While my sins were not gross or horribly criminal, they still seemed to make a huge difference. Then there were the manipulations, the calculations, and the thoughts that eventually led to sin. I even saw the subtlest of my evil thoughts. They were all shown the way they happened. Many things that I did not even remember anymore came back to me in that "movie."

I fell for what seemed an eternity. I was feeling terribly disgusted with myself. My sorrow grew. When my repentance peaked, I realized I was watching small pranks I had played in my early years.

"That was a joke!" I screamed. "I was just playing!"

Then my body hit the floor. *Thud!*

I blacked out for a second, then I felt a surge of pain that rang through my body like a five-alarm fire. I was in trouble. It was pitch-dark. I was lying somewhere at the bottom of a hole, I couldn't move. Then I heard the music. It was the waltz! The jazz band was playing the last song of its set, an American song made famous in the early fifties by a group called the Ink Spots, "It's a Sin to Tell a Lie." This was one of my favorite songs. It could also have been my last song. I must have been lying under the jazz band's stage. While the jazz band was playing this song, the bandstand for my tango band began to ascend and bandstand for the jazz band began to descend. I was right under it. At the song's last note, it would be completely down and on top of me. I would be crushed to death.

I had to do something! Once the bandstand starts to descend, there is no way to escape. Was this to be the end of my life? Trapped at the bottom of a dark hole listening to a waltz? Were my sins so bad that I deserved to end like this? The pain in my leg was so bad I could hardly stand up, so I started crawling across the floor, frantically reaching for anything along the wall that I could grab and pull myself up. I needed to climb out of this dungeon before it became my tomb! But the walls were flat and smooth. There was nothing to grab. There was no way I could climb out without something to support me.

I was terrified. I started screaming, but that didn't do any good because the twenty-piece jazz band was playing right above me.

Then I realized that nobody would ever find me in this darkness under the stage. I would be entombed here until my body decomposed. The music playing above was close to the one-minute mark. I felt the end of my life approaching. I could hear the mechanical noise that signaled the descent of the stage. This was it. My life was over.

This way!

Just when all hope was gone, I heard a man's voice. Someone had found me! I looked in the direction of the voice and saw a glimmer of light. I could also see a bit of my surroundings. Maybe I was too panicked to have seen the light earlier. I saw a hand stretching toward me.

I reached up as well as I could, and someone took hold of my arm and pulled me up. I managed to hobble up what seemed to be a forty-five degree slope. It was like scaling a mountain. When I reached out with my other hand, I felt an indentation, a small platform, something to hold on to. I kept climbing. In the glimmering light, I could see the man's light-colored trousers. Finally when I got out from this pit, I collapsed on the floor. I saw the stage coming down beside me. If it had been one second later, my life would have been over. I watched the stage go down into the pit. I had escaped from death by a hair's breadth.

Because I was so panicked, I did not quite remember how I got out from the prohibited area but I was alive and safe. I turned to thank the man who had saved me. But no one was there! Maybe he had gone for assistance. Whether it was because of the fear or the pain or seeing my blood, I fainted.

When I came back to consciousness, I saw a lot of people standing around me. I could hear the sound of a siren.

What had happened to me caused quite a bit of excitement. When musicians and stagehands at the Mikado came to visit me in the hospital, I confessed that I myself was to blame for the accident. I told them I was ashamed of what I had done and apologized for all the trouble and worry I had caused for everyone. I had no choice but to tell the truth and accept the consequences. I also wanted to know who had helped me. The stage manager asked around, but no one came forth. There had been over thirty stagehands working backstage. I assumed that in time one of them would make his presence known to me.

When I was finally discharged from the hospital, I moved back to my parents' house because it would be a month before I could fully manage by myself.

Though my left leg was broken and I had many cuts in my face and body, my life had been spared. I could have been handicapped. It was possible that I could never have played the violin again. I was thankful to the person who had saved me.

When I returned to work in the tango band, the head of the stagehands and several security guards came to see me. They needed to learn what had happened to me by visiting the exact area where I had fallen. But I was not ready, emotionally or physically, for an investigation. To this day, the thought of my accident sends shivers down my spine, and I now have a phobia of heights. I was also still embarrassed by my wrongdoing and did not want to discuss it again. I was hoping it would just quietly fade away, but no, they were adamant. They needed to fill out the official report.

The stagehands had turned on the lights so that we could see everything in the prohibited area. Now I could see the two bandstands and where they were lowered to. We looked down into both pits. They were plain, black, boxy holes. I couldn't understand what I was seeing and asked if the forty-five degree slope had been taken out or changed.

The stage manager just looked at me. "What are you are talking about?" he asked. "We didn't understand how you got out of the pit. There's no way you could climb up, even if you were not injured."

I was confused. "But where are the small lights?" I asked.

"What lights? There are no lights in here."

Now I was more confused. "But there were small lights where I climbed up. From the bottom to the top."

Then I looked down and saw the bottom of the pit more clearly. It was not the flat surface I had dragged my body across. The bottom of the pit was a grate over an uneven floor with huge nails and metal pieces sticking up. What I had felt under me was a solid surface. I stood there staring, completely stunned.

"How did you climb out?" someone asked.

"I told you. A man came and helped me. He pulled me up."

"How did he know where to find you?"

"I was screaming. He heard me. He happened to be there."

"No one could hear you with the band playing," the stage manager said. "No one comes here at night unless there is a problem, and we had no problems that day. We don't know who helped you. No one has claimed they did."

Someone else spoke, "What did he look like?"

"I didn't see his face," I said. "It was too dark. I'm sure he was one of your stagehands. He was wearing work clothes."

With each word, I felt my voice getting weaker with uncertainty.

"Look," the stage manager said. "There is no way anyone could reach you. The walls don't slope, and it's twenty feet down. Do you understand?"

The severity of my injuries proved that I had fallen down from a great height. The stagehands and security personnel confirmed that, but there was no explanation for my survival.

A miracle had happened. Someone had come to save me in the last moment of my life. Who was he? I know now. Although he looked human, he was not a man.

And how to explain the forty-five degree angle of the wall I crawled up? Unless you are a bug, it is impossible to walk or crawl straight up but that is what I did. Somehow, within seconds, *lights and a forty-five degree wall were created.*

What happened at the moment of impact? Yes, it hurt, but I felt like I had landed on a sort of cushion. I landed on a smooth surface. If I had fallen into the pit with those huge nails or sharp metal bits sticking up, my injuries would have been a hundred times more severe. It would have been instant death. *The space was also altered and changed to help me survive that fall.*

And there was more. I felt like my spirit came out of my body for a split second when I hit the floor. I saw my own body lying in that deep pit, but what I saw under me was some thin fabric. The actual color of this floor was black, but the floor I saw under me was white. It also emanated a dim light, so I could see my body and my surroundings. This white material covered the entire floor. It was only for a second when my spirit came out, but I have a photographic memory of what I saw. It is just like a picture taken from above. It was rectangular in shape.

The "time" issue was another mystery. It was truly inconceivable. I also think about what I saw in that one second. I viewed the scroll of the first twenty years of my life. What would the scroll look like after the next twenty years? At the end of my life? In the process of growing up, it's inevitable that we will collect sins or at least transgressions. Was my accident a warning to change my life?

And one last thing I must think about. In my adult life, I do not go into any prohibited area. But on that night, I was somehow strongly drawn to that area under the stage in the theater. I knew *the others* wanted me to understand the mysteries that belong in their world. That accident might have been predestined. And help was also provided as I was promised, for the same way I had died and gone to hell.

The incredible manifestation that was miraculously created saved my life. All of my peculiar experiences seem to have been created in the other world, in another reality. What happened to me is beyond my comprehension, but it really happened. And I had witnesses in this incident.

My life had been saved twice. Both times, I was saved by light. Light was the key to my deliverance. And both times, I fell into places where no human could help me escape. Someone must have been watching over me. I still remember the alien's words: *We will be watching you.*

For whatever reason, against all odds, my life was spared.

Mystery Man in the Death World

MY FIRST LOVE BECOMES MY LAST LOVE

In Japan, the birthdays of people who reach the age of twenty are celebrated in January. You wear a kimono and visit the Shinto temple. But instead of celebrating this important day, I was busy preparing for a long ride to Tokyo in the super-express bullet train. It was the New Year break at the university, and I was at home with my family. As the train pulled out of the station, I settled in for the ride that would change my life.

I first noticed him as I boarded the train. He was very different from the showy, outgoing men I was moving among in the social world. He was seated alone and had a serious demeanor. He looked to be in his mid-thirties. After a few minutes, he changed seats and sat next to me and began to read a book. The book was German philosophy.

We were both en route to Tokyo. As we began to talk, I learned that his name was Tanahashi, and he was a professor at the University of Tokyo, where his specialty was existential philosophy, a deep and heavy subject. He told me he had studied in Heidelberg, Germany, after receiving his doctorate in Japan. I wanted to hear about his life in Germany, but he carried on nonstop about existentialism. It was almost as if he was giving me a lecture, though I had never been interested in philosophy. But now, I had to admit that I found it fascinating. I had to take a deep breath every minute or so because his words were filling my soul. No one had ever spoken to me like this. No, I stand corrected: it had happened once before…the man in the white robe. But he was not a human being, whereas Tanahashi was very human, and he was sitting right next to me! His lecture was eerily similar to the one I had heard in the death world. No one had touched my soul before the way he did. I couldn't understand my feelings, but something was certainly happening to me.

And then, as if I were struck by a bolt of lightning, I knew that he was the man I wanted to be with for the rest of my life. It was crazy. I had just met him; I hardly said a word because I knew almost nothing about his subject. But it didn't matter. I was sure about this.

We decided to have lunch and walked to the dining car. The train was running at full speed through snowy scenery that I might have enjoyed observing from my window. But I could barely take my eyes off of Tanahashi. We barely spoke during our meal, but my heart was filled with joy and contentment beyond words. And my mind was flooded with wild thoughts. I was imagining what it would be like to be his wife. I felt as if time was stopping and I was alive in a perfect moment with this man. I knew that this was love. It was the true love that one is ideally supposed to have. Tears filled my eyes but they dried as soon as he finished his meal and began to speak again about existentialism.

With the conductor's announcement that we were about to reach our destination, I knew the train would pull into the station and my dream might come to an end. I was nervous. Was this it?

"Do not become a mediocre person," he was saying. "Do not be satisfied by a lukewarm life. Strive to become the person you were meant to be."

These were his last words to me. They were almost the same words I had heard in the death world. My mind was racing. The world was spinning. It was time to bid him good-bye, and I couldn't bear the thought. What could I say or do? I was too shy. I had so much respect for him that words failed me.

"Here is my card," he said. "Please call me."

I was shaking when he placed his business card in my hand. He smiled, turned, and walked away. I couldn't move. I stood frozen to the spot until he was gone from my sight. I was certain that he was the man I wanted. And now I had his business card, with his home and business addresses and a telephone number.

From the moment I met him, my view of life changed. All I could see was him. I lost all interest in socializing with the wealthy men in the Ginza who could show me a good time. Tanahashi had said he wanted me to call him, but I lacked the courage to do so.

I became a woman possessed. Instead of calling him, I started walking past his apartment building on my way home from work. I never knocked on his door, but just stood behind a tree a short distance from his building and gazed at his window. I did this several times a month. I also visited his university. I could have searched for him after class and innocently bumped into him, but even that would have been too bold for me. I settled for walking around the campus and knowing he was close by. Once or twice, I drummed up the courage to pick up the phone. I even dialed the number. And I always hung up on the first ring.

This lasted for nearly a year as I fantasized about being married to him, having his children, and living a humble philosophical life with him. When I pictured myself with him, I saw myself as a different woman, one who was softer and more idealistic. I worked in the men's world and sought to make my position equal to theirs. I wanted anyone to think I got my musical work solely because of my talent and often came across as tough, but that was because I valued my independence and was making my own way professionally. I was not the typical demure, submissive Japanese woman. So I accepted what I had and rationalized that my longing for Tanahashi was good.

But things changed from the best to the worst. One night, I saw no light in his apartment. I went home, but I could not sleep. I changed my routine and began standing outside his home night after night. But there was never a light in the window. I finally decided to visit him during the day. I encountered the elderly woman who was sweeping by the gate in front of his building. It was a very intense moment for me when I asked if she knew where Tanahashi was.

"He moved out. He got married."

Though I had imagined what she said in one of my worst scenarios, at that moment, hearing the words out loud, I almost fainted.

"He was the most sincere person I ever met," she went on in a happy voice. "He devoted himself to his studies and hardly ever went out like other men. I was his landlady. I used to ask him why he doesn't get married. He said that he couldn't find the right person. He was content to just continue studying. But wouldn't you know it, someone at the university introduced him to a woman who was well suited to him."

I had heard enough. I thanked her and walked away. My tears did not stop for hours.

Hours, days, weeks, months passed. I closed the book on that chapter of my life. Still, the love remained, and to this day, he holds a special place in my heart. To this day, I have yet to meet a man who means as much to me.

In time, however, I have come to understand that my not approaching him was not simply caused by my fear that he would not respond. In all honesty, I was aware of what I was doing. Did I really want to marry him? No. He was a professor. His study and work were anchored in Japan. If I were meant to be with him, I would be stuck in Japan. In my fantasy world, I could picture myself as his bride; in reality, however, I was fully aware that I had to follow the guidance I had received from the other world.

GERMAN PHILOSOPHY

It was a warm, early spring day. The distant mountaintops were covered with snow and the cherry trees on campus were starting to bloom. My girlfriends and I went to the park to catch up on our lives. I remember one conversation with my best friend, Yuki, who said, "Love changes everything." I was surprised to hear her say that. She was the top student and a pianist who always accompanied me. We were scheduled to graduate in a year and had been discussing traveling and visiting foreign countries. But while I was busy working, her outlook and priorities changed. She now had a boyfriend and was talking about marriage.

Everybody agreed with Yuki's statement. I, however, had no idea what they were talking about. I knew what love was, but I had never thought that way. Nor had I ever thought of sacrificing my ideals or aims in life for love. So I kept silent.

Then something captured my whole being. My eyes went to the snowy mountains in the distance, and I felt a sudden, compelling urge to study German philosophy. But where on earth or in the depths of my mind had this idea come from? I had never thought of this before. We were talking about love, but this sudden flash hit me and woke me up as if the snow from the mountaintop had suddenly fallen on me.

And then, it hit me clear as a bell. It must be love.

German philosophy. Professor Tanahashi. It was love, and now I understood what my friends were talking about. I had lost him permanently, but I had apparently never gotten over loving him. If I studied his subject, then I could better understand him. And through this connection, I could become a source of pleasure for him. Love is indeed a powerful thing.

The crazy idea of studying philosophy stayed in my mind. I would be finishing my studies at Geidai Music Academy soon, and then I would be able to study philosophy. Even though philosophy would consume a lot of time, I was determined to make it work. My feelings for Tanahashi were still strong enough to make me do it. I guess Yuki was right. I was discovering, to my amazement, that love does change us.

I applied to Waseda University, one of the very best private universities near Shinjuku. I took two years of philosophy courses and totally enjoyed being on a new campus. Everything I had dreamed of and longed for in university life was coming to me. I was popular. And what did I have to thank for leading me into such a positive and joyous period in my life? German philosophy.

Yes, my life was rosy, but I was also behind in my studies. I had to write a graduation thesis at Tamagawa University, but I didn't have a clue as to what I would write about. I toyed with the idea of German philosophy because I felt a sense of superiority studying such a difficult subject, but in reality, I wasn't doing so great in class. Philosophy was simply too hard for me. Reading it gave me headaches. While my purpose in attending this university was my love, I did not need to stress myself with this difficult course of study. German philosophy was obviously not a topic to tangle with.

So I decided to write about Beethoven. This subject was both realistic and inspirational. I had read a lot about Beethoven. One of my favorite books was Romain Rolland's 1903 biography, *The Life of Beethoven*. I also knew Beethoven's works and played some of them quite well. His composition, Romance 1 in G major, a violin piece, was one of my favorites. Beethoven's life, especially his loves, also touched me. Yes, Beethoven would be the perfect subject for my graduation thesis. I felt it would not take too long to write about him.

Now that a lot of pressure was off my mind, I was relaxed and continued happily from day to day. It was on one of those happy days, when I was sitting in my German philosophy class and daydreaming about Tanahashi, that my world changed again.

I am that which must always overcome itself.

I almost fell off my chair. These words, spoken by Professor Mizushima, woke me out of my daydream. I felt like I had been struck by lightning. These were exactly the same words that I heard in the death world.

The professor gave the page in our text. Holding my breath, I looked at the page. My heart stopped. There was a photograph. I was looking at the same face I had seen in the death world. The man in the white robe—it was Friedrich Nietzsche. Prior to this day, I knew nothing about Nietzsche. I had heard the name, of course, because he was a world-famous philosopher. Professor Tamahashi taught the works of Heidegger and Nietzsche, but I had never connected the famous philosopher to the man I had met in the death world. He had lectured to me, and then he had answered all my questions. Memories of our meeting were whirling through my mind as I tried to listen to my professor's lecture on Nietzsche's life and philosophy.

Nietzsche was born in 1844 in the small German village of Röcken in the central part of Germany. He was the first-born son of a Lutheran pastor. When he was five years old, his father, Karl Ludwig Nietzsche (1813–1849), died from a genetic brain ailment. Friedrich studied classical and Greek philosophy at the University of Bonn. At the age of twenty-four, he was appointed to the chair of classical philology at the University of Basel in Switzerland, the youngest individual ever to have held this prestigious position. He was greatly influenced by the philosophy of Schopenhauer, whose thought was influenced by Buddhism, and was also a friend of composer Richard Wagner, who acknowledged him as a musician as well as a scholar. Nietzsche never married. He traveled throughout Europe and completed the first part of his most famous book *Thus* Spake *Zarathustra*, in a mere ten days while he was in Nice, France. He died in 1900 of the same brain ailment that killed his father. After his passing, his work gained much notoriety.

As the child of a pastor, Nietzsche had great interest in the subject of Christianity, though in his adult life, he became opposed to lukewarm Christianity. But he was not opposed to Christ. Professor Mizushima emphasized that most people did not understand Nietzsche. Nietzsche had recited Bible verses in his youth, and he did same thing in his old age. That is not what an anti- Christian does. I was shocked to learn that because I never heard any such thing in the death world. Nietzsche also broke through traditional concepts that dated from the Middle Ages by bringing a new insight into how to look at life and go beyond. His major theory was the *Ubermensch*, or the "beyond man," "superman" in English.

How to exceed as a human being and attain to higher worlds—this was exactly what I had heard in the death world. It was also what the celestial being had told me. The words I was now hearing from my professor sent my head spinning.

"Fly to your sky with your own wings," said my professor.

These were the words that had brought me back to life. I closed my eyes.

After this lecture, I could not even stand up. What I had just learned was not easy for me to accept. I had been thinking of the man in the white robe as one of the aliens. Why did he appear to me? What connection did he have with me? I had no interest in his philosophy. I am Japanese. He was German. There was absolutely no connection between us.

But then, I began to understand my attraction to Tanahashi. My obsession with Tanahashi led me to discover Nietzsche. Tanahashi was the bridge. Now I understood why I had met Tanahashi. I was beginning to put the pieces of this puzzle together but the direct connection to Nietzsche was still a mystery to me.

Nietzsche was a controversial figure. His philosophy was much discussed and argued. That worried me. I didn't need any complications in what seemed to be a perfectly happy life.

Considered a genius, Nietzsche was ahead of his time and recognized as such by a new generation. In 1896, Richard Strauss composed Also sprach Zarathustra, Op. 30, in English, *Thus Spoke Zarathustra*. This work was inspired by Nietzsche and has been part of the classical repertoire since its introduction. The opening fanfare, "Sunrise," has become known to the general public thanks to Stanley Kubrick's famous 1968 film, *2001: A Space Odyssey*.

After I came back from the death world, I made up my mind to only speak about things people can easily relate to. I decided I should not talk about anything related to my having met the man in the white robe. Now I knew that man was Nietzsche. Now I also thought that studying his philosophy might not be a good idea. Being an entertainer, I thought I should avoid complicated subjects that might affect my personality.

Since I had left my hometown, my new life had been keeping me busy on this plane, engaging in study, work, and social life. All the activities that surrounded me diminished my thoughts of that mystery man who had been my savior.

But as the days went on, however, my thinking began to shift. I came to understand that if it were not for Nietzsche in his white robe, I would not be here today. Do we not owe something to someone who saves our life? Do we not owe some sign of respect to that person, regardless of whether he is alive or dead?

Nietzsche was no longer alive on this earth, but he was certainly living somewhere else. If not, he could not have appeared to me.

So, I said to myself, not only is he living somewhere else, he is very likely in the higher realm. His appearance and all the positive results he brought to me prove it. His message, how to exceed the human realm, was the subject I had been dealing with since I was little. If I could learn even a little more about my subject by studying his philosophy, I thought it would be worth it. Also, by studying his philosophy, I felt I was in some way showing my appreciation of him. Tanahashi also studied Nietzsche. I had to study.

Studying his work, I thought, this could be the aliens' purpose too. Why Nietzsche? The answer to this question became clear to me now. I knew Nietzsche belonged in another world and that he had something to do with *the others*. He had appeared when I called *the others*. He had appeared and saved me for some greater purpose. For these reasons, I needed to study his work in order to find some key to unlock the mystery that *the others* gave me many years ago.

AUTOMATIC WRITING

After I discovered who the man in the white robe was, another change took place in my life. I had always dreaded the thought of speaking in front of a group of people. Now I suddenly found myself speaking spontaneously and fluently on many subjects. I was amazed at how my speaking ability had improved immediately. I was also amazed by how I was talking about things beyond my knowledge. It's funny, but this was like when I was with the girl spirit. Back then, even the principal of my elementary school had been surprised by my bold speech. Now I was being bold again, but at a higher intellectual level. Just as the girl spirit had brought me many changes in a year, this period also lasted for a year or so. I was passionate in my conversations. And I freely entered into classroom discussions of various subjects and debates in philosophical groups and spoke with great persuasive power. I even talked on the stage. That was really unbelievable.

My opinions were accepted. My peers were impressed by my views and insights. People suggested that I should consider including our philosophical discussions in my thesis.

By this time, I had about five months left to finish my graduation thesis. Propelled by the words I heard, I wrote my first few pages very quickly. But as I continued to work, my writing and thinking slowed to a snail's pace. And then, I hit a brick wall. The subjects of death, hell, reincarnation, my ancestors, and aliens could not be included in my thesis. I needed to approach this project in a more scholarly manner.

I devoured Nietzsche's books. *Beyond Good and Evil. Thus Spoke Zarathustra. The Will to Power. Human, All Too Human*, Existential philosophy is one of the most difficult schools of philosophy. Nietzsche's work is often placed at the top of the difficult list. Existentialism is the most misunderstood philosophy in the world. Professor Mishima emphasized that we must be careful in reading Nietzsche's books. Just turning the pages, he said, could prove dangerous because Nietzsche pursued his thoughts and pushed them to the edge, working with his genius brain to establish his unique philosophy. I was aware I was approaching his work in the wrong way.

Page after page of my writing ended up crumpled and tossed into the wastebasket. With my shallow thinking, I started making mistakes again. Working with Nietzsche's philosophy was beyond my ability. I became impatient. I wanted to quit. I went back to Beethoven while I still had time. He was a safe subject that others could easily relate to.

The clock read midnight. I had finally settled on the topic of my thesis. With renewed determination, I laid a new blank sheet of paper on my desk. I stared at it, waiting for something to tell me how to start.

And then, the unexpected happened.

I heard a lecture. It was the same lecture I had heard in the death world. Now I knew who was speaking, though he did not appear in person this time. My ears were tuned to his voice. At the same moment, I saw my hand moving. It was writing by itself. My hand was moving so fast I could not even follow the words I was writing. Then I figured it out—*I* was not writing. The writing was automatic. It was as if someone else was controlling my hand. I wrote page after page.

This phenomenon has a name: *automatic writing*. A spirit or force uses our hand to write, and the writing is fast and does not involve our personal thinking. Beethoven mentioned in his diary that he heard music all the time and was inspired to write it down. He did not copy what he heard, but created the music in his own way. It took him a long time to finish each of his works. Mozart also felt compelled to write what he heard all the time in his head. He composed fast and completed a volume of work with little effort. It was said that he must have heard the music of heaven. He said that he was copying what he heard.

In my case, the automatic writing happened around midnight when I was alone and working on my thesis. It continued this way for several weeks. The first night, I heard a long lecture, but after that, each nightly lecture lasted only a few minutes. I wrote fast and completed many pages. Except for those incredible minutes of automatic writing, I always felt frustrated in my attempts at writing. I am not a patient person by nature, but as time passed, I started to realize that I was being forced to learn. In the death world, I had understood what I heard. I felt that my understanding was profound. Otherwise, I could not be enlightened. But when I came back to this plane, I could not recall everything I had heard in the death world. Now I began to understand what I was writing through what I was transcribing. This was not only material for my graduation thesis, but it was also an opportunity for me to truly understand my subject. It was the beginning of my serious personal education to understand *how to exceed the human level.*

The way the thesis was completed remains a mystery. It could be said that my work was done supernaturally. My graduation thesis, "Development of the Consciousness of Art by Nietzsche," was awarded the highest honor at the university. It was suggested that I continue my studies and acquire a master's degree. My professor thought I had a profound understanding of my subject.

I was finally about to finish my four years of university coursework. Although I still had one more year at Waseda, the major pressure was gone and I started to relax. One beautiful day in the early spring, I went to visit my friends in the lodge behind the university where I had lived. I wanted to say good-bye to them. Class had ended early, and it seemed like a perfect day to stroll through some of my favorite spots. I was lured back to one of my favorite hills, covered with tall grasses and small flowers. The sun was shining down on me. I looked up at the sky. It was so quiet it was as if the world were standing still.

And then...

We are watching you.

This was the voice of the alien. It came from the sky.

I froze.

THE PLAN OF THE ALIENS

Twelve years earlier, I had heard these words for the first time. Although years had passed and I had not heard from *the others,* I still knew they were there, still observing me. My life had been saved twice, which I accepted as undeniable proof that they were observing me, but hearing their words again confirmed their existence somewhere near me.

My mind traveled back to the day in the rice field where I had first met *the others*. I had seen and explored and moved through many different worlds since. *The others* brought many paranormal events, and my life took an unbelievable path. It felt like someone from the other side wanted me to go through the various paranormal experiences. Because they also knew that I could never handle things that belong in other worlds by myself, they also helped me when I needed help. It seemed as if *someone* was sending different individuals to me when I needed help along my life's path. It seemed to me that someone was orchestrating systematically various events for me to experience. These paranormal events started in my childhood with fabulous experiences and then went on to more complicated matters as I grew older.

I had often wondered who was orchestrating my life.

There have been many nonhuman beings in my life. I knew I was destined to be involved with them, but who was the giant puppeteer? Of course it was God. I believe that nothing can happen without God's permission. But was I being led by a nonhuman mastermind? Was I under the control by some intelligent mind in other world? Perhaps this was not something my mind could understand at this moment. I am grateful that I have been guided along the path prepared for me by the aliens and that I have also been guided to their world beyond the human realm. This is the path they are encouraging me to take. In my university years, I studied this subject through Nietzsche's philosophy. In 1994, I would work on the same subject through the yogi masters in the Himalayas. It became a major interest to me throughout my life. I would use all kinds of methods to learn what the celestial being had brought into my life.

After I finished my graduation thesis, I became a much more studious person. For the first time in my life, studying made me content. I kept enjoying debates with people in the philosophical group. Though my deep feelings for Professor Tanahashi never changed, my focus dramatically shifted to *the others* again.

Later in my life, I would hear more of these words, *We are watching you*, when their vehicle appeared in various countries.

With graduation approaching, the major topic on everyone's mind was the future. Like my friends, I needed to set realistic goals. Many girls had met their future husbands when they went back to their homes during breaks. These marriages were family arrangements. My parents had also acted like matchmakers, of course, so there was always some new man for me to meet. But I never met any of the men my parents found. I learned that marriage is a state to which most females aspire. The need to create a new generation must be inherent in female nature. Both of my sisters and my mother possess this nurturing female instinct, but alas, it appears not to have passed on to me. I wonder where my different point of view comes from. Well, yes, I know. *The others* are responsible. I clearly remember how everything changed when I met them for the first time. I totally lost any feeling for human regeneration. And so, marriage was out of the question for me. My path would be my career.

My life in the professional world of Tokyo was still going full force. I had radio bookings and appeared on television on major shows broadcast nationwide by NHK, the educational TV stations. When I appeared on *Music Around the World*, I played the Argentine tango.

But it was a time for me to go to Europe. I had to do precisely what the violin tutor on the other world had told me I would do. I had also been seeing visions of Europe since childhood. There was no doubt in my mind that I would revisit the place where I had lived in a past life. Also it is important to visit Heidelberg, where Tanahashi had studied.

Unfortunately *the others* had not come back to see me during these five years. I was disappointed, but I was grateful for my unexpected musical career. I now believe that my path was led by the celestial violinist.

I felt that Tokyo held a key that might solve my mystery regarding aliens. I would learn this a few years later when I came back to Tokyo.

Travels Around the Earth and Through Time

TRAVELS TO EUROPE

I wanted to make my trip to Europe memorable. I saw an advertisement on TV for the first luxury cruise ship ever to visit Japan. This was a Russian ship that would set sail from Yokohama for Khabarovsk, a city in Russian territory north of China. By booking this cruise, I could go on to Moscow and visit a communist country that ordinarily would be difficult to enter. Then I could take the train from Moscow and see two other communist countries, Poland and Czechoslovakia, on my way to Vienna. I decided to study classical music in Vienna. I have been wondering where the best place to go for my first adventure in Europe and could not think any city that was better than Vienna. Vienna is the capital of Austria. It is where Beethoven, Mozart, and many other composers lived. Austria is south from Germany.

I thought it would be a good idea to become a music student instead of just a tourist.

It was early July when I picked up my violin and one suitcase and boarded the cruise ship for my first big trip. I thoroughly enjoyed my first Russian dinner, after which I watched the Russian dance show in the ship's lounge.

After two-day at sea, we boarded the plane in Khabarovsk. The flight to Moscow took half a day. This was my first time to travel by air. I loved the view of the pure blue sky as we flew at an altitude of 30,000 feet. When we descended, we could see Moscow.

While my eyes were taking in the sights from my window, a strange feeling crept into my thoughts. *This is not the first time I have flown.* As a young child, I had flown in the alien vehicle. I had seen the golden city from the window of the alien ship. It felt like an electrical shock ran through my whole being when I remembered that earlier flight. While my mind was caught up in that long-ago day, we experienced heavy turbulence as the plane passed through the thick clouds above Moscow. When we broke through the clouds, I could see details of the city below us. As we approached to the ground, the old memory I had buried was reactivated. Though the speed was different, the sensation of approaching the city from above was the same. I was captured by an uncanny feeling: there had been no turbulence around the alien ship. The golden city had appeared in one second as if I had been looking through a zoom lens.

After we landed, most of our group stayed together for a three-day sightseeing tour of Moscow. We visited the churches and cathedrals in the city and its suburbs.

Although I enjoyed visiting a new country and although I was physically part of the group, my mind was still filled with the memories of the day when I saw the golden city. The others in our group noticed my strange mood, and the tour guides worried that I might be sick when I suddenly became quiet.

When the tour ended, I faced a two-day train trip through Poland and Czechoslovakia. My eyes may have been looking at the European countryside, but my mind was still somewhere else. All I could see was the golden city.

Leaving the train station in Vienna, I faced my major challenge—I spoke neither German nor English. I had to turn my mind to my upcoming new life.

I spent ten days alone visiting the important sites in Vienna. But it was still hard to keep my memories out of my mind. I told myself I should be enjoying my new life. I also thought it was not a good idea to be alone, so I decided to go to the university, where I hoped to meet someone. The University of Vienna, a public university ranked as one of the world's best, is located on the Ringstrasse, the famous boulevard that circles the center of the city. I strolled through the campus and had lunch in the student restaurant. It was there that I met two Japanese women and a man.

The girls were music students, and the middle-aged man was a professor named Kimura. Kimura was on vacation in Vienna and taking a summer course at the university. He had studied German philosophy at the University of Bonn. Bonn, which is Beethoven's birthplace and also the city where Nietzsche studied, is located in the central part of Germany, north of Heidelberg. The Rhine River flows past both cities. There was something special about Kimura that reminded me of Professor Tanahashi. As we talked, I mentioned that I was thinking of traveling in Austria and southern Germany before returning to Vienna in September, when my studies would begin. Professor Kimura expressed genuine concern about my traveling alone without being able to speak German. We made arrangements to have lunch together the next day. I arrived early. When Kimura approached my table, he was not alone. He had brought along Sato, a young male friend he was traveling with…and thus began a new chapter and a new adventure in my life.

THE TIME MACHINE

Sato was a student at the University of Bonn, but he had moved to Vienna. We both wanted to travel for one month from Austria to southern Germany, and he was looking for someone to hitchhike with, though he was not particularly looking for a woman. He intended to do an intense trip and thought a woman might not be suited for that kind of travel. It also didn't help that hitchhiking was not exactly the kind of traveling I had in mind. Kimura had brought us together because Sato was a gentleman and was fluent in German. Also, it is said that it is easier for hitchhiking couples to get a ride rather than a single person or two or more men. Because Kimura persuaded Sato to take me along on his hike, he agreed on the condition that I would not complain if the trip became too hard. Adventure was what I was looking for, but this gave me pause. I took an even longer pause to think and rethink this proposal. Sato had already lived for three years in Germany. He had taken many hitchhiking trips and was prepared for another one. I was not prepared for anything yet.

Okay, I finally said to myself. I agreed to his requirements.

In the 1970s, the Austrian government was suggesting that students hitchhike to see their country, and the Austrian people were encouraged to give rides to young travelers. Crime did not appear to be a major problem at that time.

Sato and I went first to the charming city, Salzburg, which is at the foot of the Alps. Salzburg is the birthplace of Mozart, whose music filled the air everywhere we stopped. Then we visited Saltzkammergut, the location of the movie, *The Sound of Music*. The scenery was so breathtaking.

Next, we headed west toward Innsbruck, which lies in the area in the Alps called the Tyrol. The area is considered by some to be heaven on earth. By this time, I was glad that I was traveling with Sato. My mind was no longer filled with my memories of my past. I was now living in the present and fully enjoying it. If

I had traveled alone and by train, I would have missed so many spectacular sites. I also enjoyed Sato's company. He was intelligent, and we had a lot of common interests and many things to share and discuss.

After we visited Innsbruck, we headed into Germany, where Munich would be our last stop before we returned to Vienna. We had ten days left and were now entering a scenic tourist area in southern Germany called the Romantic Road. We were still in the Alps, but the views now changed dramatically. We started to see castles, one after another. I started to wonder what my life would be like if I were to settle there. I loved the area that much.

As we were approaching our final destination, we were offered a lift to an area near another castle. The man who gave us the ride took us as far as he could on the road, then pointed and said we had about a twenty-minute walk. We were headed for the royal castle of Neuschwanstein, the most famous castle built by King Ludwig II. It is perhaps the model for the Fantasyland castle at Disneyland.

Fate works in mysterious ways. The road we took was not the highway the tourist buses took, but a small road where only private cars drove. We were also facing the back side of the castle. But the place I needed to visit was right here, and a train or a bus could have never brought me here. It was either destiny's plan or my subconscious that led me here and made the next event possible. I had no idea I would be visiting a place I had been missing.

We followed the path and reached a small alley. We were supposed to make a left turn when the alley split, but I felt the route I needed to take was in the opposite direction. Sato said that if we wanted to get to the castle, we had to go left, but I was adamant. I insisted that we turn right. My insistence surprised him, but it was not imperative that we see the castle right away. He was content to simply walk with me. It was a beautiful, peaceful walk through a countryside surrounded by tall mountains. There were no houses nearby, and we could see the castle on the mountain to our left. I kept looking around at the magnificent view.

And then, suddenly, a wave of familiarity hit me, a castle high up on a mountain, a road, the fresh air. *I know this place*, I said to myself. *I have known this place before. I was here before.*

I was standing on the same ground where I had once stood, somewhere, sometime in my past. I was remembering this place from the vision in my childhood. So much was flashing in front of my eyes. It was such a strong feeling that I almost burst into tears. I wanted to shout out, "I know this place."

I suddenly felt something very peculiar. The air was changing. The air around my head felt distinctly different. This changed air was coming toward me, but now it was no longer covering just my head, it was circling and capturing my entire body. I didn't know what was happening, but Sato also sensed a change in me and the atmosphere. He knew something was wrong, first because I had become deeply silent and, second, because my hands were up in the air waving about and my eyes were unfocused and staring into space. He later told me he was scared by what he saw and wanted to ask me what was happening. But he couldn't get through to me. He just stepped back and watched me. My upper body was swaying and I was making weird movements. Sato had never witnessed this sort of thing. He knew I was in great health and we had encountered no one and nothing along the way to bring about such a change in me.

What was I experiencing at that moment? Music. Yes, I was hearing music, and the sound of it brought back such nostalgic feelings. It was violin music. I had no idea where it was coming from, but that wasn't the point. I also had no idea when the music was being played. Now I could see people gathering in the distance, and I was being pulled in their direction. Soon, I could see it was a wedding party. There were fifty or so adults and children dressed in traditional German clothing, the bride, all in white. They were celebrating. Some people were dancing with violin music.

When I was younger, I had seen my past life scrolling as if on a movie screen. Well, there was no movie screen here. I was seeing clearly what had occurred in the past, and I was standing in the same exact space where it had occurred. It was all the same, but altogether different. I was now seeing images of actions I knew, but they had occurred more than a century before my current incarnation. Was I in a trance? Was this time moving in reverse? Was I existing in a linear way with respect to a timeline? Was I existing in the present moment and in the past at the same time?

I knew everyone in front of me in the vision. This was a life I had experienced. I knew these adults, including the bride in the white dress. I knew the children because I had been one of them. Then I heard someone calling to me under the violin music, but this calling was not in the present time. This voice was in the past. My name was different and I looked different, yet I knew it was my name. In my present life, I was twenty-four years old and Japanese. In this alternate, earlier life, I was about seven years of age and I was a German girl.

All I could do was scream, "Oh my God!"

It was the weirdest feeling, but at the same time, I felt perfectly natural. I knew this event. It had happened. It was my life. Of course, I remembered it. If I had seen something different from the actual event, I would have panicked, but what I saw was exactly what had occurred. I even knew what would come next.

And then something happened that really shocked Sato. Abruptly and with no warning, I jumped right out of my trance state. I was happy, chipper, talkative.

"Let's go!" I said. I grabbed Sato's hand. "Hurry! I want to show you something!"

Up to this point, I had never taken his hand, but I did so now with a firm grip, as a child does. It felt natural, at least to me. I can't imagine how it felt to Sato.

"But," he said, "you said you had never been to Europe."

He was very careful in questioning me, but it didn't matter because I wasn't listening to him. I had no control. All my actions from this time on happened spontaneously, not of my will, but of her will, the girl I had once been. Poor Sato, being dragged around by a girl who kept pointing out familiar spots and sights. Many hours later, he told me I had talked continuously about my German childhood.

"There are two roads over there," I announced as I led him to them.

A minute later, "Now, we turn left. I had a pony, and my father took me riding all the time on this road."

When I said this, Sato became really scared.

"And the church," I said, "the white church…I must go there!"

Sure enough, straight ahead of us stood an old, one-story, white church, and when we reached its front door, I was overcome with emotion. I let go of his hand.

"It still looks the same!" I said. I stood there, unmoving and silent, with tears in my eyes, for about five minutes.

Sato knew I had never been here before, at least not in this life. He was beginning to understand that my trance state must have been caused by something that had triggered a past-life regression, if not a temporary state of psychic possession.

And then, suddenly, I started to run as if something serious happened. My eyes were fixed. After about five minutes, I stopped again. I stood still, staring into space. Then I changed our route. There was no path, but I stalked into the bushes. I pushed them aside and went on until we reached a bubbling brook. My countenance again underwent a complete change. My gaze was transfixed, and now, I was trembling.

Sato could take no more. This place was in the middle of nowhere, hidden from public eyes. He decided he had to do whatever he could to get me out of my possessed state. He shook me, but I have no memory of it. My entire being was somewhere else. I slowly came back into my current body.

The trance had lasted for nearly an hour. I was clearly in a state of confusion, totally dazed, unable to talk. I had absolutely no idea where we were. When Sato asked if I knew the way to the castle, I had nothing to say. So he took over and led me along until we reached the alley where my trance had begun. We hardly uttered a word until we reached the foot of the castle. When we came upon some other tourists, I was almost back to my normal self.

Neuschwanstein Castle is large and very tall. We climbed up to the highest tower, where there is a stunning view from the observatory. One side of the castle faces the Alpsee Lake, whose water is as calm and blue as a crystal mirror. The other side is a panorama of magnificent fields surrounded by woods. We took pictures and chatted and I seemed to be no different from any of the other tourist enjoying the day.

All was fine and normal, that is, until my eyes abruptly went out of focus again. I was remembering this view very well and seeing it from very far above. Then I was far above everything, floating high in the air. My spirit was leaving my body. I felt dead cold. I was now experiencing the time of my death from that earlier German life. I froze.

But Sato had had enough of my going off somewhere. There were lots of tourists around us, so he yelled out, "Fantastic view!" Then he slowly led me down the narrow stairs. We walked a short distance away from the castle to a quiet spot on the meadow and sat down on the grass. We were silent for a long time, but the silence was finally broken when Sato asked me what had been going on. He told me how concerned he was, how worried and at times scared by what he had seen.

I owed him some sort of explanation, but the problem was how to begin. How could I tell him when I wasn't even sure what had happened? We'd been traveling through Germany for over a week, but it wasn't until we reached this area that I saw the scenes from my past. But Sato was Japanese, and we Japanese are all familiar with the subject of reincarnation.

"It was like a playback," I began. "As if I were in a time machine. I felt like I entered the past." He looked stunned. "I knew my immediate past life was German," I continued, "but I didn't know the exact location until now. But it was right here! It was violin music that took me into the past. I spotted one little girl, and I remembered her face! The little girl I was looking at was *me*. You must have seen how strange I looked in those moments."

Sato kept his voice calm. "When was this past life?"

"If my logical brain is correct, maybe somewhere around 1850. Could be less. I knew this many years ago…you read about these things in science fiction magazines or watch stories on television, like episodes of *The Twilight Zone*."

We remained silent as we both tried to digest what I was saying.

"Did something happen in the white church?" he asked. "I truly felt you knew that place and the church held something special for you."

His questions were simple. They forced me to think, but I couldn't come up with anything else. Being thrown off-guard like this and floundering around for some sort of logical response seemed funny to me. I knew I had an answer. I knew exactly why I had wanted—*needed* to see that white church. I had overwhelming feelings. I knew I had had those feelings in the past. Back home in Japan, the university across from my parents' house had a small white church. It was a special spot to which my eyes were always drawn. Today, I finally found the remembered white church and the reason for that attraction. The answer was somewhere near, but I still could not quite grasp it.

I asked him a question. "You saw that I led you to that church? I knew the way?"

"Yes," he said. "You knew the way very well. So well, you frightened me. I thought you might be possessed."

"Yes. Maybe I was...by her...I mean, by me." I could sense his uneasiness.

"You talked about riding a pony," he said. "With your father."

"Did I say that? I don't remember saying that out loud. But it's a memory I've always had since my childhood...in this lifetime. But if I said that, it confirms my memory of that past life."

He had another question. "What happened when we reached the brook? You stood as still as a statue."

"It was my death. I saw my death."

For a few minutes, I could not speak.

"This is serious," I finally managed to say. "We hear how our soul leaves our body after death." I paused to think about how to say this. "The view from the castle...I saw my soul departing from my body. I was looking down at my body while I was floating high up above it. It was the same view that I was seeing today from that observatory."

"So," he said quietly, "it was not a good death, I presume, from your reactions."

"Unfortunately not. I might have committed suicide...back there...in the brook."

"Do you know the reason for that?"

This was not something I want to get into, but I felt I needed to finish this conversation. "This is the memory I have had for many years," I said. "I once lived in the southern part of Europe, where the weather was warm and the sun was bright. I lived there for many years, but I came back to Germany because of a serious problem. Something to do with family and my serious sickness. Up to this day, I only had a lovely memory of my childhood here. I did not know my traumatic death also happened here."

A few days later, when Sato and I arrived in Munich, I hardly remembered anything about the other cities we had visited on the way to Munich. As we had only one day left for sightseeing,

I was trying to get myself together and be done with my strange moods and silences.

I felt sorry for Sato. He had put up with so much with me as a hiking partner. We tried to celebrate our last night together with a beer at a lively Bavarian restaurant filled with happy music. Finally, we stood in front of the youth hostel we were staying at and said our good nights. We made plans to meet for breakfast.

Next morning, when I cheerfully made my way to meet Sato, I found him sitting on the sidewalk in front of the restaurant holding his head in his hands. All of his belongings had been stolen. There was no way he could travel to Vienna without his passport. It was a devastating blow. We had been traveling in heavenly places, but a youth hostel in a major city is far from heaven. He decided to stay in Germany and find work and then, hopefully catch up with me in Vienna. He accompanied me to the train station and sent me off.

Now, sitting alone, I could not stop thinking about what I had been through. I told Sato things about my death in that earlier life, yet there was much more. The memory of this suicide attempt was something I did not want to remember but it came back after I met *the others*. I clearly remembered my thoughts during the final day of my past life. I saw myself in a living room near a large wood-framed window. The house was built with bricks and there was a huge fireplace near the dining table. It was a medieval style, two-story house. There was no one else in this house at that time. I had been sitting for quite a long time, just staring outside. It was autumn. Through the window, the forest looked almost yellow. Then, all at once, I stood up, went into the kitchen, picked up a large knife, and put it in a sack. Then I left the house for the last time. I turned back once for a final good-bye. I had special feelings about that house. Perhaps it had belonged to my family.

I walked through the woods, and I could still sense my feeling of being dead cold. This scary feeling was so real that even though it happened in another lifetime, I still retain the sensation of that day. I thought I would walk until my life was depleted. I don't remember how far I walked, but I know I finally sat down on the ground. The sun was coming through the tall trees and the air was crisp. In my last moments, I wanted to be at one with nature. I wanted my last sight to be of yellow leaves under the placid blue sky, the autumn color that I like the most. I assume I came to that brook. I have no idea if I used the knife, but I know I had an intention to commit suicide.

It's funny. In this life, I cannot use a kitchen knife. I cannot even hold one in my hand. If I even see one, I get shivers. People laugh when I cut vegetables with a small fruit knife. I became aware of the knife issue when I was about five years old and Mother accidentally left a kitchen knife on the table. She always put the knives in a high place to make sure her daughters would not touch them, but one day, I walked into the kitchen, and my eyes went right to that knife. My heart stopped. The fear surged through my entire body. It was only one second, but I saw the image of my death. I saw the body lying on the grass. I saw the knife.

It's also strange that when I faced suicide in this life at age seventeen, this same memory came to me. History has a tendency to repeat itself if we do not do anything to change it. Two late autumn days, and I felt the same kind of cool, fresh, crisp air and gazed at yellow trees against a blue sky.

My memory of the medieval, two-story, brick house was linked to the foreigners' house at the university across the street from my parents' house. Nice is a city in the southern part of France, where the weather is warm and the sun is bright. In this life, I was led by the aliens to live in Nice, which also held a secret from my past life. I would learn this later.

Finding my past-life home was one of my purposes for coming to Europe. I had intended to travel through various parts of Germany to find the old home I was missing. I had even been thinking I would travel alone because it was my personal journey, and I wanted to experience deep meditation on this sentimental journey. Who would have imagined that I would discover my old home so soon? It was totally unexpected. I assume I needed to know about my past life before I started my European life. I had accomplished something I had to deal with in this life. It was part of my incredible journey of self-realization. Now I better understood that I had to finish my unfinished work from that life in this life. I had been thinking that if I found the place I was missing, I would live there. But my new life would begin somewhere else, after I learned of my suicidal death.

I am glad I traveled through Germany with Sato. If I had traveled alone, I would not have had a witness to this strange experience.

MY MUSICAL AWAKENING IN THE VIENNA WOODS

Professor Kimura was waiting in Vienna for Sato and me to return. It was the beginning of September. I gave him the sad news that Sato had been robbed and thanked him for bringing us together for a successful trip. As our conversation continued, Kimura expressed his concern about my accommodations, since I was still living in the hotel. He took me to the student union at the university and showed me the ads for student housing. One AD that had caught his attention was an offer of free rent in exchange for babysitting from eight to ten o'clock at night. Kimura thought this would be a good opportunity for me to learn German. A bonus was that the house was in the Vienna Woods, an area I already loved.

We boarded a bus to the house. The whole trip took nearly an hour, but we were in what looked like a dream world. Mr. and Mrs. Gillar were night-school teachers who needed someone to put their children to bed. I moved in the next day. My charming room faced the Woods, where I saw deer grazing.

Strolling in nature is my favorite thing to do, and it could not get any better than the Vienna Woods. The leaves of the trees were turning to gold. The memory of the girl spirit came to my mind. I met her among golden trees while I was strolling on the mountain. She took me to the heavenly golden world. That was the last time I saw her, but then I met the celestial violinist. I had been a faithful violin student since then. It was strange when I thought about those days. The time machine experiences now were also strange; My vision had started with violin music. Did music have something to do with my past life?

At the conservatory, the former concert master of the Vienna Philharmonic, Walter Barylli, became my professor. I felt greatly honored. I also applied for a class in German for international students at the University of Vienna, where I had met Professor Kimura.

Soon, Mr. and Mrs. Gillar introduced me to their relative, a nice conservative guy named Rudy, who was studying Japanese culture.

One night, Rudy invited me to a charming Hungarian restaurant in the Vienna Woods. It was a comfortable autumn evening, and the yellow and red hillside beyond the Woods looked like a romantic painting. We sat outside in a garden under a grape arbor and gazed at the sunset. The sky started to change to rosy pink. It was a picture-perfect evening. Though my German was still poor, it was fun speaking in my first foreign language. I felt like I was living in a happy dream.

At that moment, I heard music playing. Although it was intended to add to the ambience of the night, it did not evoke a romantic feeling in me. What it did was arouse a part of me that had been dormant for a long time. This was the music I had forgotten for many years. It was the sound of a violin coming from some far-off place, yet playing here and now. Something deep inside me awakened, my heart skipped a beat. My date was speaking to me, but I didn't hear him. I had to understand what I had forgotten for so many years. What was this music?

And then, I saw six musicians enter the patio—two violinists, a cellist, a bass player, a clarinet player, and a cymbal player, all of them in costumes with shiny, blue vests with golden linings.

They were Hungarian gypsy musicians playing music I had never heard before in my life. Or had I? The nostalgia would not let up.

The first violinist came to our table and started to play a serenade for us. And then, I made the connection. *It was the intense music with deep emotion that the celestial violinist had played for me. On the other world. As a child, more than half a lifetime ago.*

In the Hungarian restaurant in Vienna, this violinist was playing a song called "I Would Become a Tree if You Were the Flower of That Tree." It would later become one of my very favorite songs. After dinner, Rudy took me dancing in a romantic garden, but I don't remember our conversation. All I heard that night was the music that kept playing in my ears.

The next day, I decided I had to learn gypsy music. I did some research and learned that one of the most famous gypsy violinists played in a restaurant called the Mathias Keller, which was located next door to the Viennese State Opera. It was, I was told, an outstanding restaurant patronized by members of the Viennese Philharmonic and the opera singers, who often went there for dinner after a performance. I was intimidated, but I went there alone because I wanted to concentrate on the music. There were no other young people, only me, sitting alone. But I didn't care. I was mesmerized by the violinist. The actual sounds I was looking for were not exactly gypsy music, but it was the closer than any other music I ever heard. I waited for the band to finish their performance, and—it was midnight by now—I fearlessly approached the lead violinist and told him how much I was impressed by their music. He was a world-renowned gypsy violinist named Sandor Deki Lakatos. His father, Sandor Lakatos, performed in Munich and was one of the most famous violinists of the day. In the Lakatos family tree were many generations of the renowned violin virtuosos.

I asked Sandor Deki Lakatos if he could give me private lessons, but in spite of my fervent desire to learn from him, he said no. The next day, I went back and took my Japanese girlfriend

Kuramitsu, a piano student who spoke German fluently. I thought that my first approach had not been effective because of my poor German. Yet even with the help of my friend, I was still politely denied. I persisted. I went back to the restaurant every night. He saw me each night, and each night, I was disappointed again.

A week passed. I decided to try a different approach. I took my violin to the restaurant and played for a few minutes as an impromptu audition. I had never before showed this much interest in music, nor had I had that much determination to get what I wanted. My desire to learn this music had become an obsession. This was scary. It was not the me I knew. Playing the violin had been the means I used to fulfill my desire to travel, but now things were different. *I was different.*

I played a song called *Zigeunerweisen* ("The Gypsy Way") by the classical composer Pablo de Sarasate. It is a very difficult piece. I needed to show him I could play violin well. But he still was not swayed.

"We gypsies are not allowed to teach persons who are not gypsies," he told me. "Music is our legacy. We do not even teach our daughters, but only pass our music on to our sons."

I decided it was time for their legacy to expand. With my adamant, even reckless, hounding, I finally persuaded him to seek approval from his father to teach me. It was a long shot, my not being a gypsy and a woman, to boot, but at last I prevailed.

"Are you serious?" Lakatos kept asking me. "This is our ethnic music. We gypsies play gypsy music because it is in our blood."

The Viennese people around me were saying the same thing to me. But my determination was never swayed. I started my private lesson and continued for many months. And then, Lakatos let me play with his band for my training.

By now, nearly a year had passed since my arrival in Vienna, and I had no intention of leaving, even though I lacked the money to live there. My one-year student visa would expire soon, so I had no choice but to apply for a scholarship. I learned that I was the first Japanese person ever to receive a scholarship from Austria. I was stunned that I was even accepted, but I sensed that I needed to stay in Vienna a little longer. My celestial violinist must have had more plans for me in Europe. Then Professor Barylli offered me an opportunity to work with the Vienna Radio Orchestra during the summer vacation. This job was at the Schönbrunn Castle, where Mozart played the piano at the age of five. It was the castle where Princess Maria Antonia, who grew up to be Queen Marie Antoinette of France, lived. It is the most fantastic castle in Vienna.

My experience with the Vienna Radio Orchestra helped me to get the job at the MGM Grand Hotel Orchestra in Las Vegas in 1982. I started to work with Dean Martin, and then later I played with other famous stars like Bob Hope and Julio Iglesias for two years. Finally, Liberace helped me to become a headliner. I was practicing between shows in the back stage of MGM. He heard my practice and came to talk to me. It was an unexpected surprise. He normally passed by this area just before his show time. But on this night, I had an opportunity to talk to him. He persuaded me to create my own show. This was how my new career started.

The job at the MGM Grand led to my becoming a headliner on cruise ships, a career that lasted over twenty years.

Finally, in 1984, I created my unique and exciting solo violin show, adding gypsy music and country-and-western songs, coupled with humorous dialogue, gimmicks, costume changes, and dancing. I traveled around the world on cruise ships that took me to hundreds of countries. Until 2009, I did over five hundred cruises on some of the world's most luxurious cruise lines, including the *Royal Caribbean*, the *Princess*, the *Queen Elizabeth*, and others.

In my show, I used the technique I call the dancing violin, and the sentimental music linked to gypsy music that is something I learned in the celestial world. Classical music is not suited to cabaret shows, but gypsy music is. It is lighter. And romantic music with sentimental feelings. It is also lively and goes with dancing. Audiences were charmed and fascinated when I danced and spun while I was playing the violin. This was not a common thing for a violinist to do. I have often wondered if the aliens sent the yellow butterflies to teach me how to spin and play. I knew those butterflies were not the ordinary insects we see every day. I believe they did.

When the celestial violinist played, I was mesmerized by his sounds. He sounded like the super high-technology sound systems used today in huge auditoriums. I never thought a violinist could perform in such a way, but I have been using high-technology sound systems since I started to perform on cruise ship. Perhaps his performance showed me what I would be doing in my career.

Of course, without Mother's efforts and Father's financial support, my career as a violinist would never have happened. Also teachers, professors, Lakatos and finally Liberace's help brought me to this point. I can never thank enough to all of them, but I can say that my successful career, however, came from the things I learned in the celestial world. It is true that aliens took a major role in creating my career. There are many violinists, but my special techniques surely led me to success.

Vienna started to become *my* city. Something I never expected happened. I was offered Viennese citizenship and a permanent position with one of the largest symphonic orchestras in Vienna, the Vienna Volksoper, or People's Opera Orchestra, which played in the second biggest opera house in Vienna. It was the greatest honor I had received to date in my life. If I had taken the offer, I could have settled comfortably with an important position and security, but I knew that the destiny the aliens had prepared for me was different. In spite of this great privilege, I had to decline the honor. I had no second thoughts.

Also, there was a change in me. Playing in an orchestra or a band no longer interested me. Now I wanted to play solo. After I had gained some confidence in playing gypsy music, I started to think about going back to Japan to begin a new career.

I thought I could establish myself as a gypsy solo violinist in Tokyo, something I could never do in Europe because there were already too many gypsy musicians.

Rudy and his parents were sad because he wanted to marry me. But living in charming Vienna Woods and having a loving family was, however, not my destiny.

Before I left Europe, I visited Heidelberg, the famous romantic city and home of a famous university. My train arrived early in the morning, when the city was shrouded in fog. I stood on a bridge above the Rhine and looked at the university where Professor Tanahashi had studied. My crush on Tanahashi had led me to study German philosophy and had brought me to Europe. My attraction to him was unreal. I only have such an attraction to the aliens. Though my path and career were guided by otherworldly beings, he definitely participated in an amazing way. I believe that Tanahashi was also sent to me by *the others*. I knew right away that my attraction to him was not a merely human feeling.

Being a solo violinist was not something I had ever imagined I would be, but I had finally started to have an ambition in music that would last my whole life. It is unusual for a violinist to be a popular entertainer, but what I saw in the celestial world and what the celestial violinist said would happen, did happen.

CHAPTER 12

Back to Japan, Back to Mystery

When I left Vienna, I knew what my focus should be. I needed to be in Tokyo to establish my new career as a solo violinist. My determination was firm, but I knew the money I had was not enough to live on for very long. I had no idea where to go. I started making phone calls to my friends, but I was unable to contact any of them. I suppose they had all married or left Tokyo. Rent had been increased so much that I still could not find something I could afford after a fervent search for a few weeks. I even thought about going back to the tango band. I knew I could get a job with them, but that wasn't my desire any longer. I had to focus to my path that I was destined to. I started to play on the streets and parks. I lived in a tiny, wretched room. It was one of the most miserable times in my life. I missed my beautiful life in Vienna and wanted to go back. I already knew how difficult it was to start a new life in Tokyo, but I had a strong urge to come back to Japan. I thought my urge was for my musical career, but there was an another serious reason I needed to be in Tokyo at this time. I was brought back by the aliens. I would soon learn the reason.

One day, I placed an advertisement, *Gypsy Violinist Taught by Famous Gypsy Violin Virtuoso in Vienna*. It worked. I got a manager. Then I held an audition to get a good pianist to be my accompanist. I selected a very talented pianist named Sasaki.

After a few weeks of intense rehearsal, my new career began. Sasaki and I put on gypsy costumes and started our concert tour. Our unique music made us popular. After six months of concerts, my manager got us a job at the Palace Hotel, which is located in front of the emperor's palace in Tokyo and is one of the most prestigious hotels in Japan. Hotel people loved me to stroll from table to table and play near the people, just like gypsies did. Gypsy style was unique in Japan in those days.

A year later, Sasaki and I were offered a job at the Inter-Continental Keio Plaza Hotel in Shinjuku. This was the biggest hotel in Tokyo, with fifty floors. The sky restaurant we played had a fantastic panoramic view of the city. All my efforts were being rewarded. I had finally established myself as a gypsy violinist. My career was moving in a positive direction, and once again, I was ready to settle down for a while. I decided to move to a better apartment near Shinjuku.

A SPIRITUAL MANIFESTATION BY MASTER GOI

The apartment I found in a nice residential area named Nishi Ogikubo was brand-new. The building was bright white, which struck my eyes because it is rare to see white among the brown wooden houses so common in Japan. It was quite far away from where I was working, but right away, I took this one without a second thought.

When I moved in a few days later, a strange thing happened. It was early in the morning and still dark when a voice woke me up. *May peace prevail on Earth.*

I opened my eyes. There was a man standing next to my futon. I wanted to jump up, but I could not move. I looked up at him.

Even though my room was dark, I could see him clearly because an aura of white light surrounded him. He looked Japanese and had short black hair, deep, dark eyes, and a slim figure. I could tell that he was a highly spiritual person because he was dressed in a gorgeous, long, purple robe with a gold stripe on the chest. In Japan, purple is considered a highly spiritual color. He wore special socks that matched his kimono. His socks were white and shining. His feet were on the floor. He was standing there, holding a small incense pot in his left hand. I thought he looked like a saint.

He chanted *May peace prevail on Earth* three times while he began sprinkling powder on me. Within minutes, all my fear was gone and I began to relax. My eyes remained fixed on him as he moved around my futon very softly. He was with me for about five minutes, then just slowly vanished into the air. I fell into a deep sleep.

When I woke up at my usual time, I had slept well, but the vision of the man was still clear in my mind. I had never heard the words he recited before. Although he was a spirit, he had seemed so real that I felt as if I had been hypnotized. I was entirely at peace. It was a very strange experience.

The first thing I do every morning is make coffee. That day, the electricity in my apartment was not working and all the lights were off. I called my neighbor, but she said there was no electrical problem in her apartment. I waited thirty minutes to see if the electrical power would come back on, but there was no change. I checked the circuit breakers but they were in the normal positions. I was now concerned and decided to report this problem to my landlords, Mr. and Mrs. Kobari.

The Kobaris were a very nice elderly couple who lived in the house next to my building. Their daughter and her husband also lived in my building. They had an office, but since it was Sunday, the office was not open, so I went to their house. As soon as I opened their door, I jumped in astonishment. Hanging on their wall was a large framed picture. It was the man who had appeared in my bedroom.

"Is something wrong?" Mr. Kobari asked me.

"I cannot believe this," I said, pointing at the picture, "but that man appeared in my bedroom while I was sleeping last night and he said, *May peace prevail on Earth.*"

The Kobaris jumped to attention and immediately called their daughter. Soon, we were all sitting together, our eyes fixed on the picture on the wall. The man I had seen, I was told, was the founder of the spiritual organization called the World Peace Society.

"His name is Masahisa Goi," Mr. Kobari said. "When we built this apartment, we did a ritual to purify the ground and buried his picture and few other items containing his power. His prayer is *May peace prevail on Earth.*"

I was stunned.

"He is still alive," they said. "This had to be a spiritual manifestation."

Then they showed me the picture they had buried in the ground. It was tiny and showed only a white light against a dark background.

"When his picture was taken," they said, "this light appeared instead of his face. His teaching has a lot to do with white light. Thus his organization was also named the White Light Association, *The Byakko Shinko Kai*, in Japanese." Mrs. Kobari added, "Because of Goi's teachings, we had painted our apartment building white. His temple is also bright white. You should visit it. It's in Chiba. We will take you."

I was so astonished by everything I had just learned that I almost forgot to tell my landlords about the electrical problem in my apartment. But when it came time to take a look, all the lights in my place were shining brightly. I was embarrassed, but they seemed to understand what had occurred.

"Goi seems to have some different currents in his body," they said. "This incident has to be an effect generated by him. Various electric problems were reported in his organization."

I finally had my morning coffee. I was glad everything was back to normal. After coffee, I fixed my room. I slept on a futon mattress in the center of the room, and every morning, I moved the mattress into the closet, which was the typical Japanese way of arranging things. This morning, I noticed something shining on my blanket. I looked closer. It was very fine gold powder. The powder was also on the floor where Goi had walked around me. I scooped up some of this powder and showed it to the Kobaris. It was, I learned, incense that he sprinkled, and it had not looked golden at the time. I had just assumed the color of incense was brownish, an earthen color, but this had somehow changed into golden powder. Not only that, but I had been lying under my blanket and had felt the sensation of the powder directly on my body. How could that be? And there was another surprise—when I took off my nightgown, I saw golden powder on my chest and arms. I was wearing a long-sleeved nightgown, and my whole body, except for my head, had been covered by the blanket. How did this powder get on my body? And finally, the man was a spiritual manifestation. How could a spirit leave something tangible and material?

The appearance of this man was also something I could not easily dismiss. I did not know Goi's actual height, but he had looked taller than a normal human. His golden stripe on his purple robe stuck in my mind. Buddhist monks wear this stripe, but his was very shiny, highlighted, and I had seen words written on it, though neither Japanese words nor using the Latin alphabet or any other languages I had ever seen. While I was looking at him, I kept wondering what language it was. Later, I learned that this language belonged to some other world.

That night, I told Sasaki about my visit from Goi. It was the first time I had brought up a paranormal subject with her because nothing strange had happened to me until now. Sasaki replied that her father was interested in the supernatural and that it was his side business. I knew that her mother was a piano teacher, but I didn't know about her father. Our backgrounds were, in fact, quite similar. Sasaki also had two sisters, a family of four women and one man, just like mine, and the women's side involved music. But there was one difference. Her family accepted supernatural matters. That was because of her father could not take normal medical treatments and had to search for alternative treatments. He had investigated supernatural fields and established his company, which created natural medicines. Sasaki was still living with her family, and I soon became friendly with them. Her father took an interest in my story and invited me to various meetings of groups interested in the paranormal. Being friends with Sasaki's family stirred up my old interest in other worlds.

When I was in high school, people had begun discussing unidentified flying objects (UFOs) on TV. Now paranormal subjects were a booming industry, and there were many TV programs dealing with them. While I was in Vienna, I had received no information about what was happening in the world because Viennese television at that time had only two educational channels, and not many people had TV sets, not me, not any of my school friends. Now back in Tokyo, I started to see all kinds of interesting things on TV. A little boy, for instance, became famous because he had been visited by aliens and received supernatural powers. Aliens had come to him in his room and also were seen outside his house, which was out in the country. Sasaki's father had visited the boy and witnessed how he could bend forks with verbal commands. Strangely, however, the boy's parents never saw the aliens, but a friend of the boy, a little girl, saw them in his room. The aliens almost flew up to the ceiling when she walked in. The girl described them as being small in stature. I saw these two children on TV. She was only six years old, and there was no reason for her to lie about this event. This happened before the release of the 1982 movie, *ET: The Extraterrestrial*. These two children had never implied that the aliens who visited them were scary, but spoke of them as friendly beings.

Other kinds of aliens were also being reported, but what I was seeing on TV was not like my experiences, and even though the TV reporters were collecting personal experiences from other people, I didn't tell my story because I wasn't supposed to do so until the right time came. When I saw a TV report that someone else had met aliens and ridden in their vehicles, this was the first time I had ever heard about such a thing happening to someone else. I felt that my experiences were being confirmed. I thought it was good that people were becoming aware of the existence of aliens, not only sighting them but communicating with them too. I thought that now, people would believe my experience. I also began to understand that there were many kinds of extraterrestrials, and I had met just one kind among many. This confirmed what I learned on the other world. *"There are many beings that exist in this universe. Our spiritual level determines our next destination."*

Though I accepted the invitation of Sasaki's father, I did not visit Goi's temple in Chiba. Too many things were happening to me in Tokyo. Why should I go to Chiba, south of Tokyo, a trip of more than an hour? The truth was that Goi was a spiritual leader and the landlords had buried his picture in the ground, probably right under my apartment. This man appeared to me because I was (and still am) sensitive to a spirit. It was understandable.

A SHOCKING ALIEN EVENT

Early in September, Ishiguro, another friend, invited me to his home for an Obon party. There were about twenty people in attendance, and while we were chatting, Ishiguro's mother approached me. Out of the blue, she spoke to me.

"You will have an unexplainable message from somewhere soon," she said. "It will come through an electric device. It will feel very much like an electric shock throughout your system."

A message? Unexplainable? That made me curious. I soon learned that she was an ascetically trained Buddhist and could psychically tune into people. I also learned that she normally did not talk about supernatural things in public. From the moment I arrived in her house, she had not given any predictions to anyone else, but suddenly, she interrupted her casual conversation to speak to me.

"I don't understand this," she said. "This is very strange." She tried to get a better picture in her mind, but it was difficult. Everybody was wondering what was happening to her. As I found out later, she normally did not talk this way. After a few minutes of deep silence, she raised her head and said in a more cheerful voice, "But don't worry about it. It will end right away. You will not be injured. All is fine. But let me know what happens. I need to know this."

"Is it something bad?" I asked her.

"I don't know about good or bad," she said, "but be aware of electrical devices during this month."

I had had all kinds of strange phenomena in my life, especially during the time of Obon, and this warning seemed a little intense. But Ishiguro's mother had also said it would not be bad because it would end right away and no harm would occur.

With the good food and the fun, I soon forgot what she said.

About a week later, I was on my way home from work. It was just before midnight, and I was walking through the Sinjuku railway station when a piece of paper came flying at me, blown by the strong wind. It somehow attached itself to my foot. I shook my foot, but the paper did not let go, so I reached down and picked it up. It was a flyer for a film. It read, *Aliens, Higher Beings*. That caught my attention. With my footprint etched on it, the paper was not clean, so I looked around to see if I could find a cleaner one. Maybe people were handing them out, but I did not see anyone nor any other papers on the ground, so I guessed that someone must have dropped it. Around the train station, you can find all kinds of advertisements and flyers.

I had seen flyers about UFOs many times, but at this point in my life, I was not thinking about any of those things. Aliens did not visit me anymore. I assumed that they would never come to the big city, only to remote areas where there were no people around. *Now is not the time for aliens*, I said to myself. My focus now was on music.

And yet, somehow this flyer caught my attention. I looked at it again. It gave the location of a meeting in Chiba at ten o'clock the next morning. I would be free tomorrow morning. I asked an attendant at the station where the location was. It was a long distance away, he said. Chiba prefecture is large. I decided not to go. I would have to get up before seven o'clock to get there. I am a night person. I get up at ten o'clock in the morning.

But I woke up at six o'clock. Since I had decided not to attend this meeting, I tried to go back to sleep, but I lay awake. This was very rare thing for me. I wasn't even sleepy. *Well*, I said to myself, *since I cannot sleep, okay, I'll go.*

The travel time took me nearly two hours, much longer than I planned. I was already not in a good mood when I arrived at the train station for this meeting. It was a remote area near the ocean, and after I got off the train, I couldn't find where the meeting was being held. I had expected there to be a big lecture hall near the train station. Every place I went with Sasaki's father, there were many people walking to the meetings, and placards and signs were always distributed everywhere. But here? There were no signs at all. This was ridiculous. After I walked for twenty minutes, I finally found the place by asking some local residents.

Whoever put this meeting together, I grumbled, did a terrible job. It was held in a private house, and there was no indication that such an event was being held, not even at the gate. What was I doing here? I found my way on time, but I was already exhausted and feeling that this meeting would be a waste of time.

When I arrived at the reception area, I was met by a couple of greeters, if I could politely term them as such. I showed them the flyer and asked if I was in the right place for this event. The men studied me, making me feel unwelcome, even though they were polite. What had I gotten myself into? I signed my name and the time I arrived on the paper they gave me: Kayoko Tachibana [my Japanese name], 9:55. I then followed a woman to the place where I would sit. This was a seat in the last row. There were about fifty people in the living room, most of whom seemed to be in their mid-sixties, and two-thirds of them were male. And they all looked very serious. Was this event tied into something to do with religion? Everybody there seemed to be meditating as quiet music played. I was sure I was in the wrong place.

As soon as I sat down, I heard a telephone ringing. The sound was loud and annoying to the people who were meditating. While I was thinking this, the same woman who had led me to my seat came over and told me that they had just received a call for me. She handed me a sheet of paper with the message from the caller. Who could have called me? I had only found out about this event late last night. I had not met anyone and had not talked with anyone. No one could know where I was going today.

"No, this message can't be mine," I said in a quiet voice.

"Is your name Kayoko Tachibana?"

"Yes."

"Then this is for you." She laid the note on my lap.

Suddenly, I was also curious about the timing of this note. It was so perfect it scared me. I read the message.

Urgent. Come back home.

That freaked me out. What could be that urgent? Had my apartment gone up in flames? Had someone been injured or died? This was crazy. Here I was, hours and miles outside of Tokyo. I couldn't stand up and leave now. Even if anything like that had happened, there was no way anyone could phone me. Besides, there was no caller's name on this note. What kind of mistake was this? I told myself to ignore it.

At exactly ten o'clock, the meeting started. There were no introductions, and I had no idea what this group was about, though I sensed that this meeting was a regular thing for everyone else.

But when a film started, I almost fell off my chair. It opened with the words, *May peace prevail on Earth.* Up there on the movie screen—it was him! The man who had appeared to me while I was sleeping!

Goi was not present in person, but this film was about him. My heart was pounding. Did this man have something to do with aliens? Surely he must, as this was a meeting dealing with aliens.

As I watched the film, I could not believe my ears. Goi said that his message was from the aliens, though he did not use the word *alien.* He said "higher beings." His description of their world was the same as the other world I had seen. In the film, there was also a painting of a vehicle with many circular windows. It was identical to the vehicle I saw in the golden world. My visit to the golden world happened when I was seven years old, and no one knew about alien vehicles back in those days. When I finally saw pictures of UFOs in books, I was in Tokyo. I will never forget my surprise. I saw various shapes of vehicles in the books, but there were exactly the same disk shape of the vehicle that I had been taken to. The color of the vehicle in the books I saw were a metallic silver gray, the same color I had seen in the machinery room, but what I had seen in the golden palace was a kaleidoscope of colors and beautifully shiny. Now I was seeing the same colors in this film. The film confirmed my experience.

In the film, Goi was explaining how the vehicle came to him. He claimed that all communication with higher beings happened through his fervent prayers and said that his guardian spirit made this possible. He emphasized this strongly. But his prayer had nothing to do with the aliens. His fervent prayer was seeking for his path. He never asked aliens to come to him. Their visitation just happened. His research for his mission had brought him this unexpected result. His mind, he said, was not restricted to one specific religion or school of thought; he just needed to know his path. He was struggling with a serious health problem, which could be one of his reasons for praying.

He also said that there are two different kinds of guardian spirits. One kind is mostly our ancestors who have attained the higher realm. Most people have these guardians. Other kind come from a much higher place and are not human. Buddhist teachings also mention such guardians, which are deities or nonhuman beings. We don't always know where those beings, or deities, come from, Goi said, or what they are, but he added that some of them were aliens, higher beings from other worlds that come to us and become our helpers. Not everybody has such a guardian, he said, but if one comes to us, our life will change dramatically and we will be led in a different direction.

I could not believe what I was hearing. All of a sudden, everything became so clear to me.

The guardian spirits had become a serious issue for me during the years after I met the girl spirit. I had always wondered why I met a nonhuman spirit. How glad I was to hear what Goi was saying. Goi told us that his guardian spirit had taken him to another world where he had learned many things that he had no other way of knowing. My girl spirit had taken me to the other world, where I received violin instruction and the path that I should be taking. The girl spirit also came to me when I was struggling with my health, and I were miraculously cured.

The messages that Goi was sharing in the film dealt with "life in all realms of creation," including our solar system, the cosmos, and the universe. *Attaining the higher realm of existence* was his main subject. Oriental belief talks about reincarnation of humans and animals. Goi was talking about reincarnation of aliens, higher beings in the various worlds in the universe. What he said in the film was the same thing I had heard from the celestial being. This had been important to me since my first encounter, and I even ended up writing my graduation thesis on this theme. Everything Goi's film said confirmed to me that my experience was right. I still remembered the words the girl spirit said: No one understands you. But don't worry. Trust your experience.

I had always kept my experience hidden, but in the film, Goi spoke openly about his. As I watched, I took a deep breath and tried to calm my mind. My girl spirit *must have led me to here.* Now, suddenly, I understood her better.

When I think back to this meeting, it makes me wonder. Many things I needed to understand were all explained that morning. I didn't know what Goi talked about in other meetings, but he had said things I needed to know in this film. This meeting had to have been prepared for me. That was for sure. This was the film I really needed to see. This was *my day.* Finally, after so many years, I had found someone I needed to meet. Overwhelming joy surged through me; gratitude, relief, and shock, all together, all at once.

But still, one thing kept nagging at me—that strange telephone message. Who had called me? And why?

As soon as the meeting was over, I went to the reception table to inquire about the phone call. I saw the woman who had brought me the message.

"Why didn't you go back to your home?" she asked as soon as she saw me. "I was concerned about you. It was marked urgent."

"Did you take that call?" I asked her.

"No. It was a reception guy."

"I think this call was a mistake," I said.

"No," she said, "it cannot be a mistake. After I seated you, I came back to the reception area. I heard the telephone ring. I saw him pick it up and talk with the caller. He wanted me to write the message because he did not have any paper. When he repeated the message, I wrote it right down. He also made sure your name was correct."

"Then this message must be for me," I said. But I was still as lost as I could be. "Was the caller a man or a woman?" I asked.

"I don't know. The guy who took the call is tied up for the next few hours, but you can call him tomorrow."

I wanted to stay a little longer to talk to the people, but as soon as the film ended (around noon), everybody left. Nobody stayed to chat. Even this made me feel strange because people normally hang around after meetings, and there are opportunities to talk. Instead, people were packing up the chairs and cleaning the room.

On my way home, my uncertainty grew. All sorts of things started to enter my mind. I began to worry about my apartment and the health of those close to me. If this call had really been for me, I *should* worry. I hoped everything was okay. I would know when I got home.

Riding in the train, I summarized the events to myself. The first time I saw my apartment, I took it without considering anything else. Goi appeared only a few days after I moved into my apartment. My landlord belonged to this organization. The flyer for this meeting flew at me. I had never gone to any UFO meetings, not even in the area where I lived. I couldn't even understand why I was going, yet I felt like I was being pulled by a strong magnetic power. And it just happened to be Goi's event. And I learned things I had been seeking for a long time.

All this was already strange enough, and this telephone call added more mystery. Someone wanted me to go home. It sounded like I should not attend this meeting. Why? What is this message about?

Who had called me?

As soon as I reached my neighborhood, I became nervous. My building looked fine. No fire. I was relieved. When I opened my door, I saw that everything was the same as I left this morning.

Another big concern evaporated. I phoned my sister Kiyo and asked her if she knew where I went and if she had called me. It was a stupid question, but I asked anyway. Of course she didn't know anything, and she said that she had just talked with Mother and everything was fine.

What was so urgent?

That evening, I asked Sasaki if she had called me. Even though I knew she didn't know anything about the message, I had to ask her because she was the last person I was with before the flyer came to me and I went to the meeting. We walked to the Sinjuku station together every night and took different trains. It was right after we said good-bye that the mysterious flyer came to me.

After I asked these two people, there was no one else to ask.

Early the next day, I called the person who took the call. He recognized my name right away and answered my questions freely.

"The caller was a man," he said. "He sounded middle-aged. He was a quiet person because his message was spoken calmly, even though it was urgent. The caller said, 'This message is for Kayoko Tachibana. Please tell her. *Urgent, come back home.* After he said this, he hung up. There was no time to ask the caller's name. Since you were the last person to arrive and the paper you wrote your name was on the top of the file, I knew who you were. The caller must have been looking for you in order to catch you right at your arrival."

When I explained the strange situation to the man, he went silent. Then he said, "Regarding aliens, there are many unexplainable things happening in our organization. You should talk about this with Master Goi."

Well, at least, I knew now that the caller was a middle-aged man. Then I remembered the words of Ishiguro's mother. This was a shocking incident. The telephone was an electrical device. I had received the message, but I was not harmed. It was brief. Everything she had said was true. I was amazed by her accuracy. But I needed more information.

As soon as I hung up the phone, I went to Kobari, my landlord. For the past six months, I had not visited Goi's temple, but now, I knew I had to go. I wanted more information about Goi and how he had met aliens. Once there, however, the reaction of the people to my story made me more confused. They acted as if they had no idea what I was talking about.

"Meeting aliens?" Kobari said. "Where?"

"Didn't you know about the film? It belongs to your association."

"I know Goi has observatories," Kobari said. "His group has been doing some kind of research for many years, but normal members are not involved."

"Does he not talk about aliens?"

"No."

"Isn't that strange," I said. "In the film I saw yesterday, he was talking so much about aliens. I need to visit his temple."

"We will take you to the October meeting," Kobari said. "I know Goi. I can introduce you, and then you can have a private meeting with him."

This was a good idea!

But now I knew something else—*the caller was not human.*

The next day, thanks to Kobari's reaction to my questions, I called the reception man again. Also, I was curious about the private house where the meeting was held. When I connected again with the reception man, I explained that my landlords had buried Goi's picture before they built the apartment where I was living. The Kobaris had belonged to Goi's congregation for many years, yet they were not aware of any alien events.

"How did you get that flyer?" the man asked me. Now he was curious about me. "If you were not connected with this organization, you should not have had that flyer. You would not have attended our meeting."

I was surprised to hear this. "I'm not a member," I said, "and I didn't know Goi was connected with the meeting. I just found the flyer in the train station."

"There were only a few flyers printed," he said, "and they were meant only for people who belong to our prayer group."

"Prayer group?"

The man was clearly getting touchy about my story and my invasion of the group's privacy. "As you saw in the film," he said, *"our prayer group brings aliens to us.* This alien issue is very serious. We only gather with selected people. We are all trained. This is not something we do for the public. We were curious about you. We thought you were perhaps a daughter of one of our members. Since you had that flyer, we could not refuse you."

Now all of a sudden, he was angry. No wonder I had been getting strange vibes about them. That explained my first negative impression. But what was happening was not my fault. I had attended the meeting without being rejected and had learned a lot about Goi and aliens. There was a mix-up. But our connection was meant to be. It was fate for me to be there.

"Could I come to your meeting again," I asked "since I already attended one?"

The answer was no. It was a pity.

At this point, I had a clearer view of this event. This meeting was a "secret event." Now this reception guy knew that the caller was not human, though he spoke Japanese. Since the message came through someone's telephone, I had a witness. That was good. But the message was still confusing. Since I couldn't figure this out on my own, I decided to seek assistance from Ishiguro's mother. I thought she would be able to answer my questions. After all, she had first brought up this subject. I made arrangements to see her right away.

"Tell me what happened," she said.

After I told her everything, she became quiet and pondered for a while. Finally, she said, "This must be from the other side, not from earth."

Though I had told her everything that happened, I had not said anything about my hunch that the caller was not human. Her words surprised me.

"The reception guy and I know now that the caller was not human," I admitted, "but I need more information. I need some kind of clue to help me understand this mystery. Why did I need to go back home? Why was the message marked urgent?"

"I wish I could give you more details," she said, "but this one…I just cannot help you." She pondered for a while. "When I got that message at the party," she finally said, "it was altogether different. Almost an electric shock. So I had to speak immediately." She paused again, then continued very deliberately. "I wonder… regarding the words, *Come back home*. Does *home* have to mean your apartment? Could it be some other place? Someplace not on earth?"

I didn't know how to react to that. I had assumed the home meant my apartment. Now, suddenly, I had a moment of pure clarity. All the communications from aliens I had during my childhood made sense, at least in my mind. I knew they wanted me to come to their world. That was the reason they came to me. I had asked them to take me to their world, but my request had not been granted. My head started to spin.

"By the way," said Ishiguro's mother, "do you know you are sensitive to electricity? Your body has a different frequency."

I nodded. "I know that. I might have been born with it, but I think the aliens did it."

"Aliens did it? How?"

I had not intended to get into the subject of my childhood. But now my mind went to the aliens' world. It was too late to take back my words. "Well," I said, "it has been a big secret, but I met aliens when I was a child."

"Really? How?"

"I was taken. I think they did something to me, though I do not know exactly what they did. But I was in an alien vehicle. There were a lot of machines in it. It is possible that those machines might have affected my body. All kinds of paranormal things started to happen since."

She nodded. "I told you a shock would come from an electrical device. Your body is accepting or drawing a different frequency to you. Do you know you are also drawing spirits because of this? I am sure you have experienced more strange things. This telephone call is just one of them."

It was true. I have had many spirit issues in my life. I knew they were coming to me and talking to me. Goi's spirit also appeared to me. And he caused the electric problem. Now, knowing Goi had the same electric effect, I was relieved. It was good to know that I was not the only one to have strange electrical effects caused by aliens. I was afraid to speak to people and kept this to myself all this time.

Ishiguro's mother's information satisfied my curiosity. She was my mother's age, but I felt I could talk to her about everything that had happened to me. Twenty years had passed since my first encounter with *the others*. Times had changed, and people were talking freely about UFOs now. That could be the reason for her acceptance of my story. Or was she always that way? Whatever the reason, today, I finally received an answer to my questions about this mysterious call.

I thanked her, and just as I was about to leave, she said, "You will go to America next year."

"America? Next year? I've never thought about that."

We'll talk again. Come to the Christmas party" she said.

When I left her house, my head was still spinning. I had received too much information too fast. Going to America had never entered my mind. I moved to this apartment to stay in Tokyo for at least few more years, so I just ignored this idea. But I had to deal with another more serious matter.

Did *the others* really want me to come back? Once, that had been my dream: to go to their world. But this dream was not something I had planned or anticipated in my adult life. I had a career and a lot of future plans now. I need more time to digest everything I'd just learned. There was no way to prove Ishiguro's mother's interpretation was correct. If the *home* referred to my apartment, the meaning of the message changed. But my apartment and family had nothing urgent about them. My parents' house was no longer my home. After my mother and Sasaki's mother came to see our performance at the Palace Hotel, they were pleased, and Mother had left me alone about getting married. Maybe Ishiguro was right. But the longer I thought about it, the more uncertain I still felt. I needed further consultation. I decided I had to ask Goi himself. He should be able to answer my questions. After all, this strange event had happened in his meeting place.

The Kobaris took me to Goi's beautiful white temple in Chiba. It was closer to Tokyo and much bigger than I expected. We sat in the front row.

As soon as Goi came on the stage, he and I had firm eye contact. I felt like I had been struck by lightning. It was the same kind of shock I had felt the first time I saw a photo of Nietzsche in my textbook at the university. I couldn't believe my eyes. Even though these two were of different nationalities, they looked so much alike. How could this be? When Goi appeared in my room, he looked bigger than a human. But now I could see that Goi was not a big person. When I met Nietzsche in the death world, he was also bigger than a human. They both emanated white light.

Goi opened his lecture with his peace prayer. He spoke as fluently as a minister or a professor on the topic of the path to spiritual enlightenment. This speech was quite different from what I had heard in his film. Kobari was right. In this lecture, Goi did not say one word about aliens. But he said, "After going through various cycles of rebirth in various worlds (not only earth), we acquire sublime wisdom." That was the same thing I had heard in the other world. He also spoke about duality, which was also one of Nietzsche's major topics, beyond good and evil. Goi said that *Shinjin*, in English, *New Man*, is equal to the *Beyond Man* (*Ubermensch* in German) of Nietzsche. Goi said, "The *New Man's* High Consciousness will exquisitely change the Earth's vibrations in the twenty-first century." Nietzsche's theory is considered to be the twenty-first century's philosophy. Goi emphasized that he was dedicated to raising planetary consciousness and committed to higher spiritual goals. Not only did these two men look alike, I thought, but their messages were surprisingly similar too. Goi's speech was very passionate. He was very energetic. I felt as if I were living through a repetition of my experience in the death world. Goi had stopped looking at me, but my eyes were fixed on him. I was now facing the person who had stirred up my life.

Afterward, when I was formally introduced to Goi in another room, he looked at me so sharply that I felt as if I were being hypnotized, just as I'd felt at the time of his manifestation in my apartment. I could not move. I could not speak. I had waited for this meeting and prepared all kinds of questions, but now my tongue refused to move. His piercing gaze continued for a few minutes in total silence. I did not know what was happening. Then I heard,

You go to America. You work with music. But someday, you will change your life. That time, you will come back to me.

America? Ishiguro's mother had said the same thing. I was surprised that these were the first words Goi said to me. I had expected to hear something more significant, like a reference to my experiences with aliens, which he might have sensed psychically. But that was all he said. He didn't even say when my life would change. And when he spoke these few words, he had already turned away from me, and then he just walked away, but not because other people were waiting to speak with him. He just went to his room. I was deeply disappointed. I had expected to receive more information about the mysterious phone call. I had not been able to ask even one question.

Seeing my dismay, Kobari said, "Goi is not a big talker in person. He only talks when he gives his speeches. You received enough information. He told you what you would be doing and also gave you the conclusion that you would come back to him again. That is good."

I never again visited Goi's temple. He said that I would come back to him. Those were his last words to me, but I never took them seriously. In fact, I thought his prediction was wrong. I never believed that I would go back to him. I was not intending to stay in Japan. I was in Tokyo only temporarily for the purpose of establishing my career. Since Goi had not spoken about aliens and I was not allowed to visit another meeting concerning aliens, what else could I do?

Until this day, the film about Goi was the only event I ever attended regarding aliens and UFOs. This visit to his temple was the end of my contact with Goi until later in my life.

But I did some research on Masahisa Goi. He was born in 1916 in Japan. The World Peace Prayer Society is a nonprofit, nonsectarian, member-supported organization founded by Mr. Goi in 1955. Mashahisa Goi was also founder of Byakko Shinko Kai, an association based on his spiritual teachings for the development of mind, body, and spirit. He wrote more than fifty books on spiritual development.

At one time, his organization was called Universe Science. In the 1960s, he built a planetary science research center, but although he built this for study, he stopped talking about aliens to the public. Only a handful of people, mostly elderly people, understood his mission. Once he tried to talk openly about aliens, he soon saw the problems inherent in this. Talking about aliens was not acceptable in those days. Instead, he emphasized his philosophy of peace and unity, *May peace prevail on Earth.*

In the original Japanese words of the prayer, *May peace prevail on Earth*, the character for "earth" includes not only humankind but also includes the cosmos, and the universe.

I also learned the history of Goi's spiritual practice. Because he was born with a fragile physical condition, his health problems led him to not only the prayer but to esoteric studies, including yoga. He devoted himself completely to his healing work. Refusing to take money for his services, he said he wished only to be of service to humanity and prayed toward that aim. His fervent prayers were answered by a heavenly call, although it was some time later that the true meaning behind this call was revealed to him. A deity from another world became his guardian spirit. Goi pursued his spiritual disciplines until he received rigorous spiritual training through the guidance of his guardian deities. After the completion of his training, at the age of thirty-three, Goi reached enlightenment and experienced oneness. I also learned that he recalled being concerned with his future career as early as the age of three.

It is very unusual for a young child to think about his or her future career, but I became aware of my calling at the age of six when I had my first encounter. I realized this deep in my core. If someone has such an extreme experience, I guess the age does not matter. My destiny became very certain. Though I do not know what happened to Goi when he was three years old, I can only assume he might have had a similar experience as mine.

Many years later, when I contacted Kobari and his organization again, I learned that Goi had died in 1980 at the age of sixty-four. That was about five years after I met him. I was shocked to learn this. If I had not come back to Japan and had not lived in the Kobaris' apartment building, I would never have met Goi.

After Goi's death, no one else in his prayer group had contact with aliens, and the alien vehicle never returned. His planetary science research center was closed, and his spiritual center was moved from Chiba to near Mt. Fuji. Mt. Fuji is of course the symbol of Japan and is known to be a holy place. The people who were working closely with Goi in those days are also mostly gone now. He did not have children. His adopted daughter took up his work to pray for world peace, but Goi's original alien message has been entirely lost.

I learned something else interesting. Goi worked very hard to become an opera singer for many years. He was also fond of the arts and literature, but his alien contacts persuaded him to drop all that and pursue his career in the spiritual field.

This made me think. Music, art, and literature are the fields in which I work. Goi said I would work with music. No one in his group, except the Kobaris, knew that I played the violin. Now I wonder how Goi knew I was a musician. Kobari affirmed that they never passed my personal information to his association.

Moving into an apartment in the Kobaris' building shattered the normal life I had been living for so many years. Finally so many questions regarding to the aliens and other world were answered when I met Goi and the telephone call from the nonhuman being woke me up and reconnected me to the alien world.

Before I left my home town, I intuitively felt that I needed to be in Tokyo. This was because I met *the others*. I thought Tokyo held the key to my alien encounters. I was right.

But that ended quickly as I suddenly became very busy preparing for foreign travel again. I would fully realize this later in my life, but for the next thirty years, I would follow a secular path and focus on my musical career.

CHAPTER 13

To the World

My next opportunity for foreign travel came to me through Mr. and Mrs. Susini, a very nice Hungarian couple who were visiting Tokyo on business. It was the beginning of November 1975, one week after I had met Goi. Mr. and Mrs. Susini heard me play gypsy music at the Keio Plaza Hotel. I was able to speak with them in German, and during our conversation, they said they could not believe they were hearing original gypsy music played by a Japanese violinist. When I told them I had taken lessons from Lakatos, they were more impressed because Lakatos was their favorite violinist. They immediately offered me a job in Sydney, Australia, where they lived and were connected with the Hungarian consulate. Now I knew that my music was even acceptable to Hungarian people. Australia was also the country I always wanted to visit. I could not afford to let this new opportunity pass.

One day soon after I met the Susinis, I was having tea with my manager, Mutou, and mentioned this new offer. She brought up a topic I never expected. She belonged to a Buddhist society and had just returned from a convention held in Las Vegas.

"You should go to Las Vegas," she said. "I do not have any connections for your career there, but I know some Japanese people there who can help you. Even just a visit to experience the different kind of life there might be good for you."

"I would love to go after my contract in Australia is finished," I said. "I'm planning to travel from now on. I would love to use this opportunity to venture to America."

Goi and Ishiguro's mother had both said I would go to America. They were right! I felt that Goi's prediction might be better than I thought.

But first, I signed a contract with a hotel in Sydney for three months, starting in January, 1976.

This was going to be a different kind of journey for me because I did not intend to live in Japan anymore. It was time for me to follow what I was told by the celestial violinist. *Travel around the world as a performer.* Once I left Japan, I would keep traveling around the world until I had covered the whole world.

I gave my landlords my departure date. I felt bad that I would not complete even one year of my lease, but I had to drop everything. Now everything moved effortlessly forward and with incredible speed. As I look back, it seems that I moved to Kobari's apartment just to meet Goi, and after that purpose was accomplished, I did not need to be there any more. Destiny was pushing me to my next step. But Mr. and Mrs. Kobari, who were aware of my strange connection with Goi, were concerned about me. The electrical problems also still continued from time to time. No one else in Kobari's building had electrical problems or received any kind of manifestation from Goi, not even the Kobaris.

After Goi manifested in my apartment, my life changed in many ways. I was constantly directed toward spiritual pursuits. But I had no interest in that path. It interfered with my career and travel. I hated these changes, in fact, and tried to stay away from paranormal matters. I knew now that Goi was responsible for many of them. He was stirring up my life. Even if I could finally answer many unanswered questions, I had a career. I had ambitions and dreams in the practical world. If I had not embarked on my musical career, I might have taken a spiritual path, but the aliens had told me to travel as a violin performer. Theirs was the advice I followed. Besides, Goi himself had confirmed that my path to America would be through music.

In December, I went to say good-bye to Mrs. Ishiguro and her son. She was delighted with my new job. "Australia will be very good for you," she said. "You really are lucky. But you will go to America too."

"Yes, I am planning that," I told her. "I've got some connections. I will cover the whole world." Then I told her my plan.

"Your life will be very interesting," she said. "you will have all kinds of things, and there will be a lot of rising and falling. The aliens will contact you again. You are watched. An antenna you have in your body catches their signal, so they can locate you wherever you go. You will also write your life story some day, so take notes of events in your life. And be sure to let me know how you are doing."

I knew *the others* were always watching me, but now I wondered where they had put the antenna in my body.

Mrs. Ishiguro was still concerned about the telephone message. She asked me how I reacted to it, but what else could I say? I had to be realistic.

I still remember what Mrs. Ishiguro said. *Someday, you will change your life completely. But don't worry about it. It's a long way to go. When that day comes, remember my words. Your real destiny comes from that day on.*

TO AUSTRALIA

There is a huge Hungarian population in Australia, and everybody around me spoke German as well as Hungarian and English. Mr. and Mrs. Susini set me up in Glenview Hotel in North Sydney.

I lived there and played international music with an Italian band five nights a week. Mr. and Mrs. Susini also arranged for me to perform with gypsies in a Hungarian restaurant on my day off.

One day, they invited the Hungarian consul and his staff to the restaurant to hear me play. Three members of consulate were fascinated to learn that I had studied directly with Sandor Lakatos, who was a great favorite among the Hungarian community in Australia. Then something amazing happened. The consul offered to sponsor me on a TV show in Vienna, Budapest, and various German cities, and possibly also in Paris. I was speechless. I had never expected such an honor, especially from the consul. It was more than I had ever dreamed of. Adding to this, I again received an opportunity to become an Australian citizen by Hungarian people's support.

These offers were more intriguing than one I received in Vienna. Australia gave me all kinds of fortune that I would never have had since. I liked Sydney. Australia is a very good country. But it was not the time for me to settle and have a good life. Fame and fortune did not interest me at that time. My focus on the aliens suddenly became firm. I decided to proceed with my original plan that the celestial beings had dictated to me.

SIGHTINGS OF ALIEN VEHICLES IN AMERICA

Las Vegas, 1976

When I arrived in America, a Japanese man named Mr. Ebisu came to the Las Vegas airport to pick me up. Mr. Ebisu was a good friend of Mutou, my manager, and also belonged to the Buddhist society that had held its convention in Las Vegas. After he took me to the Buddhist meeting, he set me up in the small motel a short distance outside the city. Back in the late 1970s, Las Vegas was entirely different than it is now. The motel was in the middle of the desert but he promised to take me to look for a weekly apartment the next day.

I woke up at 3 a.m. because of the time difference. I was glad for the warm weather in Las Vegas because it was getting cold in Australia and I did not have any winter clothes.

I went out to the pool. No one else was there. I could see the city lights in the distance. I laid down in a beach chair and gazed at the moon and the stars and wondered what was coming in my life.

After about ten minutes, lights suddenly appeared in the sky. There were about twenty of them, and they were mostly round and a little smaller than the moon, though they were brighter and whiter and lacked the shadows we see on the moon.

I sat up and watched them by myself for at least five minutes. I had no one there to call. No one else was up. The lights moved high above my head, zoomed back and forth, then all disappeared in one second. It never occurred to me that it might be an alien vehicle because its shape was completely different from the shape I knew. These were indeed unidentified flying objects. Later that day, I asked the Japanese people I'd met if they had seen the lights in the sky and if those strange flying lights had something to do with Las Vegas. But no one knew what I was talking about. It turned out to be the first of more alien visits to me.

With Mr. Ebisu's help, I soon started playing in an Italian restaurant, the Chateau Vegas, as a gypsy strolling violinist. Because I had a tourist visa, I could not work but this was training for me to learn American music. A few months later, I went to Los Angeles and San Francisco, where I played in Hungarian restaurants. I had to keep moving every few months in order to experience the whole world. Then something unexpected happened. Because of my special skills as a gypsy violinist, I received my permanent visa in San Francisco just a few days before my six-month tourist visa expired. I planned to go to Mexico, but I went to Hawaii instead when the Hungarian restaurant closed for the winter.

Hawaii, 1977

My next sighting happened in Hawaii when I was in the Hilton Lagoon Apartments next to the Hilton Hotel on Waikiki beach. I was visiting my friend. The apartment was on the twentieth floor, and the living room faced the ocean. One night, I was sitting on the balcony with a friend. My friend went to bed as the clock read 2 a.m. I stayed on the balcony a little longer, just enjoying the peace and quiet of a beautiful night sky over the ocean. It was a clear night with no clouds, a full moon, and a lot of stars.

Where I was gazing was clear, and then, a second later, a huge alien vehicle appeared out of nowhere. It radiated amazing, beautiful rainbow colors. The light was so bright that the dark sky around the vehicle changed color. I could easily see the shape of the vehicle. How amazing it was! I saw many windows, maybe fifty, but it is hard to say how big this vehicle was. The full moon looked small beside it. Doubting my eyes, I blinked several times and rubbed my eyes, but the vehicle was still there. I gazed at it for several minutes, and soon I began to think, *I know the others are there.* I screamed in my heart to them, *Come and get me! Take me with you!*

At that moment, I noticed that I was leaning over the edge of the balcony, lifting my arms to them as I always did. The reply I heard was, *Not yet. We are watching you.* I was very disappointed and angry. Then, I decided I needed a witness to this unbelievable sight.

"Wippa," I called to my friend, "come here!"

"What happened?" she asked as she came through the living room.

"Look at that!" I pointed up to the sky and looked at her for a second. But when I looked back at the sky, the vehicle was gone. It had disappeared, though I could still see the colors. "It's gone," I said.

"What's gone?" she asked.

"There was a UFO," I said, pointing at the sky. "Look! The sky is still red and yellow."

"What is that?" she asked. My friend saw only fading colors.

Within a few minutes, the colors all faded out and the sky was dark again.

It was 2:15 a.m. I had been with *the others* for about ten minutes, but I knew they did not want her to see their vehicle. I did not see their vehicle fly away. It came suddenly and went away suddenly. This was the most amazing and stunning vehicle I have ever seen on earth. It was identical to the vehicle I saw in the golden world, though the colors were different.

After this sighting, I became a strolling violinist in a French restaurant at the Hale Koa, which is next to the Hilton Hotel. This high class hotel belonged to American officers and I was honored to work there. Hawaii soon became my favorite place in the world. But although I really wanted to stay, I quit my job a year later and began traveling again. I worked at the Continental Hotel on Guam and Saipan, the Sheraton Hotel in Hong Kong, and in a Hungarian restaurant in Vancouver, Canada.

Because of Lakatos, Hungarian restaurants all over the world welcomed me. Many of the Hungarian people I met around the world took my messages to Lakatos and his father when they visited Europe. I heard that Lakatos's family were happy to hear my news. He had broken the gypsy rules and taught me his music. I met Lakatos two months after my time-machine experience in Germany. The time-machine started with violin music. It had to be gypsy music. Destiny works in mysterious way. Thanks to gypsy music, I could work in America as a gypsy strolling violinist until I became a headliner. I would never have had such an obsession if it had not been linked to the music of the heavenly violinist.

After two years of traveling, I came back to Las Vegas, where I went to work with the MGM Orchestra.

Las Vegas, 1983

One extremely hot day in Las Vegas, a friend and I decided to go to Mt. Charleston, which is about twenty miles away. We wanted to go to somewhere cool. It was early afternoon, and ours was the only car on a lonely road in the middle of the desert. Suddenly I saw a vehicle right in front of our car. It was about ten feet above us. It just appeared out of nowhere. I was looking at the bottom part of the vehicle. I could see it was a dull, silver color and had four round "legs" used for landing. I could not speak. I could not move. My eyes were stuck on that vehicle. My friend, who was driving, did not notice it, however, because he was looking at the road. He kept talking to me, but when I did not respond, he looked at me. Then he looked up at what I was looking at.

"UFO!" he screamed.

And at that moment, the vehicle flew away in total silence and with tremendous speed. It stopped in the distance ahead of us for about five seconds. Then it flew more slowly toward what I thought was a forest some distance down the road, where it stopped again for a few seconds and came straight down very slowly. When my friend and I arrived at the forest, we could see it was not a forest, but a wasteland of tall bushes and dead trees. It was fenced-in federal land. We drove around the fenced area, but it was very large and we did not see a gate or any people. Since this was government land, we later reported what we saw, but were told that UFO research had been terminated.

My friend and I both saw the same thing. The vehicle stopped three times. I could see its shape, its bottom, its top, its sides. As I write this, I remember something strange. The car I was in was traveling about eighty miles an hour, but the vehicle was always in the same place and same position as if it were hovering above us. I was watching at least thirty seconds or more. It must have been moving at the same speed as our car. The aliens in the vessel were very close to us. I believe they came to look at us, even though my friend and I did not see them.

The shape of this vehicle was similar to the one I knew. But this was a smaller sized vehicle. The huge, sized vehicle I rode in when I was a child can contain probably thirty or forty beings. The room was spacious. I saw many windows. But with the exception of Hawaii, I would see this kind of small vehicle more often in the future. I think that is because it is less noticeable in public and easier to come close to me.

Those were my major sightings in America. I had never had those kinds of sightings in Japan. Something new started to happen after I left Japan. They continued in the various countries where I traveled and lived.

Thirty Years Later

In 2008, I found the photograph of the white light that Kobari had given me while I was cleaning my room. I had met Goi in October, 1975, just a few months before I left Japan for the last time. Since then, I have moved constantly and had not seen the photo for over thirty years, I didn't even know it was still in my possession.

Goi's association is called Byakko Shinko Kai, the White Light Association, in English. My life was saved twice by the nonhuman being and white light. That's why I am still here, still alive.

As I stared at the photo, Goi suddenly reappeared in my mind. I needed to know more about him. But after so many years, even after I found the telephone number of the White Light Association, the people there told me they had nothing to do with the Universe Science group or planetary science research center. This was hard for me to believe, but they refused to even admit that Goi had done any research on aliens. I told them about the private meeting I had attended and the film about aliens I had seen there. After I also told them about the private meeting I'd had with Goi himself, one chief person finally gave me some information. I had received some literature while I was still in Tokyo, but I always felt I was being pushed away. The literature I received was quite different from what I had heard at the meeting about aliens. This makes me think that the private meeting I visited was the only place Goi might have shared his secret. After he stopped speaking on this subject in public, he might have directed his people not to talk about his secret research. Since they didn't know me, their hesitation to tell me anything was understandable. But they were enthusiastic when they spoke about his mission for world peace.

I learned that the headquarters of the White Light Association had moved to New York in 1988 and had been accepted in 1990 as a non-governmental organization (NGO) in affiliation with the U.S. Department of Public Information. They were dedicated to spreading the message and prayer *May Peace Prevail on Earth*. In 1976, Goi had made wooden peace poles upon which his peace prayer, *May Peace Prevail on Earth*, was written. His message, known as the Peace Prayer, is displayed on more than 100,000 "peace poles" in some 180 countries worldwide, including at the United Nations building in New York, as well as in the Muslim world. I saw them in Germany and France. His work is also called the Goi Peace Foundation. Many religious organizations decline after the founder's death, but Goi's work has grown in the world after his death.

Deep in my heart, I knew there were other people who had experiences with aliens in Japan. It is obvious. Aliens did not come only for me. First, I found Goi, and then later in my life, I met Seiyū Kiriyama, the monk who was the founder of the Agon-Shu Buddhist Association. Without Kiriyama's help, I probably would not be alive today, for I had another crisis related to hell in 1991. When my situation got worse, I met Kiriyama in Tokyo in 1992 and he helped see me through that difficult time. He was the helper mentioned by the alien when I had my experience in hell and was told, *The hell experience is over for now, but it will come back again. In that time, you will have a helper.* I had assumed this "helper" would be nonhuman, but it turned out to be this well-known monk.

MONK KIRIYAMA

Kiriyama gained his supernatural power through many years of ascetic practices. He learned to rescue those who had fallen into the lower realms described in Buddhism and Tibetan esoteric Buddhism, which deal with the after-death realms and reincarnation. Rescue work is common in Japan and other parts of Asia, where many monks help lay people who are concerned about their family members' and ancestors' deaths. Over ninety percent of people in Japan are either Buddhist or Shinto, which originated in Hinduism, which has a history of nearly five thousand years, though the origin of *shinto* ("way of the gods") is uncertain. Kiriyama says that many sicknesses and calamities are caused by spirits from the lower realm that are clinging to us. These spirits are mostly related to our ancestors, and when they are removed, our situation on earth changes. Kiriyama was the person I needed when I was a teenager and had my experience in hell with the ancestors of my mother's family.

When I was a teenager, I was doing serious research on the alien and spirit worlds in the library and in my hidden attic. At the same time, Kiriyama was in the middle of his ascetic practices. During the next thirty years, his organization became huge, and he gained many followers throughout Japan and the world. Kiriyama, who is now over ninety years old, has devoted his life to helping people by using his supernatural powers. To this day, he is still doing the same work and engaging in world peace missions.

In 1992, he was dealing with about 500 cases a month. When I asked for his help, he said he had never seen a case as complicated as mine. In fact, he talked about me to his followers for six months. This was unprecedented because he has hardly ever talked about one person's case more than once or twice. Because he spoke about me so long, I became known in his organization. Eventually, he began doing research on my situation and wrote a book about my unusual case. This book describes how fate is intertwined with family trees and his work in finding the solutions to generational curses.

In 1990, my life was at its peak. I was living in New York City and France, and wanted to establish my career in Europe. I never anticipated that anything bad might happen to me, but all of a sudden, awful things started happening, not only to me, but also to all of my family members, even to the families of my sisters Kiyo and Chizu. I was involved in a second suicide attempt. I already knew the outcome of suicide, yet it happened to me again. The suicide was beyond my control. Because history repeats itself, I think it must be something inherited in our family. The sons of Kiyo and Chizu also attempted suicide. Like me, Chizu's son was affected by the hell situation. He became very depressed and did not attend high school for many months. My sisters' marriages also fell apart, and Kiyo was stricken with cancer. My mother was seldom sick, but suddenly she, too, fell ill and was bedridden for several years. Though my health was good, and I was still working, I started to have sudden attacks that doctors could not understand.

Kiriyama spoke about something that had happened nearly 500 years earlier in Mother's family. It was exactly the same thing I'd seen in the movie images when I was in hell. He learned that all our present calamities were originated from that time and that the present calamity had started to happen over 200 years ago. This is true. The majority of my mother's relatives either committed suicide or died unexpectedly in tragic accidents. Because my mother's family was powerful, people were curious about what was happening. Five hundred years ago, Japan was going through a dark age. As heads of the samurai and working with the emperor, our ancestors had a lot to do with the brutal civil wars of that era.

Mother had seen strange deaths, one after another, and heard many mysterious stories in her childhood. She didn't need any more drama in her life, especially not ghostly visits by Takako. I now learned that there were many ghostly apparitions to Mother's relatives. Those fearsome appearances had also led to many of the deaths in her family. This was the true reason that she avoided anything paranormal.

Kiriyama thus confirmed my experience of hell, where I saw my ancestors. Because he is respected in Japan, my family had no choice but to accept his words, and I finally had an opportunity to show my family the true reason for my absence from high school.

The message—*The hell experience is over for now, but it will come back again; in that time, you will have a helper*—came true. It was thirty years between my first suicide attempt and my second one. Help was indeed provided to us. No one in my family died. All the sicknesses, even the cancer, were miraculously cured. Though the doctors could not find any cause for my condition, even after I spent enormous amounts of money seeking help from them, my sickness went away completely. To this day, we are all in good health. My family did another house purification using Kiriyama's method, and since then, I have seen no more ghosts in that house. I can go home without fear.

Although the members of my family continues to live as they had been accustomed to live, my life changed. Although Kiriyama gave me the key to solving my family's problems, and some of them were solved, others arose because there were still too many ancestors and their enemies. I understood it might take a lifetime of work to resolve our problems.

Now it was up to me to find a permanent solution for the questions surrounding my life. That's why I moved to the Himalaya Mountains in 1994. When I had my first suicide experience, I was passionately studying Buddhism. Now that passion came back. First, I went to India on a pilgrimage to the Buddha's eight holy places. Then I lived in Nepal and Tibet so I could study esoteric Buddhism. It was interesting to learn about Shambhala, or Pure Land, a society where all inhabitants are enlightened. Although those with special affiliation may be able to go there, it is not a physical place that we can actually find. But Shambhala is located, it is said, in the higher reaches of the Himalayas or somewhere near the Tibet area. If one has the merit and the actual karmic association, one can arrive there. It is a pure land in the human realm. The hidden land of Shangri-La, as described in James Hilton's 1933 novel Lost Horizon, is said to have been inspired by the Shambhala myth.

I also studied yoga in the Himalayas. Yogis were very much aware of the existence of aliens and their worlds. The Buddha also spoke of many beings in the universe. I learned a great deal about how the yogis view aliens, as compared to how the people in the western world see them. This became the most fascinating trip in my life.

Even though I left India after one year, I was very impressed with Buddhism and continued to study it through correspondence for six more years. I meditated for long hours and have led a celibate life for decades. I did everything I could at this time and acquired great knowledge.

In 2010, I planned to meet with Kiriyama, who lives now in Kyoto, and talk with him about aliens. He was over ninety years old and was still traveling and leading a very busy life. I assumed that, given his age, he did not need to stir up activity that might lead to a scandal. He had received many peace prizes in Japan and other countries, and even the emperor and priests of our Shinto religion had asked for his help. This was because no one could do this kind of work better than he could. Pope John Paul II had invited him to the Vatican, and he was also a friend of the Dalai Lama.

Kiriyama said that because our family's situation was far more severe than that of other families he had met, there was no way we could manage it ourselves. For this reason, he felt a responsibility to help me. I had heard that many of his followers were curious about his attention to me, because I was only one person among thousands who asked him for help. Even though he never said in public why he felt any responsibility to me, I believe he was sent to me to help me when I could not help myself. His help had been prepared more than thirty years earlier by the aliens. If not for them, I would never have gotten this kind of special care from him.

Though Chizu's son escaped death, he earned poor grades in school and could not enter the university. He does not have the career he wanted, and his life is now a struggle. In my high school days I had no help from Kiriyama or any other person. What would my situation be now if I had not been helped by the aliens? Like my unfortunate ancestors, I could be dead. But I had help, and I graduated high school and university near the top of my class. My career around the world flourished. This is how I prove the existence of nonhuman beings who help me.

Kiriyama and Goi were similar in many ways. Kiriyama also suffered from poor health in his youth and almost lost his life, but he was completely cured and regained great health. He then began healing other people's ailments. Goi's first spiritual work was curing sicknesses with his supernatural power. Both men started their ascetic spiritual practices in their youth and gained extraordinary powers. Goi's dream was to be an opera singer, Kiriyama's, to be a writer. But after they set foot on their supernatural paths, their careers went in different directions and led to remarkable results. Both were also doing world peace missions.

Like them, I struggled with sickness when I was young. My poor health was a huge issue, but I was cured supernaturally. I did not engage in ascetic spiritual practices as they did. My death-world experience and my isolation (when I was doing research on spiritual paths all alone in the library and in my hidden attic for eight months) might be considered similar to their ascetic practices. I was trained by the unseen world, whether I wanted it or not. After I came back from the death world, dramatic changes took place in me as I gained enormous knowledge and the extraordinary ability to pass all my examinations. But since I did not follow a purely spiritual path, I have never done the remarkable work they did.

Talking about aliens in public is always troublesome. Like Goi and Kiriyama and others, I hid my experiences for many years. But communication with higher beings changed all three of us. Goi's website says, *Most people believe that we experience the astral world only after death. However, this is not the case. In fact, people live in the divine world, while existing in a physical body.* I can relate to this. Goi said he heard unimaginable things in the other world. Though he did not say publicly what those things were, I can also relate.

Because my experiences in the other world happened very early in my life, I took these abnormal matters as normal, and lived a dual life.

My journeys through the Heavens and Hells of Extraterrestrial Worlds. All these things seem to be unimaginable or unbelievable, but they really happened to me. I will slowly discover what alien abduction is all about.

Unexplainable Paranormal Events

SPACE TRAVEL, URGENT, COME BACK HOME

When the apparition of Goi manifested in my apartment in 1975, I found traces of gold powder and wondered about them. I believe the golden powder was related to Goi because when he appeared in spirit in my apartment, he sprinkled powder around my bed. One day in 1993, the same kind of gold powder appeared on my hands, just a sprinkle, but enough to catch my attention. The more I gazed at my hands, the more the powder seemed to appear. Scattered specks became a film, coating my hands. This phenomenon happened frequently for about five years. The golden powder would go away when I wiped or washed my hands, but then it always came back. People who witnessed this mysterious manifestation wondered about it. I demonstrated it for a medical doctor, Dr. Shakil Khan, whom I met in 1996 on a cruise ship. He wanted to write an article about my musical show in the *"Japan America Digest"*, and during our interview in a coffee house, the golden powder appeared again. Because he said he was a physician, I told him about this mystery. It was a good opportunity to ask questions. I asked him to watch my palms. Then I began gazing at them, and the powder started to increase. Five minutes later, there was a significant amount of golden powder on my hands. Although he was greatly amazed, Dr. Khan did not have an answer. But because he was so amazed, my story became the front cover of the magazine. But of course the golden powder was not mentioned.

There are many, small things that specialists cannot explain, so how could I expect anyone to understand my major mysteries?

Goi died in 1980, though I didn't learn about it until 2008. I also learned that his death was very strange. He had started to talk a few years earlier about leaving his body when he received a message from a higher being in another world. He felt he needed to go back to that world to do his work. According to his followers, Goi never spoke in public about this message until a few years before his death. When I heard about it, my body froze. Suddenly, my mysterious telephone call—*Urgent, come back home*—in Goi's meeting about aliens and his mysterious death made sense.

After that mysterious call, I struggled to find out what it meant, and after some research, I learned that I was being called by a non-human being. I also understood what Mrs. Ishiguro had said. I was being called to come back to their world. The word "home" did not mean my apartment. But I did not understand the urgency of the message until 2008, when I learned about the message Goi had received and his decision to leave his body. My puzzle was solved. It became clear to me that it *was* indeed the urgent call I had received. I had been called to come back to *my true home*. I now understood the important work prepared for me in their world.

It took me thirty years to find out the meaning of my mysterious call.

That telephone call was my reconnection to *the others* after many years. From my first childhood encounter, I knew the aliens had come to take me to their world. I had waited for them for a long time and with all my heart, but had finally given up. My entreaties were not answered. Then, out of the blue, when I did not care any more and was having a good time in my earthly life, they finally called me. I never thought I would receive an actual telephone call from *the others*. Since I was living near the center of Tokyo and there was no remote place near my home, the telephone call was the perfect way to get my attention. More importantly, it came to me at Goi's assembly and in a meeting about aliens. Then I knew unmistakably that I was called by *the others*.

At the time, I had no way of knowing that Goi had also received a message. Before he decided to leave his body, he made the wooden Peace Poles. The Peace Poles were his major work in spreading his message to the world. He did this in 1976. It was the next year I met him. It came as a great surprise to me. This indicates that Goi and I had received the same message at the same time. He must have prepared himself for things he had never anticipated. I had heard that Goi was a friendly person, even though he was not sociable, but when I met him in person, he acted strangely. He must have known more than I imagined. Later, I learned that he had special eyes and could instantly see a person's circumstances.

I was exhilarated that *the others* had contacted me again and wanted me to come back. But how could I go to them? They couldn't just pick me up like they did when I was a child.

And they did not pick me up. But I must say this: soon after I met Goi, I lived through some very mysterious events involving out-of-body experiences during which I began to see my astral body leaving my physical body and walking in space. This usually happened when I was lying down, mostly just before I fell asleep. Each time, I saw my spiritual body rising up. First, my upper body would sit up. Then without needing to push myself off the bed, I just rose to a standing position and walked out of and away from my body. The movement was smooth and effortless. My astral body often turned back and looked at the physical body I was leaving behind, but I had no interest in that body. It was only a material body. The real me was the body that was moving with my consciousness. The space between me and my physical body was devoid of color, but I could see my body because I saw a dim light around my bed. The path I was walking along was also lit by the small lights. I understood that those lights were not real lights. Though I had a lamp near my bed, it was always off when I slept. The dim light I saw above my bed was not the light in my lamp. This was light to show me the location of my body. It had to be the astral light. The small lights were showing me the direction I must take. My spirit was walking in a different dimension.

As I remember this, I can't help but think that our spirits might be wandering around in another dimension while we are sleeping. I can say this because sometimes I went to sleep after I saw my spirit rising up and walking. I thought that everybody had this happen to them every night, even though most people don't remember it. Or, to be clearer, *we don't "see" it*. I had never seen myself before. This was the only time I witnessed what my spirit was doing.

The more my spiritual self walked, the farther I went from my physical body. I was moving upward. It seemed like I walked for a while. Then I came to the place where I saw a veil (or maybe it was a curtain). Nothing held it up. There was no frame. It was just a cloth suspended by itself and surrounded by jet black space. The veil divided the space I was in from another, different space. Was it an entrance to another dimension? My speculation turned to uncertainty. I guess I should have been a bit elated. Perhaps this was an invitation to see something new, though not at this time. I can't help but think there is some kind of boundary our spirit cannot pass. I am certain that our spirit does not go this far while we are asleep. In my experience, my astral body did not often reach this veil. But even when my spirit body was at the veil, I hesitated to go through it. Venturing where one does not necessarily feel welcome, pushing the boundaries of the spiritual dimensions...what if what's on the other side is death? Even for a spirit.

The veil looked brown in color and was soft to the touch, but it was not easy to pass through. A spirit should be able to pass through any place, I would guess, because they are not impeded by the physical. A stone wall would offer as little impediment as air. But not here. I felt resistance coming from the veil. There was no opening. I wondered where the entrance might be, but I could not find it.

When I looked back at my physical body, it looked very small. And then, when I started thinking about what to do, I was immediately pulled back to my physical body. I usually woke up with a jerk. I often screamed and lay awake for a while and thought about this experience. At last I got used to the idea of having this space odyssey.

But sometimes I passed through that veil! I willed myself to pass through and my determination did it. Then something astonishing happened. *I found myself in the universe.* Yes, perhaps this sounds ridiculous, but I saw a white cord behind me. The cord was attached to my lower spine. This cord, I thought, must be the connection between my spirit and my body. Maybe we all have it when we go out into space and the universe. The cord was bright against black background and was waving and coiling. I saw the earth at the far end of the cord.

I was astounded when I found myself in the universe, and yet I was calm, too. I was not just floating but moving toward some place. Once in a while I looked behind me and saw the earth.

Most of the time, I kept moving, but eventually the earth caught my attention and I felt I needed to go back. When I had traveled this far, it was an enormous shock when my astral body zoomed back into my physical body. My body was greatly shaken and my breath was almost cut off. I had to work on staying alive by controlling my breathing. Many times, I was so astonished, I sat up without knowing it. It was a scary moment. I was sweating all over my body. This happened more than a dozen times.

My desire to remain on earth and my concern for my parents always brought me back to earth. I was twenty-eight years old, and I felt that there was some important thing I needed to learn on earth. So I decided it was okay to stay here. If I have accomplished my mission when I reach old age, however, I will definitely not fly back down to earth. If I do not intend to come back, I know the cord will simply break loose, and then I can leave my physical body naturally and go to the next place without suffering.

This is not committing suicide. In the past, it always happened without my intention. I never wished for it. *This is also not dying,* even though people may find my dead body. This is leaving the body, just as Goi did.

For at least six months, I left my body practically every night. This happened because I was called to come back. Yet I was not forced to leave the earth. *I had a choice.* Because I kept leaving my physical body, I began to understand Mrs. Ishiguro's words that I was called to come back to their world.

I know that if one door closes, the next door opens, but I never thought it would take my whole life until the next door opened for me. I always thought they would take me back someday or I would travel through space again to get to their world. To this day, however, this travel has not happened, even though I have tried hard.

As I grew older, whenever I fell into calamities and when I started to face physical limitations and problems, I often regretted that I had not left the earth during those nights. When I was young, I also did not know I would be caught up to this world and lose my way so greatly. I also have not yet carried out the important mission on earth that I was told to do in the golden world. This guilt devastates me. If I left the earth, I would not have to face all these problems. But if I intentionally tried to travel through space, it would become a suicide attempt that might lead me back to the hellish world. Now I no longer have a choice. I know they do not want me to come back after this time. I must finish my work on earth.

I have no idea what experience Goi had, but I am quite certain that he had an experience similar to mine. When Goi passed, he was sixty-four years old. He had given up his musical career and devoted thirty years of his life to his mission of bringing the earth to a higher vibrational level. I am sure he felt he had come to the right time to go back because of the urgent call he received, even though his health was good. I knew I belonged to the golden world when I was only six years old, and I have been missing that world ever since. This is why I understand Goi's decision very well.

When I look back on my nighttime space travel, I realize that that might have been my time to move on to the next stage. I had already gone through many paranormal events and learned a great deal about other worlds. I also became a violin performer and traveled many countries, but instead of derailing my path, I should have left my body because I was called with such urgency. I was disappointed in my choice later in my life, but at least I gained more knowledge through this stunning experience and I began to understand what my alien abduction was all about.

In 2013, when I visited Goi's sanctuary at Mt Fuji, I heard that Goi felt it would be more important for him to do alien's work than remain on earth to do the same work he had been doing. This was confirmed by his followers.

Goi was the only person that I knew of who shared very similar alien experiences. It is obvious that we were guided by the same aliens and visited the same golden world. Though we shared the same experiences, beings in other worlds are individuals. They're different and have different paths, just as we have. Goi and I were guided by different individuals, which made our paths different. The important thing is that our lives were motivated by the different forces than the earthly one. We became aware of the higher world and its beings and the path leading there.

UNEXPLAINABLE ALIEN EVENTS

We all know that there are many unexplainable things in this world. Although humankind learned more in the 20th century and made more scientific discoveries and adaptations than at any other time in history, our knowledge is still limited. When I was a child in post-war Japan, we did not have washing machines, and, though it's hard to believe now, the radio, with its terrible static and noise, was the only electronic entertainment we had. Back in the early 1950s, who could have imagined the world we live in now? No one could have imagined we would have computers and satellite technology. That said, how can we ever guess what the world will be like 100 or 500 years from now? It is far beyond our imagination. What was once science fiction has become today's reality. Who knows—someday, communication with extraterrestrials (the higher beings) might become a normal thing.

Many mysterious things have also happened in the history of Japan. Scholars say that our ancient clay figures, the *dogu*, could be the oldest artwork found so far on earth. They look like astronauts. The ancient Japanese people might have thought that the beings who came from the sky were gods. The origins of Japan are mixed with the tales of gods and goddesses who live in heaven, and there is a possibility that beings from other worlds have intervened in our world. They might have participated in the development of human history in ancient times. Those ancient visitors to earth are surely different kinds of aliens from the scary aliens we see in science fiction movies and the tabloids. If they participated in human activities and contributed to the development of human culture, they must have been higher, better beings from somewhere else.

The mysteries in my life related to aliens that began during my childhood continued as I grew up and traveled to and lived in other countries. I have had an opportunity to review these mysteries in my adult life.

Vancouver Canada, 1982

An experience I had in January of 1982 in Vancouver, Canada, for example, was something science cannot currently explain. But it confirmed many of my childhood experiences.

It was midnight. My Hungarian friend George and I were walking near the beach after work. No one else was there. George was my pianist in the Hungarian restaurant where I was playing gypsy music. By day, he was a high school science and math teacher. The snow was deep that night and the sky was clear. Suddenly we saw an extremely bright white light high above of us. It was about three or four feet long and it remained still for about five seconds.

"UFO!" George screamed. Later he told me that he had never believed in the existence of UFOs before, but that's the word he screamed. I couldn't speak because I instantly knew *the others* were there.

Even though we could not see the shape of the ship because the light was so bright, we could tell it was a UFO. As soon as George screamed, it flew away at tremendous speed. This was like my UFO experience in the desert outside Las Vegas, but much faster. This time, we saw another white light in the sky. This second light was very high in the sky and far away, but it was much brighter than the moon. It stood still, and then the first light (which I am sure was a vehicle) collided with the smaller light, and then we saw big sparkles in all directions. We didn't hear any noise. No longer were there two vehicles in the sky. Now there was just one bigger vehicle, almost twice as big as the first one. It stood still for some seconds, then sped away and was gone. From beginning to end, this experience lasted a little over fifteen seconds. George and I both saw this.

The two vehicles crashed together with tremendous energy and merged without breaking. No fiery aftermath, no debris raining down from an overhead collision. How did this happen? When I think about how long it takes a space shuttle to dock with the International Space Station, I can hardly speculate how two ships can unite as I believe they did in the time they did. There must have been aliens operating both vehicles, and there might have been more beings in them. I am sure they didn't die in the crash. I suspect that the aliens on those ships might have been heading to their home somewhere in the universe.

An extremely strange UFO-related experience had happened to me two weeks before that sighting in Vancouver. It was another unexplainable incident in my life. I am reluctant to write about it and have seldom spoken of it because I didn't need people to think of me as a crazy woman. But I decided to write about it here. My decision is not only because this would prove some of my childhood experiences, but it is also good for people to know that this kind of mystery can happen in our world.

Two weeks before George and I saw the UFOs in the sky, I found a wooden statue in the snow in front of my apartment. It was after midnight on a beautiful, full-moon night. The statue was about three feet tall and looked a bit like a totem pole. Totem poles are normally painted with different colors and many faces, but this figure was plain brown wood and only one face. The face rather looked like the big faces on the Easter Island statues, but this statue had a long body like a totem pole. The face was much more unworldly and absolutely expressionless. It looked like a strong man.

I picked it up and, for a moment, George and I stared at it in silence.

"This is the strangest face I have ever seen in my life," he finally said. "This must be from the other world."

I agreed with him, but didn't know what to say. Finally, I said, "I'll take this to my apartment to keep as a guardian."

"I would name this strange guy Arthur," George said.

So I did. Then I set Arthur in my living room. Soon I noticed something strange about him. I started feeling like he was watching me. I felt his eyes on me. I even saw his eyes moving. So then I set Arthur in a corner of the foyer outside my apartment. I thought that was a good place for him. "You stay here," I said to Arthur (like we say to a dog) when I went to work.

Four hours later, I came home. I didn't see Arthur. Had someone taken him? The statue had no value. Who would want it? The quiet, four-story apartment building I lived in was for adults, so there were no children who might take things. Each floor had only two apartments. I was on the third floor. My neighbor was a nice, quiet, old man, and we had few visitors. You needed a key to gain admittance into the building.

I looked for Arthur, but didn't see him until I opened the door to the emergency staircase next to my apartment. There he was. I put him back by my door and made a sign. *Please don't touch.*

The next night, the statue was still there, so I thought my sign was working, but the night after that, he was gone again. This time I found him halfway down the stairs. I was getting uneasy. A day later, when my neighbor came back from shopping, I asked him if he had moved my statue. He strongly denied touching it.

The next night, Arthur disappeared from the hall again. I went all the way down the stairs to look for him, but he was nowhere to be found. Very confused. I finally went into my apartment.

My heart stopped. There was Arthur, standing in my living room where I had first placed him. He was in exactly the same spot!

I placed him outside again and decided to talk to the building manager the next day to find out if he had put the statue in my apartment. He didn't live in this building, but he was the only other person who had a key. I wondered how he knew the exact spot I placed Arthur in my room. The next morning, when the building manager was cleaning the floor in front of the elevator, I watched him. He did not touch my statue. Then I asked if he had put my statue in my living room. He said no and that he never went into my apartment.

This was making me crazy. I couldn't handle this alone, so I called George and asked him to come to my apartment. Normally, he rang from downstairs, but this time, I brought him up. We both looked at the statue before we left for work. When we came back at midnight, Arthur was missing from the hall again. When we found him inside my apartment, George insisted the building manager had done it.

On other nights, we found Arthur in the emergency staircase, sometimes perched halfway up the stairs in the stairwell. Arthur moved around, but he always went back to exactly the same spot in my living room. Every time Arthur moved, it was always at night. And while I was at work. I was glad about that. If he had come into my living room while I was home, I might have had a heart attack.

George became very curious and came home with me every night to see what Arthur was doing. Every time Arthur had moved, I put him back outside my door. But he managed to move from place to place.

"You moved again!" I berated him like the owner of a misbehaved cat. "Why are you moving?" I can't remember, but I wouldn't be surprised if I'd waited for him to answer me. "Do you like my living room better than outside?" I guess I was very scared by Arthur's ability to move by himself. But I had already had a near-lifetime of extraordinary happenings, and in the end, Arthur was just a poorly behaved statue not doing his job of standing still.

This nonsense continued almost every night for two weeks. It made George crazy, too. It was a terribly intense time for George. Being a teacher of science and math, he could not accept a moving statue. One night we found Arthur in my living room again. We stared at him for a long time, curiosity mixed with uneasiness. Arthur still had no expression on his face. Arthur was, I knew, something more than a statue. I just didn't know what. But George, a man prone to science, someone who adheres to the laws of physics and not psychics, saw Arthur differently. Objects in motion tend to stay in motion, but a statue, something stationary and without self-propulsion, *must* remain stationary. And Arthur defied that. It scared George.

Finally, George screamed, "I do not know what the hell is happening here. This is very wrong. I cannot take this outlandish thing any more. Throw that statue away!"

I did not know what to do. I also wanted to through Arthur away, but somehow I could not do it. I wanted to keep him as my guardian. So I kept him to this night.

The following night, George and I saw the alien vehicles in the night sky. After we went back to my apartment, Arthur was gone! I looked everywhere for him, even in the baggage storeroom, but I never found him. He was permanently gone. Did Arthur fly up to the alien vehicle? Did the aliens take him back?

After seeing the alien vehicles, I realized that they must have been responsible for Arthur's relocation and disappearance. Then, I remembered what had happened to me in my childhood. Just like Arthur, I was relocated from the playground to the forest and to the field. I understood that the relocations in my childhood were done by aliens. But there was still a question. Did this solid statue actually pass through the solid door of my apartment? I understood my relocations because I was relocated through the air. But Arthur's relocations were different.

I also remember what happened to the small disks in the fields I had seen when I was six years old. They all disappeared. After I realized they belonged to *the others*, I figured out that they went back to their big vehicle. I assume that Arthur's disappearance could be the same as the disks. *The others* must have taken him back.

I am certain of one thing: *the others* came to see me. There is no question about it. It is possible they sent the statue to bring their message to me. Arthur's unearthly face showed me that he belonged to the other world.

This otherworldly happening made me think of so many things. Arthur reminded me of something else that happened a long time ago. When I met the celestial violinist, I saw a big brown tree. Its solidity and earthly color did not belong to the shining golden world. Then a violin appeared. It was made of brown wood, and I believe it manifested from that tree. Arthur was also made of brown wood. It seems to me he was also manifested from that tree. I cannot forget how I puzzled over that tree when I was in the golden world. Brown solid wood and golden transparent world.

Now another thought flies into my mind. Goi's peace prayer, *May Peace Prevail on Earth*, was written in the peace pole, plain brown wood. And the incense that Goi sprinkled around my bed was brown and made from plants. But this brown powder changed into gold powder. I believe this kind of transformation symbolizes the transformation of earth to the golden world. I still think Arthur was a messenger from *the others* sent to tell me they were still watching me and encouraging me along the path from earth to the golden world. Transformation *is* their message.

Nice, France, 1992

In Nice in November 1992, I was alone on the beach. It was a quiet evening. As always, I was admiring the beautiful ocean and the sunset as the sky turned a golden yellow. It was so fabulous, I felt like I was entering another world. Then I started to see a billow of cotton clouds gathering in the sky. A lot of them. It was unusual to see these clouds in the late autumn.

Suddenly a strange feeling came over me. Though I didn't know why, something was very different. It grabbed my attention. I looked up. There was a huge, thick, grayish-white cloud above me. I watched it for a while, and then I was suddenly looking at the bottom of a vehicle. It was a small ship, similar to the one I once saw in the desert outside Las Vegas, could be smaller. Then I saw maybe ten small discs like those I'd seen in Japan. Next I saw more tiny discs coming down from the center of the vehicle. I jumped up. I knew *the others* were there. Then some of them came down right in front of me. They were so near, I could see exactly what they looked like. They looked the same as the ones from my childhood but they were a little bigger, about five inches long. Then I began trying to catch them—and almost did—but they disappeared, some of them moving away from me, behind me, others flying away. I leaped into the air in an attempt to catch a disk higher above me. I was hoping *the others* would take me back to their ship. Unhappily, it was not to be. I watched all the disks as they flew back to the mother ship before I could touch them.

I couldn't help thinking that those disks were living beings that had very good eyes, not just tiny vehicles. They could definitely see me reaching for them, but they did not want to be caught. I know the disks belong to the aliens, but what are they made of? They are strange living creatures, or maybe transparent vehicles, that our science does not understand. Though I was not taken to their ship, this was a similar experience to the ones in my childhood. In Nice, however, I saw the ship and witnessed disks coming from it and going back to it.

After about ten minutes, I did not see the small disks any more. They had probably all gone back to the mother ship. But now I didn't see the vehicle, either. I studied the clouds above me for a long time, but I did not see the vehicle fly away. When *the others* came near, I sensed a difference in the air. Now the strange feeling had gone away, the sky returned to normal, and I saw the clouds starting to fade. A half hour later, only a few clouds remained.

I have seen the appearance and disappearance of the alien vehicles many times. Every time, it has happened right in front of my eyes. That evening in Nice, it was cold and hardly any people were on the beach. If there were other people present, they did not see the vehicle because it was hidden by the clouds. The tiny disks are hard to see in the daylight, even when they are nearby, because they are somewhat transparent. But their vehicle is very noticeable. I was stunned by what I had seen and said to myself, "Can *the others* even control nature?" I can accept their ability to control the tiny disks, but the clouds confused me. It was not easy for *the others* to visit me in the middle of the city, but they came without people noticing them when I was on the beach. This was the same beach where, in 1988, I had heard alien voices saying they were coming to see me.

My history of alien encounters started with the tiny disks when I was six years old. Since then, my life has been never the same. And now, some forty years later on an autumn evening in Nice, my life had changed again. I ended my secular life. My mission, which had been given to me in the golden world, now became clear. Even as I was always guided on the path *the others* wanted me to take, they never forced me. I was free to take any path I wanted to. But when my focus went too much to the secular world, I received warnings. That's why I've had so many sightings. Paranormal events are my wakeup calls.

Nice is a special city. It is a city where the aliens come to visit me in very special ways. It started in 1988 when three alien vehicles radiated white light on me. My mother (who was with me) could not take this light for even a few seconds, but I stared at it for fifteen minutes without becoming blinded. I knew ahead of time that they were coming and told my mother about it. While I was in the light, I had a deep communication with *the others*. They were not happy of my life style and reminded me of my mission on earth.

Peru, 2001

In 1998, an outbreak of stomach flu began that spread to many cruise ships and continued for many years. I became ill because I had been traveling around the world for so long and was exhausted. A Persian friend on the cruise ship where I was working at the time suggested that I take a vacation in Peru. She had just come back from Peru and said the land had renewed her energy. She introduced me to her sister, who could show me around.

My first experience with aliens in Peru happened in a tiny village called Chilca. When I arrived in Lima, Peru's capital city, in February 2001, it was summer there. I asked about some quiet place near the Pacific Ocean where I could rest before I started traveling again. A man I met in a restaurant told me to go to Chilca, where there were miraculous ponds that heal the body. (He said nothing about UFOs.) It sounded perfect, so I went to Chilca right away and checked in at a small hotel.

This was my first night in Peru.

"Wake up! There's a UFO near your window."

It was 4:45 in the morning, when the wife of the hotel owner banged on my door and shouted. I let her in, and then we stood on my balcony and watched the UFO fly away.

It was a clear night. I could see lots of stars. There were no airplanes. The UFO was the only moving object we could see in the sky. When we saw it, it looked about six inches long and was sort of flat. There were no blinking lights like airplanes have, but a few minutes later we saw some metallic brightness. The vehicle moved slowly and swerved to the right and left. This was the first time I had seen an alien vehicle moving so slowly. We watched it for about fifteen minutes as it flew away and became smaller and smaller. I noticed that it looked like a star in the distance.

The owner's wife turned to me and said, "UFOs come toward the ocean late in the night because they don't want people to see them. And they leave early in the morning. They fly in this direction."

She also told me that she and her husband had watched the vehicle for a while before she came to wake me. I was on the second floor in a corner room, the only room facing inland instead of overlooking the ponds, which are on the Pacific side. I had been offered a room with a better view of the ponds, but I intentionally took the corner room. I must have known (unconsciously) that the aliens were coming to see me because I was the only guest who asked to awakened.

I had gone out to swim to the healing pond as soon as I'd arrived. While I was swimming, I overheard people talking about alien visits to this village at night. Before I went to sleep that night, therefore, I told the owner and his wife that if a UFO came, I would like to see it. Who would have expected me to be called during my first night there?

The owner always gets up at 4:30 in the morning to start breakfast for his guests. When he went outside, he looked up and saw the vehicle. He came back inside and brought his wife outside so she could see it, too. But the vehicle was already flying away. They hesitated to wake me but because even though the vehicle was quite high in the sky, it seemed to be hovering near my window. They thought I should know about this.

I heard later that the owner had never seen a UFO before, so this sighting was a huge topic of conversation that morning.

Because of the timing and the location of the UFO, they decided that I had attracted it. When I came down to have breakfast, many people came to talk to me. I learned a very interesting story about this village.

The water in the ponds at Chilca contains heavy salts of various minerals. These ponds are called the *miracle lagoon* because many sicknesses are healed there and barren women become pregnant. People say the minerals were brought there by aliens who have a base under the Pacific Ocean.

Frequent sightings are reported. People come to the beach in this village and stay all night in hopes of seeing UFOs. The police are on duty to keep the people safe. A few days later I tried to stay on the beach all night, too, but the police officer I met in that night sent me to my hotel.

This happened around 10 p.m., and there were perhaps thirty people around me. They'd brought camping gear. I thought staying on the beach was not dangerous and asked that policeman why I couldn't stay. He said that the aliens might take the people away. Such cases had already been reported. Groups of people were allowed, he said, but not one person alone. When I asked if he had even seen a UFO, he said he had seen many. He also described how they arrived. He said the vehicle dived into the ocean in a split second, but there was no water displacement. It was, he said, as if the ocean did not move while a vehicle pierced its surface at full speed. He also said the UFOs made no noise. I understood that, for I never heard any sounds that came from their vehicles.

People in this village live very simple lives. Chilca is a poor village. There are small hotels and guest houses around the ponds, plus a few tiny shops and primitive restaurants. But I loved the healing ponds, and the beach was fantastic, so I stayed in Chilca for several weeks.

While I was there, I also met a few people who had ridden in the alien vehicles. One of them said he had been dropped in a remote area a few days after he was abducted and intended to write about his experience in a book. Even people who had been taken had nothing bad to say about the aliens. The healing ponds benefit many people, the villagers say, so these aliens must be good ones.

Peru is famous for UFO visitations. I saw the tiny disks again in a small village called Aguas Calientes (Hot Springs), which is near the famous Inca ruins of Machu Picchu in the Andes. The tiny disks appeared at night in the valley and emitted white lights. I saw them once when I was walking with a local man. Their movements were too quick to be insects, and they were much bigger and brighter. The man knew they were not fireflies and became curious, so he climbed up the mountain to see better. Though he could not get closer to them because they flew higher, he said he had never seen anything like them before.

A few nights before, when I was walking alone, I saw about twenty of the disks flying together about fifteen feet from me. At that time I had no idea what they were. While I was watching, maybe ten of them flew toward my chest, which startled me. Though I didn't feel anything, they seemed to hit my chest. This all happened within a minute, and then I did not see them any more. They were all gone. Because of their quick disappearance, I felt that they might be the tiny alien disks. This was my first time to see the disks at night. When the disks were flying, I saw straight, thin white lines behind them. They were apparently a sign of their velocity. Those lines made the man I was with curious. Though I told him nothing, he said, "They are maybe the small UFOs."

Another UFO-related experience happened to me on the Nazca plain in Peru. The Nazca lines, which are a famous tourist attraction, may have been created by aliens. It is said that those lines were made between AD 400 and 650. Maria Reiche (1903–1998), a German mathematician and archaeologist, conducted some research on the Nazca lines. After her retirement, a relative took over her research. I met her relative, a nice lady, in the restaurant near the lines. Because I often performed my musical show in Germany and spoke German, we got along right away and because I told her that I was not allowed to stay on the beach alone at night in Chilca, she led a UFO tour for some of her friends and me.

The UFO incident happened after midnight in the desert. The German researcher and her friends (including two men) were there with me. We lay down on the ground and looked up at the beautiful, star-filled night sky. We saw many falling stars. Then suddenly a huge, bright, white light began flashing, a slow, rhythmic shimmer. Then another light flushed in the opposite direction, and soon they were flashing from all directions and we were surrounded by the lights. Although we did not see any of the vehicles themselves, their lights shocked us. We got up and tried to drive away, but our car would not start. We had two choices. We could either sleep out here in the desert or walk to the highway, and the walk would be a long one because the highway was far away. But on the highway, my friends said, we might get help. Because it was a warm night, I did not mind sleeping there, but the group decided to walk. It turned to a crazy tour, not having our car this time of night. Many hours later, and with the help of the police, we finally got back to town. Later, I was told that when the alien vehicles appeared, car engines often would not start.

These local people were familiar with UFO activities. Though they did not hear bad things about aliens in this area, they were still afraid. As we walked that night, we felt as if something might happen. I believe that though the good aliens might be there, it is human nature to be afraid of mysterious visitors from outer space, especially when they come to visit us at night and in the remote desert.

I also saw the ship flying in zigzag movements in the sky. The ship was so bright that I could see it was silver-white, even under the bright sun. After about a minute, the ship flew away at the same speed as I'd seen in Vancouver. I had this kind of sightings not only in Peru but also in other countries. Peru is the country of UFO visitations. I never had as many UFO-related experience in such a short time in any other country. I am glad I had so many different sightings with witnesses. It was a good trip. I enjoyed Peru.

Back to Nice, 2001

After five months of visiting various sites in Peru, I went back to Nice. It was there that a miracle occurred: I became an artist in one day. Specifically, a painter. This is how it happened. I was painting the wall of my room when I noticed a stain on my living room wall. I picked up the white paint and tried to paint over it. But as I methodically began to cover the stain, I found myself almost unconsciously painting something else. My hand was moving without my intension. I was struck by a sudden inspiration. My desire to paint artistically was enormous.

I immediately went to an art supply store and bought materials to paint with, and then I painted nonstop with watercolors and oils for months. Even though I had no experience as a painter, I painted effortlessly and with enormous speed. Sometimes I woke up in the middle of the night and painted. I painted boldly on a big canvases without drawing anything first. Most of the time, I didn't even know what I would paint. The burning desire I had at that time was unreal. It was definitely not my own desire.

In just a few months, I had over a hundred paintings. A few months later, my first sales started in galleries in France. Since 2001, I have done nearly forty exhibitions and several one-woman shows with 100 paintings. These shows were written up in the *Miami Herald*. Normally, several artists exhibit together in those big galleries, but because I painted in different styles, my exhibition became a one-woman show. No one thought just one person had painted all those pictures. My paintings were also accepted in The Schacknow Museum of Fine Arts in Florida. Nowadays, I am doing exhibitions in Los Angeles. The *Los Angeles. Register* wrote a big article about me titled "Local artist an otherworldly talent." I have also been offered a position as an assistant to an art professor in France.

This blending of my talents and I believe my attraction to art has a lot to do with my visit to the golden world. The inspiration I had when I saw the amazing nature there was enormous. That was the only time I ever had a desire to paint. Because music had occupied all my time, the seed of art did not grow and blossom in me until later in my life. My desire to paint must have lain dormant in me until I arrived at the right time and the perfect place for it to grow. I believe the UFO-related events in Peru must have activated this dormant seed. I can only account for this kind of miracle to alien intervention. When I paint, I feel close to the golden world because the colors I saw there flash into my eyes and I want to create them on canvas. In the art business, I am what is called a colorist.

My new career, which I love more than music, happened through supernatural intervention. It was September 1, 2001, when I began to paint. Ten days later, the Twin Towers in New York were attacked. Because of this, many cruises were canceled, so I started to perform in Florida, where there is a lot of work in the winter. I also began exhibiting there. Because I had less musical work, I gained more time to paint. I painted for four years until I moved to Los Angeles to reestablish my musical career in California.

I know the consequences of connecting with the supernatural. I have also come to realize that every time an alien vehicle appears to me, my life and my career change. I knew that they came to warn me, but that was not the only reason. It's hard to believe that I got so many miraculous and unexpected results.

Because I was so ordinary, people noticed what happened to me and wondered about it.

For example, my life in the United States began after the UFOs appeared to me during my first night in Las Vegas in 1976. I received a permanent visa two days before my tourist visa expired. It is not easy to receive permanent visa, but it happened to me. I'm sure it was thanks to silent alien intervention. I was about to go to Mexico, but that plan changed. In 1982, following the strange event in Vancouver, I got a job with the MGM Orchestra in Las Vegas. Thirty classical violinists auditioned for one opening, and I was the only one who was not a member of the musicians union. Because my being hired was so unbelievable, people thought I was a friend of important people at MGM, but I didn't know anyone related to MGM. I later met Liberace in Las Vegas, and the direction of my musical career changed.

After the visitation in the desert near Las Vegas in 1983, I became a headliner on cruise ships. People wondered about that because I had never done such shows. Normally, entertainers rehearse and perfect their show for many years by doing lounge shows. Also, most headliners on the cruise ships were male and there were very few Asian performer in those days. But my headliner career started in 1984 and lasted for more than twenty years. The ships took me around the world. The prediction of the celestial violinist was finally fulfilled.

The day after the three vehicles shone their lights on me in Nice in 1988, I purchased a condo. I did this in three days, even though in those days the foreigner who did not have a job or relative in France could not buy the real estate. Against all odds, I bought the condo and my European life started. France held the key of my alien encounter because of my past life. I was led to live there. When the small disks-appeared in Nice in 1992, my life changed again, this time in a spiritual direction. After the sighting in Peru in 2001, I became-a painter.

Finally in 2007, I saw a shining white vehicle hovering in the sky above a beach south of Los Angeles. Even though I was planning to leave America and settle permanently in France, Southern California became my permanent home. I found the perfect condo near Los Angeles. My direction changed again. Then my writing career started. When I did my musical show for a movie group in Hollywood, HBO wanted to make a movie about my career as a single, female, Asian solo violinist. Though the producer did not know anything of my hidden story, his offer became a push to write my real story. Since then I have been writing several books.

THEIR MESSAGE

There are many people in the world who do not want to believe anything beyond science. I have noticed this, especially among the intellectual people I've met. For example, my friend George in Vancouver was an atheist who had never believed anything beyond science. But he saw the statue we named Arthur, and now he no longer thinks we are the only intelligent beings in the universe. *Seeing is believing*. After our miraculous sightings of the UFO and then Arthur's arrival, who could continue to think humans are the only intelligent beings in the universe? George's great curiosity made him do research and take an interest in matters beyond science. Supernatural power does not belong to science, but supernatural power is real, and we can experience it. George even started to think about the existence of God.

I became interested in God because of my alien encounters. All my life, ever since I visited the golden world, I have been obsessed with it. But how could I go there again? If they would pick me up again or if I traveled through space again, that would be great! But if neither of those things happened to me, I had to discover some other means of getting to that golden world. My desire to go there turned me to the spiritual path. If I get caught up in secular, worldly matters, as I did for nearly twenty years, that surely does not get me to the heavenly world. The celestial beings I saw and met were godly beings. I needed to be spiritually cultivated.

The celestial beings created many miracles, but they are only one kind of what must be many advanced, intelligent beings. If they can make such miracles, how much more can God do? As I pondered this, another thought came to me: *The others* are not always available for me. They only come when they want to come. I can only guess when I might see them again. Maybe they will come again when I need to change my life or career. Or when I need their warning. Who knows? They appeared randomly in the past, never when I wished they'd come. In everyday life, I need to rely on more certain things and the greater power than them. God is omnipresent. I can also learn the way to the heavenly world when I study sacred teachings.

I often think about the Book of Genesis. As we read, Adam and Eve were cast out from the garden because they did not follow God's word. They used their own judgment and did what they wanted to do. It is written that suffering and death then came to us.

I realized that no matter how advanced one is and how high one's IQ is, our human abilities are very limited in comparison to the other beings I met. It's also good to remember that any kinds of aliens who are visiting on earth have more advanced technology than we humans have. The people who do not accept other forces must depend on themselves. I believe that we humans should not be quite so independent.

I also realize this. Whenever I rely on my own abilities, I fail. All the things I did my own way led to nothing. It was like the time when I was writing my graduation thesis on German philosophy. I was trying to write from my own knowledge, but I seemed to be getting nowhere, so I quit. But when I was connected with the supernatural power, I wrote with tremendous speed and without my knowledge. I achieved a high academic score. Likewise, how could I paint when I had neither the skill nor the desire to paint?

Supernatural intervention *created* my desire and ability to paint. Many times in my life, even when I made desperate efforts, I could not help myself. But when the supernatural power entered me, everything changed.

In fact, my life was saved not once but twice by nonhuman beings when humans could never have saved me. I was saved, first, when I entered the hells and, second, when I fell into the pit in the Mikado Theater in Tokyo. I also owe the aliens my gratitude for the miraculous healings of my childhood ailments, those illnesses that doctors could not cure. My financial independence through my musical and painting careers also the results of alien intervention.

If I had denied the fact that paranormal events have happened to me, I'm not sure what I might have accomplished in my life. I do not know what kind of medical condition I would be in now. I do not even know if I would still be alive.

Since I was six years old, I have dealt with the natural and supernatural, normal and paranormal issues. I have always had two worlds in me, and I have struggled with them. But when I had communications with the aliens during my childhood, I had many miraculous experiences that improved my life. Because I was born with many physical ailments and I was less than average in school, I depended on the aliens' miraculous powers. The paranormal life became my life. My spiritual path was set when supernatural and illogical matters motivated and pushed me to achieve higher realm of existence.

But after I was saved from my crises and overcame many of my faults with alien help, I became an independent person. I even became a logical person. I like to do things on my own and succeed through my own efforts. I became proud to live this way. I walked a logical path that anyone could understand. I adapted to this world and was accepted by the people I met and with whom I worked. It was such a good feeling for me that I glued myself to the secular life and clung to worldly success and worldly happiness.

Eventually, my life would take a turn. I was led to the wrong path. Then I hit the proverbial brick wall and fell. For instance in 1982, I lost all my investments in properties in Las Vegas because of a plot by my partner. After he died, I had to take responsibility because of the papers I signed when I did not read English. Not only did I lost my investment, but I also lost all my savings when I took that responsibility. It was very hard time in my life. Because I could not survive otherwise, I went to the cruise ships where I could live and eat while I was entertaining. Another disaster came after I failed in my career in Europe. That led to my second suicide attempt in 1991. During the time I was planning to commit suicide, I heard a clear voice that said, *I have a perfect plan for you.* It sounded like the echo that comes when we shout into a well, but it came from above and flowed through the top of my head and straight to my heart, where it sank in deeply. I had never heard this voice before and have not heard it since. The voice was so powerful that I stopped thinking about death.

I believe this was God's voice.

As Kiriyama said, because of our family's cursed fate, those calamities fell into my life, one after the other. My cursed fate is not ended even to this day. When I met the nonhuman being in the golden world when I was seven years old, he said: *Your life is not easy. But we will help you.* They have been miraculously setting me on the right path again and again. It has seemed to me that I have been shown what the result would be if I depended on my own ability and walked my own path. After I fully understand of this and ended my secular life, *the others* did not come to me as often as before. Their warnings had succeeded. Since then, they seem to come only when I need to change my life and career again. I wish they would come more often, but I can not take their warning any more.

As the year passed, I started to understand what the aliens' message was. The more I understand what human life is about, the more I understand about higher beings. I can see that I have been led along the path that they wanted me to follow, even against my plan. The big map of my proper path was drawn by them. They are super-intelligent beings. Their plans are better than mine.

It is wonderful to know that there is something more than science and logic helping me.

MANY WORLDS, MANY BEINGS, MULTIPLE UNIVERSES

I learned about the Raelian Movement not long ago. Here is another case of communication with extraterrestrials. This movement, which is worldwide, also speaks of higher beings. Rael (formerly Claude Vorihon) met aliens and traveled to their world in their vehicles. That's the same thing that happened to me when I was a child. He met nice-looking aliens, and so did I. Although his aliens look different from mine and the concept and message that Rael received was different from mine, his story tells us that many beings exist in this universe.

Have the earth been visited by aliens?

I have always believed that our lives are not limited to this earthly plane. It is not logical to think that we are the only civilized beings in the vast universe. In the Bible, it says that *God created man in his own image.* If we are supposed to think human beings are God's only creations in his image, this sounds very wrong to me. The Old Testament also tells us that God came to regret having created us and once wanted to destroy the human race. The great flood in Noah's time is one example of God's anger at the wickedness of human beings. The sacred books of India, the Vedas, also says the similar thing.

Did God create only miserable creatures? The answer must be *no.* There must be many other godly beings in the universe. I think that if we believe we are the only intelligent beings in this gigantic universe, it is an insult to the Almighty God. God created the universe, and as amazing as it is, there must be innumerable amazing beings also existing in other spheres. I strongly feel that we are only part of his creation. I believe that God created the universe for his creatures to abide in. According to the Bible, it is said that *God created the heavens and earth*. He also said that he *made the world to live in, not to be a place of empty chaos*. If he created only human beings that live on this earth, what is the reason for the billions and billions of other planets that also exist?

I often think about our planet. After my experiences in hell and in my own death world, I see earth as a mild and beautiful planet. But there are many natural disasters here. We are often threatened by what are called "acts of God" like tornadoes and floods and earthquakes. Also, there are many hellish situations on earth. Most human beings and many carnivorous animals survive by killing and eating other beings. Killing is inevitable on earth. We face sickness, old age, and calamities in our short lives on earth. The Buddha began his spiritual practice by seeing human life as one of suffering. Is our earth the only planet where civilized beings can live and suffer?

There must be many other, much better planets and places where higher beings abide. I saw one, a golden world that was bright without the sun. The Bible mentions three heavens. Paul, who wrote one third of the New Testament, said that he was taken up to the third heaven, though he did not know whether he was in his body or out of his body at the time. The Old Testament says that *God created the heavens*. This is a plural noun. If there are many heavens, there must be many hells, too. Between heavens and hells, there must also be many other worlds.

The Buddha spoke of many beings, both visible and invisible, that exist above and below the human realm. He told us that all beings have their own characteristic traits according to their karma. The Bible also says that both visible and invisible beings were created by God. Our physical eyes are only capable of seeing material objects, but some people can also see spiritual forms. People have testified that they have seen angels. Other people will swear to having witnessed a ghost or a haunting. I know that various spirits exist. Through my experiences, I know that many beings are interacting with each other in intricate ways. Some are helping us. Some come to us to ask for help. Just because our human eyes cannot see invisible things, we cannot conclude that invisible things do not exist.

During my experience in the fiery hell, to which I traveled as a teenager from my bedroom, I came to recognize that other dimensions can be mixed in with this earthly dimension, though we may not be aware of them. Another dimension might be the spiritual world, but it could be something else. The universe might be constructed with more very complex and many-dimensional matters than we can imagine. This is one of the great mysteries of my life, but it seems to me that the other dimensions are connected to this world by some sort of tunnel. Otherwise, my experiences could not have happened. But they happened many times in my adult life.

My adventures in hell went on for about one year. I had enough time to study what had happened to me. But the hell was not the only place I experienced from my room. I actually went to many other worlds. Some of those places were very nice and beautiful, but since hell was so dominant, the other worlds were overshadowed. My experiences in multiple universes lasted for about two years. They started around the same time as did the ghostly apparitions.

One of breathtaking place was a place I call the Blue Paradise. This scene has never disappeared from my mind, and I later tried to paint what I saw there. Although I am still trying, it has proved difficult to paint the golden world because the city was not three-dimensional and the colors were transparent. To fully convey that on two-dimensional canvas is impossible. Don't think I haven't tried. It is, however, possible to paint this paradise because the scenery resembled an earthly setting. Yet this paradise was more than earthly. The colors were brightly shining, and I felt as if the mountain, the flowers, the birds, the river, and everything else were rejoicing. It was an ecstatic world with exceeding joy. I saw several big, blue birds coming near me, and when I tried to follow them, I crossed over jet-black space. After I walked a few steps there, alas, I was suddenly back in my room.

I assume that this jet black space is the tunnel to the other dimension. When I entered hell, I often noticed I was passing through this space. It felt to me like a vacant space or maybe a vacuum tube.

Another place I entered and liked looked like a tropical island. After passing through the tunnel, everything changed. Suddenly I felt the temperature change. Although it was a bitterly cold day at home, in that place I felt warm. I heard birds singing. The black space had no life, but here, everything was alive! The colors were incredibly vivid, much brighter than on earth. I found myself in a grove of trees. I saw big red flowers along the river in the distance. When I walked toward the river, I touched the trees. I sensed the feelings of the trees. Then I put my hand in the water of the river. The cold water felt good because this place was warm. I resisted coming back to my cold room and tried to prolong my stay for even a few more minutes. I visited this paradise several times. I was so happy here. Every time I went there, I could not stop smiling. These brief moments of happiness inspired my obsession to live on a tropical island on earth.

There were many other places I entered the same way as I walked to hell. Many times, I knew ahead of time that I was about to enter some other place because the air changed. It was similar to the atmosphere I felt in Germany when I had an uncanny "time machine" experience. But traveling out of my bedroom, I guess, did not involve time travel. What I noticed was something bizarre in one spot in my bedroom. My leaving didn't always happen there, but I walked into other dimension more frequently from that spot than from any other spot in the room. I felt I was almost sucked in there.

I tried to investigate these outlandish phenomena by asking my sister Chizu to stand in that spot and also to walk around in my room. She asked me what this was all about. What could I tell her? Sometimes I worried she might disappear while I was testing the door to the other worlds. If that happened, I thought, she would come back because I always came back. Though she never disappeared, I got used to traveling and even gained some control over it.

If I entered places I did not like, I tried to come back to my room quickly by jumping or running hard enough to break through the invisible wall. But if I liked the place, I wanted to stay there. I often tried to think of way not to come back when I was in a place of contentment. If I walked, I might step into my room, so I stood still. But it seemed like I was pulled out from the front of my body by some force.

My traveling to other dimension was not an out-of-body experience. I had to be completely awake and walking or standing for the traveling to begin. Sometimes it happened while I was cleaning my room or doing something else. After I got used to entering the other places, I tested myself by hitting my face, pulling my hair, pinching my arm or leg. Sometime I saw bruises on my arm because I had pinched too hard. I did these things to make sure I was not dreaming. I needed to know my physical body was in another place. If I lost consciousness, I might find myself lying on the floor. But every time I came back, I had full consciousness and was standing up. My eyes were wide open. Sometimes I found myself climbing on my bed. This happened when I was climbing a hill in the other world. I experienced these incidents with my physical body.

My visits to hell lasted nearly thirty minutes, between nine o'clock and nine-thirty at night. I always saw the clock in my room and made sure what time it was and how long I was in hell. But some other visits were shorter, only a few minutes, sometimes only a few seconds. These visits cannot be my imagination because they happened so frequently. These travels were entirely different from my visit to the golden world, which lasted nearly six hours.

This traveling between worlds was part of my life until I left my parents' home. I have asked scientists and other people to explain what was happening, but no one has had any answers. I concluded that my room had to be an entrance to another dimension and the gate to the other dimension must have opened up during those few years because it never happened any other time. This phenomenon might be called *kamikakushi* (a Japanese word meaning "hidden by God") or a deformation of embedded spaces described by Einstein. This was terribly confusing, but these things really happened in my bedroom. It is true that the facts often distort the truth and that truth can be stranger than fiction.

Then came one more very special visit to heaven that changed my life. I believe that this had to be an out-of-body experience because I was sitting in my room and looking at the sky from the window. I was almost in a trance-like state. My physical body did not experience this visit to another place. When this happened, I was sick from the awful hell experience of my ancestor. My body was heavy, I ached all over, I was depressed. I was not expecting anything good to happen to me. But suddenly I found myself standing in a great light. I immediately felt the heaviness and pain leave my body. I was startled. I did not know what had happened to me. The light was too bright for me to see anything. I was immersed in an indescribable fresh aroma. I had already experienced this revitalizing air in the golden world, but now I felt a great contentment, an unexplainable peace. All doubts and negativities were gone. It was a feeling of completion. I thought this kind of perfect peace comes only from heaven. I knew this was heaven. I did not doubt it. I still remember this sensation.

I started to walk cautiously, and then I noticed I did not feel any weight. When I looked at my feet, I could not believe what I was seeing. I was walking on top of light! The pebbles on the ground were emanating light. The pebbles looked like precious stones, rounded and shining in different, subtle colors. All kind of colors were blended softly. I felt like I was walking in the air. Yet it was more than the air. I was getting the healing vibration coming from those precious stones.

When I looked up, I did not see the sun. My eyes were not blinded; it was just too bright for me to see anything. But I sensed there was something there, a place that seemed to be made of exceedingly bright, white light. Somehow I sensed that I was not allowed to see this glorious place. It is more than I could handle.

I felt I had to pass through this area and go some other place in this heaven. As I kept walking, I started to see some kind of structure. It was an enormous landscape, I felt like I was in the open air.

The longer I walked, the better I could see because the light gradually became dimmer. I saw enormous houses and mansions far away and marveled at them. I felt that these were the private houses. I didn't know if this was a city or a palace. I did not see anything from nature, like mountains, lakes, or trees. Maybe my eyes could not see anything but those mansions. I asked myself, what kind of people live in houses made of light? What kind of lives do they have? All sorts of questions came into my mind. Where were the living beings (or angels) of this world? Because I didn't see anyone, I became curious. I kept walking. Then I suddenly felt a different sensation under my feet. Where I was walking was not as soft as before. I looked down. My feet were near the ground, and the shining pebbles were less and smaller. I became a little uneasy. I saw some smaller mansions here and there and could see the colors, but the atmosphere was no longer white. I finally stopped walking and looked around. That's when I saw three men standing high in the air. They did not have wings. They looked like saints wearing white robes, their hair shiny white, and they were smiling at me. Then the one standing in the middle raised his right hand and said, *Not yet.*

And at that moment, I was back in my room and feeling sick again. This happened only once, but it became a life-changing experience. My experience of heaven was too real to be unreal. This, I thought, could be our next life. The golden world is another heavenly world that exists somewhere in the universe.

The longer we live in this world, the more our minds become adjusted to this world. All the sacred books tell us not to make this mistake. The Buddha said that when we understand the system of rebirth, we should strive to go to higher realms, at least higher ones than earth.

But what would happen if we fell into the hell that I visited? Those hells are neither imaginary nor fantastic. I've been there. They are real worlds that also exist somewhere, and I think it's hard to get out once we fall into them. If those hells really exist, we do not want to go for even a day. I experienced two hells. They were similar to the circles of hell in the *Inferno* section of *The Divine Comedy* by Dante Alighieri, the famous late-medieval Italian scholar. *The Divine Comedy* is considered the greatest work of literature composed in medieval Italy. The *Inferno* describes the poet's journey through hell where he sees the people consigned to the nine circles of suffering. The worst hell is a fiery inferno, a place beyond human imagination. Both the Buddha and Jesus strongly warned us about this abyss. Today, most people do not want to believe in the existence of hell, but it is better for us to avoid the paths leading there. I tremble to think about what might have happened if my second suicide in 1991 had succeeded, This is why I must tell what I learned in hell. It is an example to people who have not had this horrendous experience. However, I am not saying that all suicides lead to hell. I can only relate my own personal experience. What I write about really happened to me. These things might happen to others.

I have learned through my experiences that this world is only one journey in the long journey of our soul. We are now experiencing human life in physical bodies that are best suited to this earth. If anyone could see the heavenly world I saw, they would lose all interest in this world. Awareness of other worlds changes our thinking and the purpose of our lives.

MY RELATIONSHIP WITH ALIENS AND HIGHER BEINGS

Aliens have played a major part in my life, and I have been highly motivated by them. They are my friends and teachers who have helped me and educated me. And they have been much better friends than any human friends I've ever had. It seems strange to say this, but it's true. No human could lead me the way *the others* have. Humans can know only so much and can do only limited things. Hardly anyone can teach me about another world outside this earth.

Although I met some nice, very wealthy men that I could have married and had a comfortable life with, I always knew that marriage was not the aliens' purpose for me. For this reason, I have stayed single all my life. But I have never been lonely. I don't even know what loneliness is, because I've been so close to the nonhuman beings since I met them that I've never missed human relationships. Knowing *the others* were always watching me and helping me, I have preferred to stay single. This is not sacrifice, but arises from pure friendship that is also a working relationship. Because I know their purpose, I chose this life. It is like the monks who devote themselves to the spiritual path without marriage. They are happy to choose to live a spiritual life. If we become too attached to the human life, we have a reason to become human again. Buddhism says this cycle of rebirth and reincarnation. It is a law of causation. This is why it's good to attach ourselves to God and the higher beings if we want to end the cycle of our human lives on earth.

I am attached emotionally to *the others*. My attraction is obviously to the celestial beings, but it is *the others* who still appear to me and have done so since my childhood. They are visible to anyone here on earth when they appear, because they have physical bodies. The celestial beings are spiritual beings and sometimes can become our so-called guardian angels.

I have often wondered who was orchestrating my life. *Someone* was sending various people to me at times along my life's path. It must be someone in the golden world, but I still do not know who does this. I know that God uses people to guide us. In my case, I believe nonhuman beings are also used. After my first suicide attempt, I thought, *God never gives us things we cannot handle.* If a problem cannot be solved by human beings, then God will send us nonhumans to assist us. Nonhumans are also God's creation. God controls what he created. This is not difficult to understand.

WHAT I UNDERSTAND ABOUT ADVANCED NONHUMAN BEINGS

As the years have passed, many of the puzzles I had struggled with resulting from my otherworldly experiences started to come clear. For example, when I was a child, I was curious about celestial beings and *the others*. They were two different beings. I did not understand how these beings were connected and how the things they did were connected. I now think that *the others* are cloned beings. The beings on the vehicle all looked alike, and they looked like robots. When I think now is that they are not real individuals with emotions and souls. I suspect that they were created to do work for the higher, advanced beings. Because *the others* were created by the celestial beings, I had an immediate connection when I met them in their vehicle, and felt that I had known them for a long time. While I was in their vehicle, I remembered an ancient time when I was not human. The world that I probably lived in at that time was the golden world but I was not living with those robot-like beings. This I know.

The celestial beings who have souls and emotion can only come to me in spiritual form like the girl-spirit I met. When I was a child, I needed to see the tangible beings and to have the three-dimensional experience to understand this complex issue.

How about Arthur, the brown statue? He had no expression on his face. *The others* also had no expression on their faces. I believe that Arthur was a replacement for *the others*. It was hard for *the others* to come to the center of Vancouver, so they sent Arthur to me. Arthur brought me their message: *We are watching you.* Because he could not talk like *the others*, he kept coming back to my living room and watching me. He did his work. I believe the advanced beings have the technology to create material things. I believe Arthur and *the others* were created by them.

When I was a child, I also thought *the others* might be servants who came from heaven to take me back to their world. That's what they did. I visited the golden world. I needed to understand what the heavenly world was about in order to get a firm conviction of the purpose of my life. I was told that I would live as a human being for only a little while. They are more eager for me to come back to their world than I was to go there because I continued living an earthly life and began to forget my origin, especially during the times when my life was going well and I was happy living on earth. *The others*, the cloned beings, must be the servants who can travel to the earth to bring messages to us.

I believe that we will soon discover many new things that will surprise us. Many visitors, both good and evil, from other worlds are coming to earth. They're doing their work. Some of their work is for their purpose, and they use us for their research or they might be doing some distractive work. Those are the negative cases. But that is not all. For instance, the Book of Ezekiel in the Old Testament mentions the fiery chariot from heaven and different beings.

I also think about the star that led the wise men to the birthplace of Jesus. The Bible says that the star appeared to the three wise men and led them to the place where Jesus was born. The star did not move. Comets move, but it is almost impossible for a comet to lead people to an exact location. The alien vehicle, however, looked like a star in the distance. Surely the aliens can lead us with vehicles that look like stars. In our history we can find much help from the heavens. I speak not only god's angels. I speak of the aliens that have been visiting earth since ancient time for good reasons. They are helping us, even individual person, like us can get help from them.

There are many religions on earth. A spiritual path should lead us to the peace and a higher stage of existence, but there are so many conflicts and wars between religions.

Goi's fervent prayer was to find the path he should walk. He saw the conflicts of the many religions and wanted to open to himself to the path without any restrictions. He was guided by the higher, advanced, nonhuman beings. Nietzsche also fought against medieval European Christianity and spiritual laws. His book, *Thus Spoke Zarathustra* tells how to rise above the human realm. Mahatma Gandhi studied many religions and walked a path of nonviolence. This is something I identified in the celestial world.

My alien encounters opened my eyes to the universe and beyond. I believe that fundamental questions, such as *What is human life all about?* and *What path do I take?* can be answered when we see the bigger picture.

When I was a child, I wanted to have witnesses because I wanted to prove my paranormal experiences were real, but I never had any. I guess the post-World War II days weren't the right time to bring the subject of other worlds into this world. But when I became an adult, witnesses appeared. I also started to have a proof of my childhood experiences. That is because it is a time for me to talk. Without witnesses or proof, no one would believe me.

I believe I have had almost every kind of paranormal experience possible. Yes, it is very rare for one person to have so many, but because someone in another world wanted me to go through the other-world experiences, I had them. I was being trained for something I could never be trained for in this world.

I now believe my life was planned before my birth. I also believe the author of my life comes from another world. I know my life was used for the purpose of the advanced nonhuman beings (aliens). Because planning and using my life were for their purpose, I believe the aliens have been observing and helping me. I was destined to work for them. I was told this in the golden world and have known it since I was seven years old.

After I left my home in Japan, my life became very active. It is active to this day, which is why I cannot afford to spend my time on mere fantasy. A child's imagination and fantasies do not usually carry over into adult life, but the things I experienced with aliens have never left my mind. In fact, the older I get, the more the things I took for granted in my childhood have come back and stirred up memories. If my encounters with aliens were merely my imagination or fantasy, what could be the explanation for their many visits and the unexplainable events that happened to me? I moved all over the world. Many times, I didn't even know where I was going next. Yet *the others* always found me. My trip to Nice happened without any planning on my part, but they found the hotel room I was sleeping in. I knew ahead of time during that night in Nice that they were coming and purposely left the window open. Are these coincidental events? I don't think so.

My life has taken me all around the world. I have traveled to 110 countries and lived in fifteen of them. I performed on more than 500 cruises and in famous theaters in America and Europe. Though I have done many things in my life, I have never taken any recreational drugs, not even marijuana. I hardly drink alcohol (only a glass of wine once in a while). I work mostly on cruise ships and in hotels, which are careful about what kind of people they hire. I was offered Austrian and Australian citizenship before I received American citizenship. I have established myself and earned recognition around the world. I have credibility. Yet I am saying my story is true. The alien encounters and the paranormal experiences I describe really happened to me.

My experiences are hard to understand. I know this. I know I cannot prove many of them. My major at the university was German philosophy, and I also studied Indian philosophy for seven years. The original Buddhism, which is found in Indian philosophy, is a profound philosophy based on logic and science. I have a logical mind. I am not a fantasist or a fanatic. I was a New Yorker for twenty years, though I was often away, so I know what the logical world is. I am definitely not an easy believer. This is why I have had a great struggle with Christianity. But I have discovered something beyond logic and science. Now I know it is well worth devoting myself to the path I have begun to understand.

The time we live in now is quite different from the time when Goi lived. He stopped talking in public, but I do not have to stop. Many years have passed. I have finally realized the urgency of my calling. At this point in my life, I no longer care what people think or say about me. I delayed doing my assigned work because I was afraid of people's reactions that might have a negative effect on my good career. But that does not matter any more. I don't have much time left. I need to do everything I'm supposed to do. So I wrote this book to tell my experiences, which I have never shared before and was afraid to share.

This is my start.

However, it is important for you to know that even now it is hard for me to tell my hidden story. I still have my musical career and people respect me. Also my passion now is painting. I am dying to paint, but I do not have much time because of my mission. I'm not only sacrificing my desire, but I must also endure the ridicule and derision. Yet I have resigned myself to do what I need to do.

I have lived in a competitive world in the entertainment business. My career kept me busy. I was always distracted from my mission and the idea of my real origin. What matters now is where I will end up. I solely must focus on this subject now. I cannot afford to fail.

My final conviction, however, applies to many people. Where we will end up after this short and troubled life on earth can be one of the most significant topics. We all die, sooner or later. This is certain. It is better to be prepared for the afterlife while we are still engaging the practical work of living on earth.

I remembered my true origin, the time when I was living as a nonhuman. But if I had not met *the others*, I am not sure if I would have fully remembered. This made me think. Even though you are not aware of it, yours could be the same situation as mine.

I am someone who happened to discover this secret through aliens. I am bold enough to tell this to the world. This is my mission. I am not merely doing my work. I am destined to do this work on behalf of the advanced nonhuman beings. Hardly anyone understands this yet, but time will tell. I believe that interplanetary actions and multiple universes hold important keys to our future and for our lives.

Lately, because I am not traveling much, I have time to watch TV and get the news. I was recently stunned to learn that the subject of aliens draws mostly negative comments. It might be true that terrifying things are happening and those cases might be more numerous than good cases in the last century. It seems like my kind of experience is still not commonly known. But it is not very rare, either. Recently I have been connected to the prominent speaker Mary Rodwell, principal of ACERN(Australian Close Encounter Resource Network) in Australia and co-founder FREE(Foundation for Research into Extraterrestrial Encounters) in the USA. She has researched three thousand cases and knows about many cases like mine. If alien abductees were not getting hurt, physically or mentally, most people do not talk openly about them. I, myself, could not talk about mine. We generally keep our lives and abductions hidden. If people were injured, they need to report it. That is the reason bad cases became commonly known. This is why I am encouraged to protest.

To this day, I still hear the words *We are watching you* whenever their vehicles appear. They are still encouraging me to be courageous in my mission and complete the human life for the better place.

I hope my speaking out and writing this book brought you a new perspective. Some readers may have had similar experiences to mine and can relate to me. But others are still hiding or afraid to talk about their stories. My book may help them step out. The more people talk, the faster the preconceived ideas change. The people who became aware need to work together to change the old belief. We have entered a new cycle. According to the Mayan calendar, it is a new era now, and soon beliefs will start to change. It is the time to begin our mission.

EPILOGUE

This book is based on paranormal experiences that happened to me during my childhood in Japan and in my adult life in sites around the world. Because of the difficulty in explaining these complicated issues, I have given considerable detail and background in many chapters. I could not, however, write everything that has ever happened to me on my mysterious spiritual path. I intend to write more in another book one day.

Even though I decided to disclose my extraordinary life in this book, it was not easy. I was reluctant to write about things because of the reaction I knew I would get from certain quarters. I also thought about omitting some events or moderating some things that really happened. After giving this more thought, however, I wrote about the events of my life truly as they happened so that the reader might better understand what I have experienced.

I have worked all my adult life as a professional musician and have traveled a great deal. I never joined any paranormal associations and purposely avoided discussing such topics after I left Japan. I do not know any person who knows what I know and have not met anyone like Goi, although I believe there are more people like him, I have never searched for such people. Because Goi appeared to me in spirit, I met him and received much information from him. Otherwise, what is in this book is all my personal experiences. This book was not written to support pre-existing belief systems.

My reluctance to discuss my experiences before now has been largely due to the degree that they challenge my own rational mind, and I am only going public now that I feel I understand the "big picture". *This is a book* about my spiritual *awakening inspired by encounters with other worlds and their inhabitants.* My experiences have been so profoundly moving that I believe my vocation at this stage of my life is to let others know truthfully about my encounters.

ABOUT THE AUTHOR

Julliena Okah was born in Japan where she was encouraged by her family to follow a music career. Later she studied music in Vienna and art in France and is recognized as a world class solo violin virtuoso and painter. She became a headliner with her own unique and exciting solo violin show on major cruise ships for some twenty years. She has performed at famous concert halls and theaters around the world, even at commercial venues in Las Vegas and on numerous TV shows. Her oil and watercolor paintings hang in art galleries and with private collections worldwide. She is a graduate scholar of German philosophy. She traveled throughout the world and has lived in 14 countries. She studied various Indian creeds while living in India and studied Christianity in America. She resided in New York City and Nice France for 20 years before moving to Southern California.

Cover Painting ("Blue Paradise") and all paintings by Julliena Okah.